FOUR
QUEENS
AND A
COUNTESS

Four
QUEENS
AND A
COUNTESS

Jill Armitage

AMBERLEY

First published 2017

Amberley Publishing
The Hill, Stroud
Gloucestershire, GL5 4EP

www.amberley-books.com

British Library Cataloguing in Publication Data.
A catalogue record for this book is available from the British Library.

ISBN 978 1 4456 6916 8 (hardback)
ISBN 978 1 4456 6917 5 (ebook)

Typesetting and Origination by Amberley Publishing.
Printed in the UK.

Contents

1

Four Wardships and a Wedding

Even in her lifetime Bess of Hardwick was considered by many to be the stuff of legend – charismatic, forceful, determined yet romantic. She was born in 1527 into the relative obscurity of a small gentry family whose ancestors had been established at Hardwick on the Derbyshire/Nottinghamshire border for at least six generations. They had acquired Hardwick, a freehold tenement established in the early thirteenth century within the manor of Stainsy which originally occupied the whole of the adjoining parishes of Ault Hucknall and Heath, at a time when it was still early enough to call themselves de (of) Hardwick after the name of the manor. Hardwick means sheep farm, a clue to the hilly, wooded pastureland on which it is based. It was to play a large part in Bess's story.[1]

The Hardwick Ancestry

One sunny August morning in 1485, forty-two years before the birth of Bess of Hardwick, a significant battle was fought in Bosworth, Leicestershire. It lasted only two hours, with fewer than a hundred men killed on either side, but among those slain was King Richard III. As the crown of England was placed on the head of the victor, Henry Tudor, Earl of Richmond, he was hailed as the new King Henry VII of England. The Tudor age had begun. Understandably, local men played a significant part in the battle, and among them was John de Hardwick from just over the border in Derbyshire. He is known to have fought bravely and guided the

7

Tudor army safely round the edge of a marsh which adjoined the battlefield.[2]

As a knight, John de Hardwick was entitled to wear a coat of arms. The Hardwick arms consisted of a silver shield with a blue saltire cross. Along the top of the shield was another band of blue on which were three five-leaf devices in silver. The crest consisted of a stag standing on a mound, dressed in gold with a collar of red and silver roses round its neck. It is described as 'verre eglomise panel of the arms of Hardwick, and Talbot impaling Hardwick, surrounded by fruit and flowers'.[3]

Being a knight was a great honour. The king would award lands and manors in return for knight service – a fully armed knight and his servants to act as soldiers for forty days a year. Knight service ensured that the Crown could call on landowners up and down the country to help fight the constant battles, and provide an army quickly and cheaply. However, there was a price to pay. If a landowner could not provide knights and soldiers for the king's army, the king had the right to collect scutage, a tax in lieu of military service which was used to enable the Crown to pay for troops. There was also an additional worry for Tudor landowners like John Hardwick, who had fought so bravely at Bosworth: if he died before his heir was twenty-one, the underage child could not fulfil the requirement of knight service so the Crown would demand something in its place – usually a wardship.

But the Battle of Bosworth brought an end to the Wars of the Roses and peace reigned. As the country became more peaceful it was no longer necessary for men to provide knight service, but the Crown, ever keen to keep its rights and a lucrative side-line, retained the wardship of minor heirs. This was one of the king's ancient 'feudal incidents' or rights of royal prerogative, dating back to the feudal principles of seigneurial guardianship. It meant that any land that the family owned could be taken by the Crown and administered by the Office of Wards, which would hold the estate and use the income as the Crown wished until the heir came of age.

In the late fifteenth and early sixteenth century there were three John Hardwicks in succession. The first John Hardwick married Elizabeth, daughter of Henry Bakewell. Their son John married

Elizabeth Pinchbeck, and it could have been either of these two men who fought at Bosworth in 1485.

The third John Hardwick was born in 1495 and was only twelve when his father died in 1507. As was the custom, the estate could have passed into wardship but instead, shortly before his death, his father gave (or said he had given) his lands to trustees. They would own the land until his son was twenty-one and took possession, and in the meantime it would remain in the hands of the widow. This was accepted and the father's last wishes were respected.

The Hardwick estate in 1507 was described as comprising 6 messuages (dwellings with land attached), 200 acres of arable land, 20 acres of meadow and 30 acres of pasture in the lordship of Stainsby, together with half a bovate of land in Glapwell, held of John Leeke's manor of Pleasley. This suggests that the estate consisted of five tenanted farms and their chief residence, Hardwick Hall. In keeping with similar buildings of that time, Hardwick Hall would have been a half-timbered house with barnyards, stables and dovecot yard.[4]

The third John Hardwick married Elizabeth Leeke, daughter of Thomas and Margaret Leeke of Hasland. Early records are often very confusing; not helped when three successive John Hardwicks all married girls named Elizabeth.

At this time, John Hardwick farmed 450 acres in Derbyshire and received rents on a further 100 acres in Lincolnshire. Hardwick Hall and more land was held in fealty to Sir John Savage for an annual peppercorn rent of 'twelve pence, one pound of cumin, one pound of pepper and one clove a year'.[5] The young family was prospering and John Hardwick began to convert the original medieval timber farmhouse into a stone manor house for his growing family.[6]

The Birth of Elizabeth (Bess) Hardwick
John and Elizabeth had one son and five daughters: James, born in 1526; Dorothy, whose birth date is unknown and who died young; Mary, born 1523; Jane, born 1524; Elizabeth, always known as Bess and born 1527; and Alice, born 1528. According to John Hardwick's will, there may also have been another baby daughter. In the Tudor period infant mortality rate was high, with 2 per cent of babies dying before the end of their first day, 5 per cent within a week and 13 per cent within a year. Since childbirth was a mainly female affair attended

by gatherings of women, if the baby was in distress and likely to die before it could be taken to the church, many hasty baptisms were carried out by midwives. This was done in the belief that an unbaptised child would not go to heaven and would thus be in danger of eternal damnation. The early baptism of a baby was considered essential if a child was sick; it was even considered a possible cure. People believed that a child wouldn't thrive until it was named, so baptism was essential for its future health. Superstition played a large part. It was considered prudent to first make the sign of the cross over an unbaptised baby before taking it in your arms. New babies were symbolically taken upstairs before being returned so that they would go up in the world rather than down. It was also strongly believed that babies should not be taken out of the house before baptism because taking an unbaptised baby into someone's house brought in bad luck.[7]

Bess's actual birthdate is not known, but it was certainly between June and October 1527. As was the custom of the day, if the baby survived those first important days a public baptism took place, and Bess was baptised at St John's Church, Ault Hucknall.

Hardwick had never acquired the status of a separate manor and remained part of the manor of Stainsby. Although early records refer to a church at Stainsby there has never been a church there. St John's Church less than 2 km away at the even smaller hamlet of Ault Hucknall dates from the eleventh century and sits between Rowthorne and Stainsby. It served the outlying villages, hamlets and farmsteads of Hardwick, Hardstoft, Astwith, Stainsby, Heath, Lound, Oldcotes, Bramwell and Glapwell. There were no chapels of ease but in the twelfth century a second church was built at Lound to serve the north of the manor.

As well as giving the baby her Christian name, the baptism involved the baby being 'crossed' with sacred oil on the shoulders and chest, the sign of the cross being made in her right hand, and the baby being dipped three times in holy water – first on the right side, then the left, then with the face in the font – the three immersions representing the Trinity. There's another superstition that says that if a child does not cry at this stage it will not live long. This arose from the custom of exorcism, which was retained by the Anglican church. Seemingly when the devil was going out of the possessed person he was supposed to do so with reluctance, so the cries and struggles of the infant at baptism were convincing proof that the holy water was driving out the devil. Sometimes a nurse was known to pinch the child to make it cry. Having thus been received into the Church, the baby was then considered safe from the devil and all his works.

During the Elizabethan period, the immersion changed to sprinkling with holy water and being anointed with oil. It was traditional for a baby to be covered with a fine white baptismal vestment called a chrisom. Baby clothes as such did not exist. From the day the baby was born it was wrapped in swaddling clothes, strips of linen that were wound about the tiny body until it resembled a chrysalis with just the head left free. That would be covered in a lace cap. The arms were bound to the baby's sides and the legs straightened and fastened tightly together in the belief that this would encourage straight limbs. Often the child would lie in its own excrement for days and was only changed and promptly re-wrapped when the miserable infant became too obnoxious to hold. The baby would be restricted in this manner until it was old enough to toddle, then both boys and girls of rich families were dressed in stiff miniature garments with farthingale, ruff and full sleeves, making them look like miniature adults. Weighed down and restricted in this way, royal children were carried everywhere by a chamberlain, so in later life many were unsteady on their legs.

As the baptism was carried out within a few days of the birth, the mother would not be present because custom decreed that a new mother must have a month's lying in. She would, however, receive women visitors in the lying-in chamber for what was known as 'a gossiping'.

In 1538, Thomas Cromwell issued a jucicial order requiring that local parishes register all baptisms, marriages and funerals, and in the 1549 and 1552 Prayer Book it was written: 'The pastors and curates shall oft admonish the people that they defer not the Baptisme of Infants any longer than the Sunday, or other Holy day next after the child be borne, unless upon a great and reasonable cause declared to the Curate.'

John Hardwick's Will and Wardship

Elizabeth Hardwick was pregnant again within weeks of giving birth to Bess, but in January 1528 John Hardwick became ill.

When he knew he was dying, John tried to repeat the same course his father had taken in order to safeguard the estate for his eighteen-month-old son James. On 6 January, he transferred all his land to his younger brother Roger and seven feoffees whom he named as his trustees. They were Edward Willoughby Kt; John Leeke Esq., his brother-in-law; Henry Marmyon Esq.; Thomas Leeke, gent, his father-in-law; Robert Peret, clerk; Ralph Spalton, yeoman; and Edward Bareford Esq. These eight trustees were to hold the land, which was to be administered for the benefit of John's widow and children for twenty years, by which time James would be twenty-one and could inherit.

John's will provided '40 marks of good and lawful money' to be found from the estate for each of his five daughters at the time of their marriages. 'Also I will that if Elizabeth my said wife be with child now, at the making of this my present will, the child to have likewise another 40 marks when it is of lawful age.'[8] There is slight confusion here as the amount was for five daughters. This would indicate that Dorothy was still alive, and there is every likelihood that there was another daughter other than Dorothy, Mary, Jane and Bess before Alice was born.

John Hardwick died on 29 January 1528, in his early thirties, and was buried in the arch between the chancel and aisle of Ault Hucknall church. No gravestone survives but some fragments of the painted glass memorial window commissioned by his twenty-eight-year-old widow have been incorporated into a nineteenth-century window.[9] The Hardwick estate was well established and Roger Hardwick may have acted as farm manager before his brother's untimely death, after which he moved into Hardwick Hall with the family and ran the estate.[10]

Despite John's early death, with Roger working the farm it continued to prosper and Elizabeth gave birth to baby Alice seven months after her husband's death. The terms that John Hardwick had requested appeared to be quite acceptable, but on 2 October 1528 an enquiry called an Inquisition Post Mortem was ordered by law. It was decided that John Hardwick had not really left a will, the chief aim of a will being to tell the survivors what the testator wants to be done with his property after his death. Note the term 'his property' – generally a woman owned nothing in her lifetime. Even an heiress had to give over her lands and property when she married, although by the fifteenth century a widow was entitled to one-third of her husband's lands. Later, the Will Act of 1540 allowed a man free disposition of freehold land, generally requiring two-thirds to go to his wife and family so that he could leave one-third elsewhere as he wished.

To ensure that everything was legal and that John Hardwick's last wishes were carried out, supervisors were appointed in August 1529, eighteen months after his death. The enquiry was delayed when Roger Hardwick died unmarried in the spring of 1530, two years after his brother, and then on 8 September 1530 the commissioners overturned the decision made by the original inquisition. John Hardwick's undoing appears to have been that he had willed land which theoretically did not belong to him. It belonged to the Crown and was held on knight service, so the gift was null and void. Seeking out that vital knight service or payment in lieu, the Master of Wards came down heavily on Elizabeth Hardwick. They took back the estate, leaving her with no income or financial support, and young James was taken into wardship. There is a possibility that the girls were taken as well, although there is no record of this.

What is on record is that the wardship of young James Hardwick was sold to a court official named John Bugby along with a quarter of the interest on the land. He paid a total of £20 in three instalments and in return acquired lands worth an annual £5 in income and the right to sell the marriage of his ward.[11]

Just over half the Hardwick estate, which included Hardwick Hall and the demesne land, was kept by the king, but provision was made for Elizabeth Hardwick and her family to remain there, paying rent to the Master of Wards for the privilege. Their situation was financial turmoil. Paying rent to Bugby for the lands he was holding, or paying for further land to farm to bring in an income, would have crippled Elizabeth financially.

To get her son and lands out of wardship she needed to find a well-disposed relative or friend prepared to raise the money. How successful she was in this is unknown. She was related to many of the distinguished families of the area; her father was Thomas Leeke, the younger son of William and Catherine Leeke of Langford and Sutton Scarsdale. His brother John inherited considerable wealth in lands and property in three counties, and made a brilliant alliance when he married Elizabeth Savage, daughter of Sir John Savage of Clifton, Cheshire and Lord of Stainsby, Ault Hucknall. They made their home at Sutton Scarsdale Hall, across the valley from Stainsby, the manor in which Hardwick was situated.

Being a second son, however, Elizabeth's father was not so fortunate. He had few expectations, but after his marriage to Margaret, daughter of William Fox of Chesterfield, they settled at Hasland Hall, and Thomas was Bailiff of Chesterfield from 1492 until his death thirty-one years later. Thomas and Margaret had two sons and two daughters – John, Thomas, Elizabeth and Muriel. He left his lands to his two sons John and Thomas; his daughters – Elizabeth, who married John Hardwick, and Muriel, who had married George Linacre of Linacre, Brampton – got nothing as they had both received their marriage portions. The Leekes of Hasland were therefore a minor branch of the Leekes of Sutton Scarsdale whose marriage partners were heiresses. They had intermarried with other country gentry, and the extended family offered opportunities which Elizabeth Hardwick was anxious to take advantage of after the early death of her husband. At this stage, with the court having taken back her estate, with no income or financial support and with young James in wardship, we can only assume what happened next.

It's possible that Alice, Bess, Dorothy, Mary and Jane were sent to live with relatives, and Elizabeth did what most widows and widowers of the day did – she remarried. With a young family, finances teetering on the brink of disaster and a son and half her land in wardship, Elizabeth Hardwick was not likely to attract a husband of rank, but her second husband was Ralph Leche of Chatsworth, a younger son of another local gentry family, with no expectations but a few leases that brought in an annuity of just £6 13s 4d. It was not enough to attract a woman of substance, but the Leches were anxious to better the lot of a younger son. Elizabeth's dower, at least, was sacrosanct during her lifetime, but she needed someone to share the responsibilities and management of the encumbered Hardwick lands until her son came of age, so the Hardwick/Leche marriage was obviously one of convenience. Because Bess was only two years old when her mother remarried, she's likely to have regarded Ralph Leche as her father; this would have been helped by the fact that she was soon to have three more sisters: Jane, Elizabeth and Margaret.

Growing up in a household of girls, many clothes would have been handed down as girls were dressed as miniature versions of their mothers. Good manners and deportment were expected of a girl growing up in the house of a gentleman, even one in reduced circumstances, but education was limited. The main aim for a girl of Bess's social standing was to prepare her for service in a noble household, or at least with a family of higher social standing than her own, with the aim of making a good marriage. In the Tudor period it was normal to send children from the age of ten into service at the homes of richer families to give them an informal apprenticeship in the ways of their betters or of court. It was beneficial for parents to place their children with well-placed friends or cousins, and through her mother, Bess had a good network of powerful connections. She was taught the skills necessary to be a good wife, homemaker and mother. She would help with the indoor chores of baking, washing, cleaning, polishing, spinning, weaving and sewing. Outside she would help with keeping bees and poultry, and looking after the dovecotes and herb garden. She would learn how to make potions and salves, soap, candles and unguents in the scented still room. Entertainment was of the homemade variety, and Bess would have learnt to sing, play a keyboard instrument like the virginal, and sew. She became a needlewoman of above-average ability. Her passion for embroidery was evident throughout her life, and many of her pieces have been handed down as treasured heirlooms; examples of her work exist at Hardwick Hall and at the V&A in London.

The financial circumstances of the Hardwick/Leche family must have been very strained, and the marriage was blighted by Ralph Leche's constant problems with money. Between 1533 and 1538 Elizabeth sued him for desertion, between 1538 and 1544 he was imprisoned in the Fleet Prison for debt, and in 1545 he was committed to debtors' prison in Derby.[12]

Bess Goes into Service

The situation was not helped by having eight or nine dependent children, so to ease the burden this may have been the time when Elizabeth married her eldest daughter, fifteen-year-old Mary Hardwick, to Richard Wingfield Esq. of Crowfield, Suffolk. Mary probably got the dowry portion she was entitled to in her father's will, although there are no records to confirm this. The second daughter, Jane Hardwick, was not so fortunate. When she was betrothed to Godfrey Boswell of Penistone, South Yorkshire, the dowry portion from the Hardwick estate to which she was entitled was refused because the Hardwick estate was not productive enough to afford it. Jane and Godfrey made their home at Gunthwaite, Yorkshire.

Ten-year-old Alice Hardwick, who had been born seven months after her father's death, was betrothed to Francis Leche, a relative of Ralph who may have wavered the dowry or come to some alternative financial arrangement. Records from this time are sketchy. Because of the lack of dowry money there were no immediate betrothal plans for eleven-year-old Bess, who was sent into service in the great household of a neighbouring Derbyshire family, that of Sir George and Lady Anne Zouche of Codnor Castle.

Lady Zouche, formerly Anne Gainsford, was a distant cousin of the Hardwicks and the Leekes, and was a close friend and lady-in-waiting to Lady Anne Boleyn. Affectionately called Nan by Anne Boleyn, Lady Zouche had been in the household of Anne Boleyn since 1528, the year after Bess's birth, at which time Henry VIII and his wife Queen Katherine of Aragon were on the throne. After eighteen years of marriage their only surviving heir was Princess Mary, born in 1516, and Katherine was growing too old to bear children. Henry was seeking ways to have his marriage legally annulled so that he could take a new wife, one young and healthy enough to give him sons. His eye fell on Anne Boleyn, who had joined Henry's court as a lady-in-waiting to Queen Katherine. She was flirtatious, but would not yield to him.

Lady Zouche would have seen the situation developing at first hand, having already been in service to Anne Boleyn for five years by the time Anne became the second wife of Henry VIII in 1533. That same year, Sir George Zouche of Codnor became a gentleman pensioner to the king.

Bess was five when the unpopular new queen Anne Boleyn gave birth to a baby daughter, the Princess Elizabeth, on 7 September 1533.

There is every reason to believe that Lady Zouche was present at the birth of the baby Elizabeth and continued to play a major part in such matters as selecting a wet nurse for the new royal baby. Bess was nine when Katherine of Aragon died and when Queen Anne Boleyn stood trial, accused of high treason. In May 1536, Lady Zouche was forced to give evidence of Anne Boleyn's alleged sexual activities. Witnesses were called, and while evidence for the prosecution was very weak Thomas Cromwell nonetheless managed to contrive a case based on a great deal of circumstantial evidence and some salacious details about what Anne had allegedly got up to with her brother.[13]

The decision was a foregone conclusion, and Anne Boleyn was executed. At the end of the sixteenth century, George Wyatt, grandson of poet Sir Thomas Wyatt and one of Anne Boleyn's first biographers, compiled his work largely based on information from the reminiscences of Lady Zouche.[14]

Following Anne Boleyn's execution in May 1536, Lady Zouche continued to serve Anne Boleyn's successor, Henry VIII's third wife Jane Seymour, in the same capacity as lady-in-waiting; however, Jane died of postnatal complications less than two weeks after the birth of her son, Edward. She was the only one of Henry's six wives to receive a queen's funeral, and his only consort to be buried beside him in St George's Chapel, Windsor Castle. Lady Zouche is identified as the 'Mrs Souche' who received a gift of jewelled borders from Queen Jane Seymour and attended her funeral in 1537.

Although the bond between Lady Zouche and the motherless Princess Elizabeth must have been very strong, there is no evidence that she remained in London after 1537. In 1542 she was granted an annuity of £10 'in consideration of her service to the King and the late Queen Jane'.[15]

Lady Anne and Sir George Zouche made their principal home at Codnor Castle, Derbyshire, where they reared eight children: Lucy, born 1511; Anne, born 1513; Audrey, born 1515; Francis, born 1517; William, born 1519; George, born 1521; Margaret, born about 1522; and Sir John Zouch, Kt, son and heir, born about 1524. In 1634, his descendant and namesake John Zouch, born around 1585, sold Codnor Castle and other English estates and moved to Virginia in America.

It was into the Zouche household at Codnor Castle that Bess was sent, and where she would have gained a wealth of experience of the ways of the aristocracy. She would have learnt to dance, hunt, hawk and provide companionship for other family members. She would no doubt have travelled down to London with the family and been aware of all the happenings at court. She could have accompanied Lady Zouche to Hatfield House or Greenwich Palace, then home to Princess Elizabeth, whose rank had been reduced to Lady Elizabeth by her heartless father. It is entirely possible that Bess of Hardwick, daughter of a Derbyshire farmer, and Lady Elizabeth Tudor, daughter of the King of England, met at this early date.

Bess's First Marriage

Bess had been with the Zouche family for around four years when her circumstances changed. There is an unsupported story that Robert Barley or Barlow, a young gentleman from a neighbouring gentry family, was in service in the Zouche household when he became ill. The story goes that Bess nursed him back to health and the two fell in love. According to Nathaniel Johnson, who wrote an account of Bess in 1692 and heard the story from some elderly gentlemen, the couple met in London at the home of Lady Zouche, where Robert lay sick with 'chronical distemper'. Bess, 'being very solicitous to afford him all the help she was able to do in his sickness, ordered his diet and attendance, being then young and very handsome, and he fell deeply in love with her'. Johnson is not the most reliable of chroniclers, however.[16]

Piecing together more reliable information, we obtain a much more plausible account of the relationship between Bess and Robert Barlow. In 1542, Bess's stepfather Ralph Leche had been involved in a legal battle with Arthur Barley/Barlow of Barlow on the Derbyshire/Yorkshire border, this being another gentry family related to the Hardwicks. Bess's great-grandfather had married Margaret Barley/Barlow. As Ralph Leche owned land in the Barlow area, the disagreement could have been due to a land deal that had gone wrong; whatever the cause of the disagreement, judgement was awarded to Leche but had not been paid. This would indicate that Arthur Barlow was either unwilling or unable to meet his financial obligation.[17]

Arthur Barlow had two underage sons, Robert and George, and there is evidence to support the claim that Arthur Barlow approached Elizabeth and Ralph Leche with the proposition that Robert Barlow, his eldest son and heir, who would inherit all the Barlow estates, should become the husband of their third daughter, Bess. Under normal circumstances an agreement would be reached and the dowry passed from the bride's family to the groom's, but both families were experiencing financial problems. As part of the wedding agreement, therefore, instead of Ralph Leche paying Arthur Barlow the wedding dowry that had been specified in John Hardwick's will, the amount owing from the court case would simply be written off. This seemed a favourable situation for all concerned; no money would change hands and both families would reap the advantages of such a union. With everyone in favour, the debt was discharged and everything was finalised for the marriage to take place in the spring of 1543. Although no church records exist from this time, there is a record at Kew; however, the ink is so faded that details such as the date sadly cannot be deciphered.

It is known that the marriage took place in the lifetime of Arthur Barlow, who died a few weeks later on 28 May 1543, at which time his son Robert was thirteen years and ten months old. There is no evidence that Robert and Bess lived together as man and wife, but it can be assumed that Robert and his new bride moved in with his widowed mother and made their home at Barlow Woodseats Hall, situated on the edge of the village of Barlow. There had been a house there since at least 1269, when it was called Barlew Woodsets, meaning 'a house in the wood belonging to Barley'. Deeds dated June 1368 and later refer to Barley Wodesetes.

There is every likelihood that Arthur Barlow knew he was dying and wanted to safeguard his estates as best he could. On his death, 'the entire estate including lands, tenements and premises, descended unto the said Robert Barlow, son and heir'. After the Inquisition Post Mortem, Robert was able to take possession of his lands in December 1543, but being an underage heir meant that the Court of Wards moved in to manage the estates and Robert became a ward.

Because Bess and Robert were man and wife, if Bess's family had been in a financial position to buy the wardship, the Barlow and Hardwick estates could have been combined; however, there was no way that Bess's stepfather could afford the £66 wanted for the wardship. Instead, Godfrey Bosville (Boswell), Bess's brother-in-law, married to her sister Jane, paid the money and Robert Barlow became his ward. It may not be insignificant that Godfrey's brother Ralph Bosville was clerk of the Court of Wards, later becoming very wealthy and buying the rectory manor of Peniston, Yorkshire, which he bestowed on Godfrey.[18]

Bess's marriage should have given her a new measure of respect and independence, but eighteen months after his father's death, Robert became ill and died on Christmas Eve 1544. The young widow was sixteen and very likely still a virgin as Robert was not yet sixteen and the consummation of child marriages was discouraged before this age.

Things must have been in turmoil in the Barlow household. Godfrey Bosville, who had paid out £66 for Robert's wardship only eighteen months previously, lost his money and any control he may have had over the estate. Because there were no children from the eighteen-month marriage, next in line was Robert's twelve-year-old brother George Barlow. There is every possibility that Robert wrote a will and named Godfrey Bosville as trustee in an attempt to prevent the estate going back into wardship, but that is only speculation. There is no evidence that such a will was written, and if it was, it was considered invalid. The estate was taken back by the Court of Wards.

George Barlow was unmarried and malleable, and this was an attractive investment for local landowner Sir Peter Frecheville, who bought the wardship, married George to his daughter Jane and amalgamated the Barlow lands into his own. The Barlow family lost control of their land and property, and this obviously had a detrimental effect. By rights Bess was entitled to a widow's dower, and could claim one-third of the income in rents and revenues from her late husband's estate, so Bess applied to the Barlow family and to Sir Peter Frecheville for her share of the income. It was refused.

This must have been a very harrowing time for the Hardwick/ Leche family. It's very probable that Bess moved out of what could be described as her marital home when her husband died and his brother became the new – although minor – owner of the estate. Until she secured her widow's allowance Bess was probably supported by her family, and there is every likelihood that she moved back to Hardwick. But other than offering her a roof over her head, Elizabeth Leche, Bess's mother, could not help Bess financially as Ralph Leche had again been convicted and sent to debtors' prison in Derby.[19]

There is, however, every likelihood that Elizabeth encouraged Bess to go for what was legally hers. She would have learnt from her own experience with the Court of Wards that sometimes it is necessary to fight for your rights. Bess went to court for her portion, but Sir Peter Frecheville disputed her rights. It has been suggested that Robert's mother, anxious to keep as much income as possible from the Barlow estate, was intent upon siding against Bess. If she testified that before he died her husband did not give his consent to the marriage of Robert, his underage son, the marriage would be null and void. Could she have done that? Could she have lied to prevent Bess being awarded a widow's pension? If this was so, Bess's split with the Barlow family would not have been amicable. Sir Peter Frecheville may have reasoned that being underage and still a virgin disqualified her from receiving a widow's pension. Had the marriage been consummated? She was probably asked to verify this, because according to her witness statement, made under oath at a court hearing in October 1546, she gave her age at the time of her marriage in May 1543 as being 'of tender years', i.e. less than sixteen.[20]

Roughly 100 years later, Margaret, Duchess of Newcastle, Bess's granddaughter by marriage, wrote a book entitled *The Life of William Duke of Newcastle*. In it she wrote that Robert Barlow 'died before they were bedded together, they both being very young'.[21]

Whether this was allowed to colour the situation or not is unclear, but a court battle ensued. Frecheville continued to refuse to pay the dowry, arguing that theoretically no dowry money had been handed over. Frecheville claimed 'every possible legal impediment concerned with the marriage of a minor to delay and fatigue the legal process'. Another part of Frecheville's justification for such delays was that some of the rents claimed by Bess were only leased, not owned by the Barlow estate, and so the case continued. His stalling worked, and it was to take Bess several years and a number of court cases throughout 1545 and 1546 to get anything. In the autumn of 1545, Frecheville offered Bess a small recompense 'at his pleasure' if she would accept a yearly sum and waive her dower rights. Worn down by worry and in a desperate financial state, she was advised by her legal counsel to settle for that. She saw no alternative, and was about to accept when Sir John Chaworth, her late husband's maternal uncle, intervened. His objection secured Bess her one-third dower rights, although the amount was about 10 per cent short of what she claimed was her entitlement. The relief must have been enormous, but she continued to fight for what was legally hers and eventually won her case and compensation, equivalent to half a year's rent.

Bess became the life tenant of a third of the manor of Barlow with 80 messuages (dwelling houses), 7 cottages, 880 acres of land, 260 acres of meadows, 550 acres of pasture, 320 acres of wood, 400 acres of furze and heath, and £8 10s 0d rent with appurtenances for sundry properties in the villages of Barlow, Barlow Lees, Dronfield and Holmsfield. Bess's dower provided her with about £30 a year, perhaps £1,500 in today's currency.[22]

It wasn't a lot of money by any standard, but it gave Bess a small degree of independence and an opportunity to better herself. She may have gone back to reside in the Zouche household, although it's more likely that she decided to move on. The Zouches were related to the Grey family, and it's very likely that through this network Bess gained a position in the household of The Lady Frances Grey, wife of Henry Grey, 3rd Marquess of Dorset. The use of the word 'The' in a title denotes royal status, and in this case, The Lady Frances Grey was granddaughter of King Henry VII, daughter of Mary Tudor, niece of Henry VIII and cousin to Edward, Mary and Elizabeth. Bess Barlow was about to be introduced into the top stratum of Tudor society.

2

Divorced, Beheaded, Died; Divorced, Beheaded, Survived

From 1455 until 1485 there was civil war in England as rival branches of the royal family fought for the throne. This period of strife became known as the Wars of the Roses (in the 19th century) due to the rivalry between the powerful houses of Lancaster and York, represented by a red rose and a white rose respectively. The final and most significant battle was fought at Bosworth, Leicestershire. The Yorkist King Richard III was slain and the crown of England was placed on the head of the victor, a Lancastrian named Henry Tudor, Earl of Richmond. The newly crowned King Henry VII married Elizabeth of York, thus uniting the houses of Lancaster and York, and combined the red and white roses in a red-and-white Tudor rose. The Wars of the Roses had ended and the Tudor reign had begun.

The Reign of the Tudors
Henry VII was a skilful leader, and during his reign England enjoyed peace and prosperity. He fathered four surviving children: Arthur, Henry, Margaret and Mary. His eldest son and heir, Arthur, Prince of Wales, married fifteen-year-old Katherine of Aragon, youngest daughter of the King and Queen of Spain. His eldest daughter, Margaret, married the King of Scotland, and his younger daughter Mary married the King of France, thus cementing England's alliances with Spain, France and Scotland.

After their marriage Arthur and Katherine moved to Ludlow Castle, from where Arthur could rule his principality, but he died within a year. It was a tricky situation, and Katherine's grief was not allowed to get in the way of state business. It was decided that Katherine should marry Arthur's younger brother Henry, who became Henry VIII on the death of his father in 1509. He was just eighteen, and she was twenty three. Common law may not have considered Henry old enough to manage his own affairs, but the Church reckoned him old enough to marry.

They married on 11 June 1509, and shortly after, on 24 June, they were crowned together. The birth of a baby boy on New Year's Day 1511 was greeted with equal jubilation, but within two months the baby was dead. From then on, Katherine's poignant story of miscarriages and stillbirths continued for eighteen years of marriage. The only surviving heir of Henry VIII and Katherine was Princess Mary, born on 18 February 1516. Her birth gave reason to believe a son would soon follow, and indeed it might have done. Katherine was again pregnant in 1518, but so too was Henry's mistress Elizabeth Blount, who bore him a son, Henry Fitzroy. Katherine's baby sadly died, and Henry openly acknowledged Elizabeth Blount's son as his own. When he was six years old, Henry Fitzroy was granted the unprecedented honour of the double dukedoms of Somerset and Richmond. Such honours signalled his place as a member of the extended royal family, making Fitzroy a potentially valuable asset on the diplomatic marriage market and prompting speculation that Henry was considering making the boy his heir. But could a bastard son be in line for the English throne?[1]

In 1527 Henry named his eleven-year-old daughter Mary as Princess of Wales, and she was to set up her own household at Ludlow Castle in Shropshire to rule the principality. It was the first time a woman had been given the title in her own right, and it has never happened since. Katherine would have been both proud and sad to see her daughter moving into the castle where she had lived as the young bride of King Arthur and where she had later watched him die.

Henry making his daughter Princess of Wales was obviously a prelude to her accession as queen regent with the Duke of Richmond as a spare. Katherine's childbearing days were almost over, and the future seemed to be set – but then fate took a hand.

That same year, a French envoy was in London to negotiate yet again the possibility of a marriage between Mary and a French prince. At some point the envoy raised a significant question: didn't the fact that Henry had married his dead brother's widow make the marriage invalid and Mary illegitimate? This suggestion had previously been suppressed, but now Henry started to consider it. In Leviticus 18:16 and 20:21, God had threatened childlessness as the punishment for any that should transgress this law and marry his brother's widow. Henry came to see this as the reason for his failure to produce a son. Katherine was getting past childbearing age, so if he wanted a legitimate son he must remarry. Based on this reading of the Bible, he began to feel that his marriage to Katherine was prohibited by the law of God and therefore invalid.[2]

Henry now had no doubt as to why he had no legitimate sons, and saw himself as the victim of a providential punishment. But Katherine would have none of this. Her own sense of honour and dignity was at stake. She was a Spanish princess, and she was not about to accept any kind of respectable retirement. Henry expected Pope Clement VII to help him annul the marriage, but he wouldn't; the Pope could hardly offend the Holy Roman Emperor, Charles V, by proclaiming that his aunt Katherine had been living in incest for twenty years, and he didn't want to alienate Henry, so he decided to play for time.

Enter Anne Boleyn

Anne Boleyn made her debut at court on 4 March 1522 as a lady-in-waiting to Queen Katherine. She was playfully flirtatious and mysteriously aloof, and quickly established herself as one of the most stylish and accomplished women at the court. The American historian Retha M. Warnicke described Anne as 'the perfect woman courtier ... her carriage was graceful and her French clothes were pleasing and stylish; she danced with ease, had a pleasant singing voice, played the lute and several other musical instruments well, and spoke French fluently ... A remarkable, intelligent, quick-witted young noblewoman ... that first drew people into conversation with her and then amused and entertained them. In short, her energy and vitality made her the centre of attention in any social gathering.' Henry VIII's biographer J. J. Scarisbrick adds that Anne 'revelled in' the attention she received from her admirers.[3]

Men were understandably fascinated by her, and Anne was soon engaged in secret to Henry Percy, son of the Earl of Northumberland.

However, the romance was broken off when Percy's father refused to support their engagement because a betrothal between his son and Lady Mary Talbot had been in place since their adolescence. This wedding duly went ahead. Anne was sent from court in disgrace, but was soon back in the service of Katherine of Aragon.

In 1526, King Henry became enamoured of Anne and began his pursuit.[4] Anne was determined to resist the king's attempts to seduce her. She refused to become his mistress, often retreating to the seclusion of Hever Castle, her family home, where she would spend months away from court. They exchanged letters, which in itself was surprising because Henry had a heavy, awkward style and hated the physical business of writing. A number of the lengthy love letters he wrote to Anne survive today, offering a uniquely intimate record of his feelings; they also suggest that this love affair remained unconsummated.[5]

Anne was determined not to repeat the mistakes of her sister Mary Boleyn, who had been Henry's mistress for a short time before being passed over for another. (It was believed that Mary's children Henry and Catherine Carey were fathered by Henry.) Anne took advantage of Henry's infatuation and the convenient moral quandary. She saw an opportunity and was prepared to take the gamble when she informed Henry that she would only yield to his embraces as his acknowledged queen. Henry was so besotted by her, and so focussed on the new Bible interpretation that explained his lack of sons, that he was determined to find a way to have his marriage to Queen Katherine legally annulled. Only fourteen years earlier Pope Leo X had honoured Henry VIII with the title Defender of the Faith because of his support for the Roman Church, but the Roman Catholic faith believed in marriage for life. It did not recognise, let alone support, the breakup of a marriage, and allied with the new Pope Clement VII's concerns given Katherine's relationship to the Holy Roman Emperor, Henry's request for an annulment was refused. Ill advised, selfish, stubborn and desperate, Henry would later split the English Church from the Roman Church, and in his 1534 Act of Supremacy he would declare himself supreme head of a new Church of England, sparking centuries of religious conflict for the people of Britain. Henry was evidently prepared to change the course of England's history in order to marry Anne Boleyn, hoping that she would bear him strong and healthy sons.

In 1531, Queen Katherine was banished from court. Her rooms were given to Anne, who began to take her place at Henry's side in policy and in state, but not yet in bed.[6] Indeed, Anne Boleyn was already able to grant petitions, receive diplomats, give patronage and exert enormous influence over her future husband on behalf of foreign diplomats. The ambassador from Milan wrote in 1531 that it was essential to have her approval if one wanted to influence the English government, a view corroborated by an earlier French ambassador in 1529. During this period, Anne Boleyn played an important role in England's international position by solidifying an alliance with France. However, public support remained with Queen Katherine. One evening in the autumn of 1531, Anne was dining at a manor house on the River Thames when she was almost seized by a crowd of angry women. Anne just managed to escape by boat.[7] She was never popular, and was referred to by some of her subjects as 'the king's whore' or a 'naughty paike [prostitute]'.[8]

In 1531, in what must have been the cruellest blow of all for Queen Katherine, Henry declared that the fifteen-year-old Princess Mary was a bastard. Henry took the title Princess of Wales from his daughter, declared her illegitimate and announced that from then on she would be known as The Lady Mary.

Henry and Anne were married in a secret ceremony on 14 November 1532. Anne soon became pregnant, and because the first wedding service may have been considered to be unlawful, there was a second wedding service, also private, which took place in London on 25 January 1533, in accordance with the book of court etiquette known as *The Royal Book*.[9] This made the king a bigamist until 23 May 1533, when the marriage of Henry and Katherine was declared null and void. Five days later, on 28 May 1533, the marriage of Henry and Anne was declared to be good and valid.[10]

Katherine was formally stripped of her title as queen and Anne was consequently crowned queen consort on 1 June 1533 in a magnificent ceremony at Westminster Abbey. Henry had spared no expense, and his and Anne's cipher, 'HA' laced in a lover's knot, could be seen everywhere. According to Chapuys, women hated the flashy ex-mistress and as she passed they mockingly chanted 'Ha Ha' in parody of her royal cipher.[11]

The Birth of Princess Elizabeth

After her coronation, Anne settled into a quiet routine to prepare for the birth of her baby at the king's favourite residence, Greenwich Palace. Previously named the Palace of Placentia, the vast complex had been rebuilt between 1498 and 1504 by Henry VII, and it remained a principal royal residence for the next two centuries. This is where Henry VIII had been born forty-two years previously.

Like royal weddings, royal births were a cause for great, elaborate ceremony, all set out in *The Royal Book*. The preparation got underway in August when the queen's bedchamber was prepared for her confinement. A thick carpet was laid on the floor, and joiners built a sort of tent frame that was draped with arras, a rich tapestry woven with gold or silver thread. It was considered advisable to exclude all light and fresh air, so a length of fabric was left hanging loose at just one small window. The queen's canopied bed and the pallet, or day bed, which stood at its foot matched the specially selected hangings. Figurative tapestries with human or animal images were ruled out because it was feared that the images could trigger fantasies in the queen's mind which might lead to the child being deformed.

Gold and silver plate was brought from the jewel house; cups and bowls to stand on the cupboard, plus crucifix, candlesticks and images for the altar. By the third week in August all was ready, and on 26 August a ceremony was held to mark the queen taking her chamber. First she went in procession to hear Mass at the Chapel Royal, which lay at the east end of the river façade, then the company returned to the queen's great chamber, where Anne stood under a cloth of state to symbolise her rank. She took wine and spices with everyone before the Lord Chamberlain called on everyone present to pray that God would give her the 'good hour', meaning a safe delivery. Another procession formed and escorted Anne to the door of her bedchamber, where the males of the court took their leave of her and only women entered. Anne's confinement had now begun.[12]

Anne Boleyn went into labour two weeks later, and gave birth to a baby daughter, Princess Elizabeth, at 3 p.m. on 7 September 1533. Heralds proclaimed the news, and a *Te Deum* was sung in the Chapel Royal, but the birth of a girl was a great disappointment and a huge surprise. All but one of the royal physicians and astrologers had confidently predicted a son. Even the letters announcing the birth had been written in advance and confidently gave thanks to God for sending the queen 'good speed in the deliverance and bringing forth of a prince'. The prepared letters announcing the birth of a prince each had an 's' hastily added, thus thanking God for the birth of a 'princes'. The traditional jousting tournament for the birth of a male heir was cancelled.

The French king had already been asked to stand as the baby prince's godfather, and a letter from Eustace Chapuys, the Imperial Ambassador, to the Holy Roman Emperor stated, 'The King's mistress (*amie*) was delivered of a daughter, to the great regret both of him and the lady, and to the great reproach of the physicians, astrologers, sorcerers, and sorceresses, who affirmed that it would be a male child.'[13]

Despite the disappointment, a magnificent christening was organised in the church of the Observant Friars. Inside the church a large octagonal stage, three steps high and with railings, was built with a reinforced central section to take the weight of the great silver font, which was brought specially from Canterbury. This font had been used for every royal christening since that of Edward, son of Henry VI and Margaret of Anjou. Over it hung a crimson satin canopy fringed with gold, and prior to the service the font was lined with soft linen to ensure the metal did not touch the delicate skin of the baby. The woodwork of the stage was covered in red and blue cloth, the walls were hung with arras, and the doors were decorated with cloth of gold.[14]

Just three days after her birth, everything was ready for the lavish christening. Early in the morning the christening procession assembled, but Henry did not attend. All the walls between the king's place and the church of the Observant Friars were hung with arras, and the way strewed with rushes. The heralds carried their tabards, attendants and male servants carried unlit torches, and lords and ladies carried the equipment needed for the ceremony, including great silver-gilt basins in which the godparents could wash off all traces of the holy oil with which the child was anointed. The Lady Mary of Norfolk carried the pearl-and-stone container that held the chrism, or holy oil. The baby's godmother, the Duchess of Norfolk, carried the child in a mantle of purple velvet, with a long train held by two peers and a peeress – the

Earl of Wiltshire, the Earl of Derby and the Countess of Kent. The dukes of Suffolk and Norfolk were on each side of the duchess. Four barons – Lord Rochford, Lord Hussy, Lord William Howard and Lord Thomas Howard – carried a canopy over the little princess. Her godfather was Thomas Cranmer, Archbishop of Canterbury, and she was christened by the Bishop of London.

As was the tradition, to exorcise the child a pinch of salt was put in her mouth from the gold cellar carried by the Marquess of Dorset. She was christened Elizabeth, probably in honour of both her grandmothers, Elizabeth Howard and Elizabeth of York. She was plunged three times into the holy water, after which she was anointed with chrism, and a chrisom-cloth was then bound over the crown of her head. As a lighted taper was placed in her hand, all the other torches were lit, the heralds put on their tabards and the trumpets rang out in honour of Elizabeth, Princess of England.[15]

People supposedly celebrated with bonfires and rejoicing, but Eustace Chapuys contradicts this in his report to Charles V on 15 September, saying that 'the christening has been like her mother's coronation, very cold and disagreeable, both to the court and to the city, and there has been no thought of having the bonfires and rejoicings usual in such cases.' Which report do we believe?[16]

Anne feared that Katherine's seventeen-year-old daughter Mary might pose a threat to Elizabeth's position, but Henry assured his wife there would be no trouble. When Mary was told to pay her respects to the new baby princess, she burst into tears and declared that she knew of no Princess of England other than herself.

For the first few weeks of her life, the baby Princess Elizabeth was held in a specially prepared nursery suite at Greenwich. However, at just three months old she was given her own household at Hatfield House in Hertfordshire. Although it was only 20 miles north of London, the country air here was thought better for her health. Elizabeth was taken in procession through the streets by her great-uncle to her new home and household. Lady Blanche Troy was appointed lady mistress to baby Elizabeth, overseeing the domestic side of her sizable household. She was put in charge of the four rockers of the princess's cradle, an important task that would keep the baby quiet and amenable.[17]

Lady Margaret Bryan, a baroness whom Elizabeth called 'muggie', became her first carer/governess; Lady Margaret had previously been in the household of Princess Mary. Further humiliation arrived for Mary when her servants and companions were dismissed and she was ordered to move to Hatfield House in a subservient role to the baby Elizabeth. To have been permanently in the presence of her successor must have been torture for the seventeen-year-old Mary. She spent days in her chamber weeping uncontrollably and became ill. She would not acknowledge Elizabeth as a princess and refused to curtsey to her new half-sister.[18]

Although Hatfield was considered to be Elizabeth's main residence at this stage, as was the custom, her household often moved around to other locations. These included Hunsdon, Enfield Palace, Westminster Palace, Whitehall, Richmond Place, Hampton Court and Windsor Castle.[19]

Anne Boleyn presided over a magnificent court. She spent lavish amounts of money on gowns, jewels, headdresses, ostrich-feather fans, riding equipment, furniture and upholstery, maintaining the ostentatious display required by her status. Numerous palaces were renovated to suit the extravagant tastes of the new royal couple. Anne had a larger staff of servants than Katherine; there were more than 250 servants to tend to her personal needs, everyone from priests to stable boys, and more than sixty maids-of-honour who served her and accompanied her to social events.[20]

During this time, Elizabeth was afforded all the courtesy due to a princess of the royal blood. Anne Boleyn chose her clothes and sewed little dresses, but Elizabeth also had her own dressmaker named William Loke who would have been very aware of the importance of the clothes made for Princess Elizabeth.

The Downfall of Anne Boleyn

Despite the opulent surroundings, Anne's relationship with her husband was turning sour. Although desirable in a mistress, Anne's sharp intelligence, political acumen and forward manners were considered unacceptable in a wife. Henry wanted a subservient queen to act in the same manner as his former wife Katherine, but Anne was a totally different character. When she dared to remonstrate with him about some woman who had caught his eye, he told her to be silent as her betters had been before her.

After a stillbirth or miscarriage around the end of 1534 the royal couple spent the summer of 1535 on progress, and in September 1535 they stayed at the Seymour family home in Wiltshire. By then Henry's waning interest in Anne was obvious, and this may have been when the king noticed Jane Seymour. Opinion is divided as to how Jane felt about being the new object of Henry's affections. Some see Jane's calm and gentle demeanour as evidence that she didn't really understand the role of political pawn that she was playing for her family. On the other hand, Jane may have willingly fallen into her role and actively sought to entice the king.

The Christmas of 1535 must have been horribly strained. Henry and his wife Anne, who was pregnant again, held court as usual, and the baby princess Elizabeth would have been there for part of the Christmas period. It would be the last time she would see her mother.

Katherine of Aragon was at Kimbolton Castle in Cambridgeshire, where she had been sent in April 1534 for refusing to give up her status or deny the validity of her marriage. Apart from a few servants, she was isolated from the world to prevent her conspiring to bring about a rebellion in favour of her daughter Mary. But the fenland climate was not good for her health, and that Christmas there were reports that she was seriously ill.

On 8 January 1536, news of Katherine of Aragon's death reached the king. Anne attempted to make peace with her stepdaughter Mary, who rebuffed her overtures; perhaps she had heard the rumours that were circulating that her mother had been poisoned by Anne and/or Henry. These began after the discovery during her embalming that her heart was blackened. Modern medical experts are in agreement that this was not the result of poisoning, but of cancer of the heart, something which was not understood at the time.[21] Katherine's body was carried in procession to the Peterborough Abbey – now Peterborough Cathedral.

On the day that Katherine of Aragon was buried, Anne miscarried a baby which appeared to be a male child. Some believe that the miscarriage was brought on because Henry had turned his affections to Jane Seymour and had made no attempt to hide evidence of his new love. Jane would flaunt her favour even in front of the current queen, and just hours before the miscarriage Anne had entered a room and been shocked to see Jane Seymour sitting on Henry's lap. Anne had become hysterical at the thought of being replaced. Whatever the cause for the miscarriage, the royal marriage was over.[22]

As Anne recovered from her miscarriage, Henry declared that he had been seduced into marrying Anne Boleyn by means of 'sortilege' – a French term indicating either deception or spells. He concentrated on finding a means of getting rid of Anne Boleyn, and his new mistress Jane Seymour was quickly moved into royal quarters. Henry decided that Anne was guilty of adultery, incest and high treason, and she was arrested while at Greenwich Palace. There was little if any evidence to support the case, apart from that obtained from a court musician named Smeaton under torture.

The case against Anne was primarily engineered by her former ally Thomas Cromwell, but it was Henry himself, bent on undoing her by any means, who issued the crucial instructions. His officials, including Cromwell, simply carried them out. The law at the time was an engine of state, not a mechanism for justice. Despite the flimsiness of the claims, a case was made against her.[23]

Historians and biographers agree that these charges against Anne were false, but they were all Henry needed to sign her execution warrant. It is thought that Anne avoided criticising Henry's actions to save baby Elizabeth and her family from further consequences, but even under extreme pressure she would not confess to any guilt.

On 2 May 1536, Anne was arrested and taken to the Tower of London by barge. According to Eric Ives, historian and author of *The Life and Death of Anne Boleyn*, it is likely that she entered through the Court Gate in the Byward Tower rather than the Traitors' Gate. In the Tower she demanded to know the location of her father and 'swete broder', as well as the charges against her, before collapsing.

In what is reputed to be her last letter to King Henry, dated 6 May, she wrote:

> Sir, Your Grace's displeasure, and my imprisonment are things so strange unto me, as what to write, or what to excuse, I am

altogether ignorant. Whereas you send unto me (willing me to confess a truth, and so obtain your favour) by such an one, whom you know to be my ancient professed enemy. I no sooner received this message by him, than I rightly conceived your meaning; and if, as you say, confessing a truth indeed may procure my safety, I shall with all willingness and duty perform your demand.

But let not your Grace ever imagine, that your poor wife will ever be brought to acknowledge a fault, where not so much as a thought thereof preceded. And to speak a truth, never prince had wife more loyal in all duty, and in all true affection, than you have ever found in Anne Boleyn: with which name and place I could willingly have contented myself, if God and your Grace's pleasure had been so pleased. Neither did I at any time so far forget myself in my exaltation or received Queenship, but that I always looked for such an alteration as I now find; for the ground of my preferment being on no surer foundation than your Grace's fancy, the least alteration I knew was fit and sufficient to draw that fancy to some other object. You have chosen me, from a low estate, to be your Queen and companion, far beyond my desert or desire. If then you found me worthy of such honour, good your Grace let not any light fancy, or bad council of mine enemies, withdraw your princely favour from me; neither let that stain, that unworthy stain, of a disloyal heart toward your good grace, ever cast so foul a blot on your most dutiful wife, and the infant-princess your daughter. Try me, good king, but let me have a lawful trial, and let not my sworn enemies sit as my accusers and judges; yea let me receive an open trial, for my truth shall fear no open flame; then shall you see either my innocence cleared, your suspicion and conscience satisfied, the ignominy and slander of the world stopped, or my guilt openly declared. So that whatsoever God or you may determine of me, your grace may be freed of an open censure, and mine offense being so lawfully proved, your grace is at liberty, both before God and man, not only to execute worthy punishment on me as an unlawful wife, but to follow your affection, already settled on that party, for whose sake I am now as I am, whose name I could some good while since have pointed unto, your Grace being not ignorant of my suspicion therein. But if you have already determined of me, and that not only my death, but an infamous slander must bring you the enjoying of

34

your desired happiness; then I desire of God, that he will pardon your great sin therein, and likewise mine enemies, the instruments thereof, and that he will not call you to a strict account of your unprincely and cruel usage of me, at his general judgment-seat, where both you and myself must shortly appear, and in whose judgment I doubt not (whatsoever the world may think of me) mine innocence shall be openly known, and sufficiently cleared. My last and only request shall be, that myself may only bear the burden of your Grace's displeasure, and that it may not touch the innocent souls of those poor gentlemen, who (as I understand) are likewise in strait imprisonment for my sake. If ever I found favour in your sight, if ever the name of Anne Boleyn hath been pleasing in your ears, then let me obtain this request, and I will so leave to trouble your Grace any further, with mine earnest prayers to the Trinity to have your Grace in his good keeping, and to direct you in all your actions. From my doleful prison in the Tower, this sixth of May;

Your most loyal and ever faithful wife, Anne Boleyn

Four men were eventually accused and tried in Westminster on 12 May 1536. Weston, Brereton and Norris publicly maintained their innocence, and only the tortured Smeaton pleaded guilty. Three days later, Anne and George Boleyn were tried separately in the Tower of London before a jury of twenty-seven peers. Anne was accused of adultery, incest and high treason, and was sentenced to be burnt at the stake.[24]

On 14 May, Cranmer declared Anne's marriage to Henry null and void. George Boleyn and the other accused men were executed on 17 May 1536. Henry commuted Anne's sentence from burning to beheading, and boasted that he was being merciful because he brought an expert swordsman from Saint Omer in France to perform the execution rather than the standard headsman with an axe. On the morning of Friday 19 May, Anne Boleyn was executed in the French style, kneeling upright, rather than prostrate on the block, within the Tower precincts. She was then buried in an unmarked grave in the Chapel of St Peter ad Vincula. Her skeleton was identified during renovations of the chapel in 1876, and Anne's final resting place is now marked in the marble floor.

3

Elizabeth's Formative Years

Elizabeth was probably at the royal manor at Hunsdon in Hertfordshire when her mother was arrested. It is documented that Mary had been moved there from Eltham at the end of January, and as Mary was part of her half-sister's household at the time it is assumed that Elizabeth was at Hunsdon House too. She wasn't yet three years old, and was probably too young to be greatly affected by her mother's sudden extinction, but her lifestyle would never be quite the same again. Elizabeth never really knew her mother, but she kept a tiny picture of her in a ring.

For the first two years of her life Elizabeth had been treated with utmost respect, but her fortunes changed with her mother's downfall. Her parents' marriage was annulled, making it as void as her father's marriage to Katherine of Aragon, and as such the law regarded both Mary and Elizabeth as illegitimate, with no claim to the English throne. Elizabeth was stripped of her title of princess, as her sister had previously been, to become simply The Lady Elizabeth.

Within twenty-four hours of Anne Boleyn's execution, Jane Seymour and Henry VIII were formally betrothed and on 30 May they were married at Whitehall Palace.[1] Unlike Henry's previous two queens, Jane Seymour never had a coronation. It wasn't until early 1537 that Jane became pregnant, and hopes were high that at last there would be a son to inherit the Tudor throne. Princess Elizabeth and her sister Mary now shared a common bond; they were both neglected by their father and ignored by the court in general.

While her mother was alive Elizabeth would have been lavishly dressed in fine clothes befitting her station, but this plentiful supply appears to have dried up on the death of Anne Boleyn. Elizabeth's carer Lady Bryan was forced to write to secretary Thomas Cromwell, stating that Elizabeth was fast outgrowing her infant clothes and there was no household money to properly clothe her. She complained that Elizabeth 'hath neither gown, nor kirtle, nor petticoat'. The rest of the letter dealt with things like Elizabeth's teething problems and where she should eat. Lady Bryan and Sir John Shelton, the male head of the household, could not agree on this. Lady Bryan wanted Elizabeth to continue to have meals in her chamber, where she would eat and drink what was suitable for her age. Sir John wanted her to 'dine and sup every day at the board of estate'. This shows that there was no real question of Elizabeth losing her royal status; the only issue seemed to be how soon she would assume it by dining in state. Understandably, Lady Bryan was anxious to know what path she was to take regarding Elizabeth's upbringing.

The Birth of Prince Edward

On 12 October, the Feast of St Edward, a prince was born at Hampton Court Palace. Henry's longed-for son was named Edward and was baptised on 15 October 1537. In a show of family unity, Mary, daughter of Katherine of Aragon, was godmother, and Elizabeth, daughter of Anne Boleyn, despite being carried herself, carried the chrisom cloth. However, tragedy soon struck. Jane Seymour was reported as very ill on 23 October, and she died the next day, two weeks after giving birth.

The king was devastated at the loss of Jane Seymour and gave her a royal burial at the Chapel of St George in Windsor Castle. She would be the only one of Henry's six wives to be buried with him. But Elizabeth didn't just lose a stepmother; she also lost her carer. Lady Margaret Bryan was moved to the royal nursery, entrusted with the care of the motherless baby Edward.

Queen Jane Seymour had always treated Elizabeth with kindness and affection on the few occasions she had been allowed to attend court, but there is no evidence that she was a mother figure to her little stepdaughter. That role went to Lady Bryan's replacement, Katherine Champernowne, a well-educated and affectionate governess who was appointed to the royal household in October 1536. The Champernownes were an ancient family whose pedigree stretched back hundreds of years. Being young and unmarried, Katherine, whom the four-year-old Elizabeth affectionately called Kat, could not assume the position of lady mistress, and the title remained with Lady Troy. Kat was a sweet, motherly lady, and was completely devoted to Elizabeth. She became an important figure in Elizabeth's life, as a friend and confidante. Kat was responsible for the intellectual, spiritual and emotional development of the four-year-old for the next thirteen years and was perhaps the only stable person in Elizabeth's early life.[2]

Henry was soon looking for another wife, and put himself forward as a suitor for the recently widowed Mary of Guise, twenty-two-year-old daughter of Antoinette of Bourbon and Claud, Count of Guise. Mary had a three-year-old son, Francis, the new Duke of Longueville, by her first marriage so was clearly capable of bearing children. Apparently Henry referred approvingly to her height, to which Mary of Guise wittily replied that although her body was big, her neck was very small. She spurned Henry's proposal, and in January 1538 a marriage contract was drawn up between Mary of Guise and the recently widowed James V of Scotland.[3]

If Henry was dejected at Mary of Guise's refusal to marry him, he didn't take long to get over it. Soon negotiations were underway for a union between Henry and Anne of Cleves, a German princess, and the two were married on 6 January 1539 at Greenwich Palace. However, the two were not compatible. Henry insisted that he had been misled over Anne's looks, and used her alleged bad appearance and his resulting lack of desire to consummate the marriage as the reason for the invalidity of the marriage. It was hardly the image Henry wanted to project – impotent on his wedding night. The marriage was annulled 9 July 1540.

Wife number five was sixteen-year-old Catherine Howard, who married Henry on 28 July 1540 at Oatlands Palace in Surrey, just two weeks after the annulment of his marriage to Anne of Cleves. Catherine was a daughter of Lord Edmund Howard, whose sister Elizabeth was the mother of Anne Boleyn. Therefore, Catherine and Anne were cousins, and Catherine and Elizabeth were first cousins once removed. Catherine's youth, prettiness and vivacity captivated the middle-aged sovereign, who claimed he had never known her like. Henry no doubt thought he was rediscovering his youth by marrying a voluptuous young woman, but instead he was preparing the ground for his own humiliation. By 1541, Catherine's well-known indiscretions with courtiers Culpeper and Dereham were causing a crisis in the royal court. In November 1541 she was stripped of her title as queen after just sixteen months, and three months later, on 13 February 1542, she was beheaded on the grounds of treason for committing adultery while married to the King.

Elizabeth's Childhood

The young Elizabeth was said to be very distressed by the death of her stepmother Catherine Howard. Elizabeth was eight by this time, and her childhood must have been extremely confusing, with people coming and going with alarming regularity – not least her stepmothers. She spent time at Greenwich Palace, where her father held court, enjoyed jousting and inspecting his fleet. There's a tree in the garden there known as Queen Elizabeth's Oak, around which she reputedly played as a child.[4]

Elizabeth was an extremely bright child, and Katherine Champernowne would have taught her the alphabet and the rudiments of the English language. Elizabeth would have learnt to write on parchment and to read from a horn book, a piece of parchment usually pasted on to a small wooden board with a handle and covered with a thin plate of transparent horn. A horn book would have displayed the alphabet in both small and capital letters. The Elizabethan alphabet contained just twenty-four letters, lacking our 'j' and 'u', which were represented by 'i' and 'v' respectively. The Lord's Prayer in English was also included in the horn book, together with the mark of the cross, so the alphabet detailed in the horn book was known as the 'christcross-row' or 'chris-cross'.

By the time she was five years old Elizabeth would have been taught a range of different lessons as part of a standard curriculum for the royal children. Katherine of Aragon had commissioned one of the leading Spanish scholars of the day, Juan Luis Vives, author of *The Education of a Christian Woman* (1524), to design a programme of education especially for her daughter Mary. This included not only the traditional female accomplishments of spinning and weaving, but a humanist academic programme of grammar and languages. Her education also ensured that she was prodigiously devout in a conventional way, but Mary was not an academic like her younger sister.[5]

Elizabeth's studies included languages, grammar, theology, history, rhetoric, logic, philosophy, arithmetic, literature, geometry and music. Elizabeth was a serious child, and had an amazing capacity for understanding which enabled her to learn new subjects with great ease and enthusiasm. Her education included further non-academic subjects befitting a lady of her rank and status – sewing, embroidery, dancing, archery, riding and hunting – and she also enjoyed playing, just like other children. Elizabeth praised Kat's early devotion to her studies by stating that she took 'great labour and pain in bringing of me up in learning and honesty'.

When Edward was five, Henry again approached Mary of Guise with a marriage proposal; this time, though, it was on behalf of his heir. On 8 December 1542, Mary of Guise had given birth to Mary Stuart (Mary Queen of Scots), daughter of James V of Scotland. Just six days later, on 14 December, the infant Mary became Queen of Scotland after the death of her father. A marriage between Edward and the infant Mary would mend the relationship between the two warring countries, but again Henry was turned down.[6]

On 12 July 1543 King Henry married his sixth wife, Katherine Parr. She was a kind, considerate stepmother who took a great interest in the upbringing of Elizabeth and Edward. Katherine encouraged Henry to become closer to all of his children. She was a motherly lady who did her utmost to give the royal children a family home. She liked to have the children around her, and did much to reconcile Elizabeth and Mary to their father. She also instigated their return to court.

During a stay at the royal court, however, Elizabeth managed to offend her father profoundly, and for this she was banished from his presence. What exactly this offence was remains unknown – perhaps a remark or question about her mother or Katherine Howard, or perhaps an opinion offered on religion or one of Henry's policies. Henry's reaction was alarming, but with Katherine Parr's intervention the episode blew over, and Elizabeth was allowed back to court.

Elizabeth and her half-sister Mary were never close. There was a seventeen-year age gap between them, they were of different religions, had different family connections and very different personalities.

The mere four-year age difference between Edward and Elizabeth produced a much stronger bond; Edward called Elizabeth 'Sweet Sister Temperance'. The two were of the same religion, and both shared a passion for learning. In 1544 Edward entered his sixth year, and as heir to the throne it was considered of great importance for him to have tutors ranked among the greatest minds of the century. It's highly probable that Elizabeth was taught by them, too. She was a gifted student and her talent was appreciated by all those who had the privilege to teach her. Jean Belmain was employed to teach French, Richard Cox (Provost of Eton) taught Greek and Latin, and John Dee taught mathematics, astronomy and astrology.

Another pupil in the royal classroom was Robert Dudley, the fifth of John Dudley's thirteen children. John Dudley was Earl of Warwick, Duke of Northumberland, and Protector of England during the reign of Edward VI. Born on 24 June 1532, his son Robert first met seven-year-old Elizabeth when he was eight years old, and they became lifelong friends. Robert was an intelligent boy and certainly a match for Elizabeth intellectually, but he had little interest in the classics. His passions, even as a youngster, were mathematics, astronomy and astrology, no doubt due to the influence of the remarkable John Dee, the noted mathematician, astronomer, astrologer, occultist, navigator and imperialist. Dee straddled the worlds of science and magic just as they were becoming distinguishable, and also devoted much of his life to the study of alchemy, divination and Hermetic philosophy. He was one of the most learned men of his age, and trained many of the men who conducted England's voyages of discovery.

William Grindal was appointed as personal tutor to Elizabeth, but died of the plague in 1548. He was replaced by Roger Ascham, a well-known scholar of the day. He was responsible for tutoring other talented students, but he regarded Elizabeth as his brightest star. As Elizabeth would have been fifteen then, her education obviously continued well past this age. Ascham praised Elizabeth for her aptitude in learning languages and for her good memory. He also remarked that Elizabeth had the intelligence of a man. This was regarded as the highest compliment in the Tudor period.

Great attention was given to the study of languages, and Elizabeth was able to speak fluently in six: French, Greek, Latin, Spanish, Welsh and, of course, English. Roger Ascham's most widely known and accepted educational device was the art of double translation. This involved translating work from one language to another, then translating it back again without losing the meaning. Ascham wrote that Elizabeth developed a style that 'grows out of the subject; chaste because it is suitable, and beautiful because it is clear … Her ears are so well practised in discriminating all these things and her judgement is so good, that in all Greek, Latin, and English compositions there is nothing so loose on the one hand or so concise on the other which she does not immediately attend to, and either reject with disgust or receive with pleasure as the case may be.'

Under the Third Succession Act in 1544 Henry bequeathed the throne to his son Edward, followed by Mary and then Elizabeth; by restoring Mary and Elizabeth in line, Henry was ignoring the laws that excluded illegitimate children from inheriting the throne of England.[7]

In 1545, when Elizabeth was twelve, Katherine Champernowne married John Ashley, a distant cousin of Anne Boleyn, so Elizabeth and Katherine became related through marriage. She became known as Kat Ashley. As well as Kat, Elizabeth's immediate household in her teenage years included Blanche and Thomas Parry – the two were probably brother and sister. Blanche taught Elizabeth some of her native Welsh language, and remained a close friend and confidante until her death in the late 1580s. Thomas Parry was appointed steward to Elizabeth and also became a devoted servant of long standing. When Elizabeth became queen she rewarded Thomas Parry's services with a knighthood, a seat on her Privy Council and the appointments of Controller of her Household and Master of the Court of Wards and Liveries. Another member of the household loyal to Elizabeth was Matthew Parker, responsible for her spiritual well-being. Mary hated him because of his Protestant beliefs, but when Elizabeth eventually became queen she made him Archbishop of Canterbury.

The Death of Henry VIII

By 1546, Henry was far from well. He had a great ulcer on his leg that troubled him immensely, and his enormous weight hindered his mobility considerably. It was becoming clear to all around him that his days were numbered. He died on 28 January 1547. Elizabeth was with her brother, Edward, at the royal palace of Enfield or Ashridge when they were told of their father's death. She and her brother cried bitterly, holding each other close. Both children knew their lives were about to change a great deal, and their tears may well have been as much from fear for the future as from grief for the death of their magnificent – if at times tyrannical – father. Both were now orphans. Elizabeth was thirteen years of age, and Edward was King of England at the tender age of nine. They were both at risk of exploitation from some of the most powerful men at the Tudor court.[8]

All three of Henry's children were taken back to court in the immediate aftermath of their father's death and plans were soon underway for Edward's coronation, which took place on 31 January 1547. When Katherine Parr, now dowager queen, took her household from court and retired to the Old Manor in Chelsea, it was considered unfitting for two unmarried ladies to remain in a court without a female household in which they could serve. Instead, Katherine Parr became Elizabeth's guardian, and Mary and Elizabeth were expected to join the entourage of their widowed stepmother. There is no evidence that Mary ever moved into Katherine's household; there is plenty of evidence to support the story that Elizabeth did.[9]

Because of the young age of the new king, Katherine, as his stepmother, had expected to be appointed regent.[10] Instead, his ambitious uncle Edward Seymour, Duke of Somerset and brother of the late queen Jane Seymour, took control to rule in Edward's place until he came of age. Katherine was annoyed at the appointment of Edward Seymour, who not only made himself the most powerful man in England but also gave himself the title Lord Protector.[11]

Edward Seymour monopolised all real power over the boy king, but he had a rival in his brother Thomas Seymour, Lord High Admiral of England, who wanted to share the authority. There was much rivalry and bitterness between the Seymour brothers, who were both powerful, ambitious men. To his contemporaries, Thomas Seymour was forceful and reckless – and also, very attractive to women. He had previously shown interest in marrying either of Henry's daughters, and he had been close with Katherine Parr before she became the wife of King Henry. Sir Nicholas

Throckmorton described Thomas Seymour as 'hardy, wise and liberal ... fierce in courage, courtly in fashion, in personage stately, in voice magnificent, but somewhat empty of matter'.[12]

Katherine and Thomas's earlier plans for a future together had been shattered when King Henry sought Katherine for his wife. She was not able to turn down the King of England, but after Henry's death she was free to marry Thomas. Because custom dictated that a royal widow, 'the white queen', must reside in seclusion for forty days to check whether she was pregnant with the heir to the throne, it was necessary for Thomas Seymour to court Katherine in secret. Many saw this clandestine approach as underhanded, a devious attempt by Thomas to gain precedence over his brother by courting the dowager queen, but few seem to have taken Katherine's feelings into account.

Katherine had been married three times previously – twice out of duty. She was a great and pious lady who had published two radical volumes of religious writing, and Henry had described her as having 'great love, obedience, chasteness of life and wisdom'. She would not have succumbed to Thomas Seymour's advances if she had not been genuinely in love with him, and there is no reason to suppose that the feeling was not reciprocated in full. Thomas and Katherine were married in May 1547, four months after Henry's death. They should have obtained permission to marry from Thomas's brother Edward, as Lord Protector, and the Privy Council, but they knew it would not have been granted. The marriage was considered too hasty by many.[13]

Edward Seymour and his pompous, overbearing wife Anne Seymour (*née* Stanhope) took the marriage as a personal insult and a means of appropriating power to gain superiority. They began to turn many people in court against Katherine and Thomas, and to demonstrate her hatred Anne procured the queen's jewels, which by right were Katherine's, and kept them herself.

The Thomas Seymour Scandal
After the marriage, Katherine and Thomas moved into the Seymours' principal seat of Sudeley Castle in Gloucestershire, taking with them the fourteen-year-old Princess Elizabeth and their respective households. Also in the household was the nine-year-old Lady Jane Grey, Edward's first cousin once removed. Being the same age as Edward and great-granddaughter of Henry VII, she was being considered as a future wife

for King Edward, and was duly sent to live in the household of the dowager queen to prepare her for her future role.

Katherine and Thomas were happy, Elizabeth was treated like the daughter Katherine never had, and for the first time in her life Elizabeth was living in a happy family unit. Thomas Seymour managed to gain the approval of the young King Edward and was forgiven for the secret marriage to his stepmother. The relationship between Katherine and Thomas was strong and loving, and when in November 1547 Katherine announced that she was pregnant, they were all ecstatic. The future looked good – but things were starting to go wrong.

There were stories that Thomas was visiting Elizabeth in her bedchamber in the morning before she was dressed. There was romping and laughter. No one knows how far these romps went, but according to the gossip Thomas became more than a little familiar, if not intimate, with Elizabeth, tickling her, slapping her on her behind as she lay in her bed, and coming into her room in his nightclothes. Her governess, Kat Ashley, thought this scandalous, and reported it to Katherine, who dismissed it as innocent fun. She even joined in the romps on a few occasions. That in itself would suggest that there was nothing untoward in their relationship. It is doubtful that Katherine would have condoned any inappropriate behaviour, and Elizabeth's ever-faithful servant Kat Ashley certainly wouldn't. In the Tudor age, bedchambers served many purposes and weren't quite so private as they may sound. Kings held audiences there, guests would be entertained there and, in a busy household where peace and quiet was difficult to find, a bedchamber would offer a quiet retreat for the immediate family and a select few. It was not unusual to have a portrait painted with the bedchamber featured in the background, as Henry VIII did in his illustrated Book of Psalms. In the portrait he is reading in his bedchamber, and it wasn't because he was short of other rooms.[14]

Thomas Seymour must have been a very romantic figure for the young Princess Elizabeth, who no doubt had a teenage crush on this handsome, bold, energetic and charming man. He is said to have snatched kisses, stolen embraces and played with her maids, which would suggest that he was a true ladies' man. Even though Kat Ashley 'bade him go away in shame', she is said to have found him more amusing than dangerous. It's doubtful that the young princess Elizabeth would have felt at all threatened by his behaviour. She would have been flattered by his attention and probably infatuated by his boldness, It was said that she bore him affection.[15]

Just what occurred between Thomas and Elizabeth will never be known for sure, but gossip and rumours tend to be exaggerated. It has been said that Thomas had a key to Elizabeth's bedchamber so that he could enter as and when he pleased. He would enter clad only in his nightshirt and gown, and if she was still in bed he'd yank back the covers and leap in. Katherine supposedly caught them kissing, or perhaps even in bed together. There's another story of a strange incident which took place in the garden. Seemingly, Thomas cut Elizabeth's gown into 100 pieces, aided and abetted by Katherine. Whether this was done as some sort of silly dare or wager is unclear, but apparently at this stage a very indignant Kat Ashley stepped in and reprimanded them all for scandalous behaviour that risked wrecking Elizabeth's reputation. There is no evidence to support these stories of familiarity, but that didn't stop the ensuing scandal. Obviously the situation couldn't be allowed to continue, and Thomas was told to cease any form of relationship with the young princess in order to prevent further upset. An indignant Thomas retorted, 'By God's precious soul, I mean no evil, and I will not leave it!'[16]

It was probably Kat Ashley who finally stopped this madcap behaviour when in early 1548 she arranged for Elizabeth to leave Sudeley Castle and the Seymour household. Elizabeth was sent to stay with Kat's sister Joan and her husband Sir Anthony Denny at Cheshunt. This started further rumours that Elizabeth was pregnant by Thomas Seymour and that she had gone to the house of Thomas Parry, her cofferer, to give birth to the child.

There was no animosity between Katherine and Elizabeth. They exchanged affectionate letters after Elizabeth left the household. Katherine obviously missed her, and even suggested she returned to relieve the boredom of her confinement, but under the circumstances that would have been rather irregular. Elizabeth sent her greetings, joining her wishes with those of the Dennys and Kat Ashley for Katherine's 'most lucky deliverance'.

Katherine gave birth to a girl at Sudeley Castle on 30 August, but six days later the new mother died of puerperal fever. She was buried at Sudeley. Now a widower, Thomas Seymour was free to marry again, and before long, perhaps in order to safeguard Elizabeth's reputation, he decided to renew his relationship with the young princess. Despite several attempts to remove her from the succession, Elizabeth was in Henry's will as his heir; she was therefore a most sought-after bride. In accordance with the late king's wishes, Elizabeth had to obtain permission to marry or lose her inheritance, and understandably Thomas Seymour wanted to know what this meant in practice. He approached the potential marriage like a business arrangement, and therefore broached the subject of finance with Thomas Parry, Elizabeth's chief accounting officer.

Because Thomas did not appear to be in any great hurry to disband his late wife's household, when news of his plans got around many claimed that he intended to keep Katherine's ladies-in-waiting so that they could attend his new bride. There is another theory, however, which suggests that Thomas Seymour was backing a marriage between King Edward and Lady Jane Grey, who had been living at Sudeley prior to Katherine's death, and that he wanted to retain the household for her (more on this in the next chapter). Whatever the reason, he was not to be at his household for long.

The jealousy between Thomas and his brother Edward was still smouldering, and although Edward Seymour still monopolised all real power over the boy king, he kept the boy short of money and luxuries. Thomas remedied this by supplying such things to the grateful young king, but his ultimate aim was to displace his brother both in the young king's affections and as his legal adviser and regent. The all-powerful Edward Seymour was not one to give up easily, however, and he reacted by banning Thomas from seeing the young king. Incensed, Thomas took matters into his own hands. On the night of 16 January 1549, he surreptitiously entered the Privy Gardens at Hampton Court. His secretive manner alerted one of King Edward's pet spaniels, and to stop the dog barking Thomas Seymour shot and killed it.[17] The next day, Thomas Seymour was arrested and accused of trying to break into the king's apartments with a loaded gun. This was interpreted in the most menacing light, and he was sent to the Tower of London.[18]

To make a case against Thomas Seymour, it was necessary to show him in the worst possible light – as an atheist, a debaucher of women and a traitor. There was no doubt that Elizabeth and her servants would be interrogated, and it's very likely that Elizabeth took advice from Sir Anthony Denny and William Paulet on how to handle this. They would have discussed strategies, and Elizabeth, Kat Ashley and Parry will have agreed tactics to cope with their forthcoming ordeal. Under interrogation they were to agree that Elizabeth was prepared to entertain Thomas Seymour's advances only subject to the agreement of the council. This advice probably saved Elizabeth from a fate similar to Thomas Seymour. She would be quite aware that under the terms of her father's will she was to receive a dowry of £10,000 on her marriage 'to any outward potentate' and an income of £3,000 a year before her marriage. If, however, she was to marry without the consent of the council, she was to lose her place in the succession and be penalised with a reduced financial provision.[19]

As expected, on 16 January 1549, Kat Ashley and Thomas Parry were detained and questioned about the relationship between Elizabeth and Thomas Seymour. The Privy Council also sent Sir Robert Tyrwhitt to Hatfield to interrogate Elizabeth, but she kept a cool head. It was obvious from her answers that she liked Thomas Seymour, but she denied any scandal or bad behaviour and swore she was still a virgin. Elizabeth confidently withstood all interrogation from Tyrwhitt and her frustrated interrogator reported of her that 'she hath a very good wit and nothing is gotten of her but by great policy.'

On 28 January Elizabeth sent a letter to Edward Seymour, the Protector, requiring the Privy Council to counter the rumour that she was in the Tower and pregnant with Thomas Seymour's child, as these were shameful slanders that the council should officially repudiate. They did nothing. Then, at the beginning of February, Elizabeth was told that Kat Ashley had revealed details of the romps and frolics that had taken place at Sudeley Castle; however, she did not let this dent her dignity.

Elizabeth's loyalty to her servants was one of her enduring characteristics. She again wrote to the Protector, this time requesting that the council be good to Kat Ashley and her husband John; Kat because of her care in bringing up the young princess, and John because he was Elizabeth's kinsman. There was no mention of Thomas Parry, whom Tyrwhitt had revealed to be an embezzler abusing his office to cheat Elizabeth. The Ashleys were released from the Tower on 26 February.

Despite the efforts to slander Elizabeth and Thomas, the court could find nothing more than that Seymour was a debaucher of women. However, next came the examination of Thomas's alleged attempt to kidnap King Edward on the night he had shot the dog. Both Elizabeth and Thomas were questioned, and although Elizabeth was not charged, on 22 February the council officially accused Thomas Seymour of thirty-three charges of treason. He was found guilty and executed on 10 March 1549.[20]

Edward Seymour had finally solved the problem of his brother, but this fratricide was more than just damaging to his reputation – it would ultimately destroy him. He was relieved of his position and his power, and his place was taken by John Dudley, Earl of Warwick, the father of Elizabeth's lifelong friend Robert Dudley.

The Court of Augmentations

Never a strong boy, King Edward was utterly reliant upon those around him; with this in mind it must have really alarmed him to be told that his uncle and half-sister had been plotting against him. However, it may have all been a smokescreen to hide what was really going on.

In 1536, during the reign of Henry VIII, the Court of Augmentations had been set up to establish a centre able to administer the enormous increase in the Crown's property following Henry's dissolution of the monasteries. William Cavendish, who was later to become Bess of Hardwick's second husband, was appointed one of its ten auditors. Ten years later, in the early months of 1546, the Court of Augmentation was winding down. When Edward came to the throne in February 1547, the Court of Augmentation became a free-for-all as avaricious councillors greedily helped themselves to land and property at the king's expense. The Court of Augmentations was mockingly called the Court of Diminutions, a reference to how it spent most of its time giving the king's property away – and Princess Elizabeth was a prime beneficiary of this.

When Elizabeth left the Denny household after the Seymour affair, she set up her own household at Hatfield with 140 servants. Hatfield was where she had been sent aged three months and where she had spent time over the years. Hatfield had originally belonged to the Bishop of Ely, but Henry VIII had used it for twenty years before formally acquiring it in 1538. Subsequently Sir Anthony Denny was given responsibility for the administration of the property, which is no doubt how Elizabeth was able to move there after leaving the Denny household in 1548. A year later, Hatfield was acquired by the now powerful John Dudley, Earl of Warwick, but six months later he returned it to the Crown in exchange for land in Warwickshire. Three months later Hatfield was granted to Elizabeth in exchange for land in Lincolnshire. Hatfield then became her principal seat. Just 20 miles north of London on the Great North Road, it was convenient, modern and commodious.

Under her father's will, Elizabeth received an annual income of £3,000 paid in instalments; then the process of assigning her lands of equivalent value began. That way she acquired dozens of manors, houses and parcels of land grouped in counties. Most were situated in an arc to the immediate north-west of London – Enfield, Ewelme in Oxfordshire, Ashridge on the Buckinghamshire/Hertfordshire border, Berkhamsted and Hemel Hempstead in Hertfordshire, and Great Missenden and Princes Risborough in Buckinghamshire. More estates in Huntingdonshire, Northamptonshire, Lincolnshire, Berkshire, Dorset, Hampshire and elsewhere followed. Elizabeth was constantly scheming to improve her property portfolio by buying and exchanging. In London she had been given Durham Palace, the former residence of the prince-bishops of Durham; this is where her mother Anne Boleyn had lodged before she married King Henry. It was a magnificent building and occupied a prime site from the Strand to the River Thames.[21] However, in 1551 John Dudley had been promoted to the dukedom of Northumberland, and to give substance to the title he was intent upon acquiring landholdings in Northumberland and the prince-bishopric of Durham. As a result of this Dudley also wanted Durham Palace, and when Elizabeth finally arrived at a settlement with him she did a swap and acquired Somerset House, Edward Seymour's palatial former home. Built in the new Italian style with its impressive frontage to the Strand, it was the largest, newest, most magnificent private house in London.

As Elizabeth and her new friends grew rich, the young king, deprived of his lands for their benefit, sank into chronic poverty.[22]

Bess and the Colourful Greys

As with our first two chapters, we once again begin with the Battle of Bosworth. Sir William Brandon formed part of Henry Tudor's personal entourage there, performing the role of royal standard-bearer. Brandon was killed defending the standard when Richard III launched his final charge, and he appears in stanzas 155 and 156 of *The Ballad of Bosworth Field.*[1]

Henry VII repaid Brandon's loyalty by educating his son and heir Charles Brandon alongside his own children. Charles formed a close friendship with the young Prince Henry – soon to become Henry VIII – that lasted all their lives, ensuring him a succession of offices in the royal household, and many valuable grants of land. He was quite charming, good-looking, and knew how to woo. He lavished attention on Henry VII's sister Mary Tudor, and his name was linked with Margaret Neville before he married his niece Anne Browne in 1508. Anne died in 1511 after giving birth to two daughters.

Even if Charles Brandon and Mary Tudor had been lovers, nothing could have come of it as negotiations were taking place to marry Mary to King Louis XII in an attempt to ensure peace and friendship with France. On 15 May 1513, Brandon entered into a marriage contract with his ward Elizabeth Grey, Viscountess Lisle, and took the title 1st Viscount Lisle. In 1514, five years into his reign, his friend Henry VIII created him 1st Duke of Suffolk.

It was on 9 October 1514 that Mary Tudor became the third wife of King Louis XII of France. She was eighteen and he was fifty-two, and despite two previous marriages Louis had no living sons and needed an heir. He died on 1 January 1515, less than three months after marrying Mary, reputedly worn out by his exertions in the bedchamber but more likely from the effects of gout.[2]

On hearing the news of Louis' death, Brandon sailed over to France to congratulate the new French king, Francis I, and to negotiate Mary's return to England. Mary was '*la reine blanche*' or 'the white queen', as it was customary to call royal widows. Custom dictated that a royal widow resided in seclusion for forty days in case she was pregnant with the heir to the throne, but in the first week of her widowhood the new king, Francis, had himself been paying court to the beautiful Mary.

Mary accused Brandon of planning to take her back to England only to have her married off again in a political match against her will. It was no secret that Charles and Mary had always been fond of each other, and she issued him with an ultimatum: marry her right now or she would never marry at all. Swayed by Mary's tears and his own ambition, Brandon risked the ire of Henry VIII and secretly married Mary in the chapel at Cluny on 3 March 1515.

Brandon's marriage contract with Elizabeth Grey was terminated and the title 1st Viscount Lisle forfeited, but there were further repercussions, not least the wrath of Mary's formidable brother. Henry flew into a rage on receipt of the news, and threatened to have Brandon beheaded. Technically Brandon had committed treason, having married a royal princess without the king's consent. The Privy Council urged that Brandon should be imprisoned or executed, but because of the intervention of Cardinal Thomas Wolsey and Henry's affection for both his sister and Brandon, the couple were let off with a heavy fine and had to pay back Mary's marriage portion in annual instalments of £4,000. She also had to return all the plate and jewels she had taken to France as her dowry, as well as the many gifts King Louis had given her, but the fine of £24,000 – approximately equivalent to £7.2 million today – was later reduced by Henry.

Charles Brandon and Mary Tudor officially married on 13 May 1515 at Greenwich Palace in the presence of Henry and his courtiers. Mary's first marriage had produced no children;

her second marriage produced four, but only two girls, Frances and Eleanor, survived.[3]

When Frances was born in July 1517, Elizabeth Grey, Brandon's former wife, was still alive; this brought the legitimacy of the child into question. However, by the time Eleanor was born Elizabeth Grey had died, making Eleanor unquestionably legitimate, with a claim to the throne superior to that of her elder sister. Lady Eleanor Brandon married Henry Clifford, 2nd Earl of Cumberland; their only surviving child was Margaret Clifford, who married Henry Stanley, 4th Earl of Derby, to become Countess of Derby. As the legitimate younger daughter of the dowager queen, Eleanor's place in the royal line was sealed, but neither Eleanor nor her daughter wanted the English crown.

Frances Brandon, on the other hand, was far more ambitious. She was only too aware that she was daughter of the Dowager Queen of France and niece of both Margaret, Queen of Scotland and Henry, King of England. In her uncle's will, Frances stood fourth in line after her cousins Edward, Mary and Elizabeth. In 1533 she married Henry Grey, 3rd Marquess of Dorset, who took the additional title of Duke of Suffolk when his father-in-law died. But Henry Grey, like his father-in-law, had previously been married and his wife was still alive when he married Frances Brandon. Although he repudiated his first wife before he married Frances, in the eyes of the law, while the first wife was alive any children from the Brandon/Grey marriage were considered illegitimate or 'tainted stock'. However, such issues had been worked around before, and with the heirs of Mary Tudor being next in line to the throne behind Henry's own children, it was worth taking every chance.

When Frances and Henry Grey's firstborn turned out to be a boy, the couple wasted no time in trying to arrange a marriage between him and Princess Elizabeth. Their hopes were dashed when their infant son died, and they went on to have three daughters: Jane, born in 1537; Katherine, born in 1538; and Mary, born in 1540. It was clear that the lack of a son was a massive disappointment. The exact date of first daughter Jane's birth is not known; her arrival would have been overshadowed by the birth of her cousin Prince Edward, the first and only male heir to Henry VIII. The name Jane was uncommon in those times, and it's believed that Jane Grey was named after Jane Seymour, the mother of Prince Edward, no doubt to gain royal approval. With children of the same age, the ambitious Greys nursed the underlying ambition that one day their daughter Jane would marry her first cousin once removed, the future King of England. Henry VIII was too wise to settle for such a betrothal when he could secure a much more beneficial marriage for his son with a foreign princess.

Bess probably arrived at Bradgate Park, Leicester, the seat of the Grey family, around 1546 as a companion/waiting gentlewoman to The Lady Frances Grey. Surrounded by wealth and symbols of status, it should have been a happy household but it wasn't. With three young daughters, it should have been a noisy household but it wasn't. Frances and Henry Grey were strict parents; the children were used to sarcasm, cuffs and criticism. Not only was their upbringing strict, but the girls were emotionally impoverished. Jane is said to have complained:

> When I am in the presence either of father or mother, whether I speak, keep silence, sit, stand or go, eat, drink, be merry or sad, be sewing, playing, dancing, or doing anything else, I must do it as it were in such weight, measure and number, even so perfectly as God made the world; or else I am so sharply taunted, so cruelly threatened, yea presently sometimes with pinches, nips and bobs and other ways (which I will not name for the honour I bear them) … that I think myself in hell.[4]

Bess had been brought up in a large household where money was short but encouragement and love were in abundance. She would have been very hard-hearted if she had not tried to alleviate the Grey sisters' unhappiness. Being only ten years older than Jane and eleven years older than Katherine, she would have been a lively companion and friend for the girls; indeed, she was to remain a close friend as they grew older.

Things changed dramatically when Henry VIII died in January 1547. As the oldest male family member connected by blood (through his wife Lady Frances), Henry Grey was the chief mourner at the state funeral. He was made a Knight of the Garter, and created Lord High Constable of England so that he could superintend the coronation of nine-year-old Edward, who was crowned Edward VI, King of England and Ireland, on 20 February 1547.

Because of her position, Bess would no doubt have moved with the family when they took up residence at their London home, Dorset House, to be close at hand for these important events. There Bess would have met some of the most powerful men in the realm, and among them was Sir William Cavendish, an elderly, distinguished and extremely rich government servant. He was also a widower.

Sir William Cavendish was a younger son of Thomas Cavendish, who was secretary to the Treasurer of the King's Exchequer under Henry VII, and Clerk of the Pipe, a senior position in the Exchequer, under Henry VIII. With his older brother George in the service of Cardinal Wolsey, William is thought to have followed his elder brother as a gentleman usher to the cardinal, but after Wolsey's fall from grace William joined Thomas Cromwell's staff. It was Cromwell who had come up with the solution to annul the king's marriage to Katherine of Aragon, and he was also instrumental in the dissolution of the monasteries. Cromwell saw Cavendish as a man with the right attitude and ambition, and Cromwell was renowned for looking after his best servants. Cavendish was instructed to assess and audit the possessions of numerous monastic establishments in what were called 'visitations'. In 1534 the leasehold of the manor of Northaw near St Albans was offered to William on extremely favourable terms, and he soon obtained the freehold of the manor and lands by an outright grant. When the Court of Augmentations was set up in 1536, William was appointed one of the auditors at a salary of £20 a year, plus the profits of the office. The profits far exceeded his salary, making him a fortune.[5]

In the dismantling of the great monasteries, the prime properties went to the Crown, who sold them on to the gentry of each shire. The remainder, too isolated or insignificant to be hugely profitable to the Crown, were available for purchase, rent or lease to members of the Court of Augmentations at very favourable rates. William Cavendish's job placed him in a position to acquire land and properties at bargain prices, and, being methodical and efficient, that is exactly what he did. At the height of the dissolution in 1537, William Cavendish and his clerks were covering huge distances and dissolving up to ten religious houses per month.

Because of the need to travel to and from London, William rented a small house in Newgate Street, just north of the old medieval cathedral of St Paul's.[6] This was a major venue for booksellers, barbers, beggars and cutpurses. To the east lay the great Tower of London, to the west were the Inns of Court, and beyond that was Westminster and Whitehall.

In October 1538 William was granted lands in Cheshunt in Hertfordshire, Thetford in Norfolk and Tallington in Lincolnshire.[7] In 1539, 'in consideration of his services', William was allowed to purchase Northaw outright, together with the manors and lands of Cuffley and Childewyke in Hertfordshire. These had all previously belonged to the great manor of St Albans. He also purchased the former priory of Cardigan in south Wales with its appurtenances, plus the rectories and churches of Cardigan.[8]

During this time William Cavendish had been married to Margaret (*née* Bostock), with whom he had five children, but when Margaret died in June 1540 only Katheryne, Mary and Ann were still living. A few months later, William was ordered to Ireland to examine the accounts of the vice-treasurer and receiver of Ireland. He stayed for eighteen months, and on his return in the summer of 1542 he married Elizabeth Parker, who gave birth to a daughter followed by a son, although both perished as infants. Elizabeth died a few years later while giving birth to a stillborn child.

In the early months of 1546 the Court of Augmentation was winding down. William had played a leading role in the work of the court, and the land 'surrendered' by the monasteries had contributed £800,000 to the Exchequer. A grateful monarch offered him the post of Treasurer to the King's Chamber. Not only was he responsible for accounting for the personal expenditures of the king, he also had to manage the household expenses of the heir to the throne, the king's two daughters and the king's current wife, but he would have to pay £1,000 to secure the role.[9] With the possibility of winning royal favour, and on the assumption that once installed he would invariably be the recipient of many lucrative perquisites such as the ability to sell favours, William borrowed the money.

On Easter Sunday 1546, William Cavendish was knighted by the king and sworn onto the Privy Council. Then, when Henry died and Edward ascended the throne, Sir William's position as Treasurer of the King's Chamber was reconfirmed at a salary of £25 per quarter.[10]

He was now a man of substance, lord of several manors in Hertfordshire, leaseholder of a fine London house and owner of a very useful portfolio of lands and properties that stretched across the country from Wales to Suffolk. However, he was lonely and had no male heir to inherit.

When Bess met William Cavendish in 1547, he was forty to Bess's nineteen years. They could have had very little in common, yet a strong friendship developed. Bess had good breeding, good connections, no dependents and a small income of her own. She was young and healthy and came of fecund stock, so there is no doubt that Sir William saw her as having the ability to provide him with healthy sons. He had already been married twice and had two daughters – some reports say three, although there seems to be an indication that the third daughter had some form of mental or physical disability that prevented her living with the family.

Bess probably saw Cavendish as a father figure who could provide for her and protect her from the financial problems and insecurities that had so far blighted her life. Marrying him would give her a title, charge of two fine houses and equal footing with members of the court. For a nineteen-year-old this was a huge leap up the social ladder.

In 1547 Bess Barlow and Sir William Cavendish married in the Grey family chapel at Bradgate Manor in Leicestershire. Sir William recorded in his notebook, 'Memorandum. That I was married unto Elizabeth Hardwicke my third wife in Leestersheer at Bradgate House, the 20th August in the first year of King Edward's reign, at two of the clock after midnight.' The time of the wedding had been carefully calculated to fit favourable astrological predictions. Bess was very superstitious about such things, and later she had an astrologer in her household. She studied astronomy and astrology, and her enduring fascination with astrology was exceptional for the time. She believed in solar rather than divine intervention, and used the term theology to refer to the study of religious ideas and teachings that were not specifically conventional. But Bess was astute and prudent enough not to express her spiritual views. After all, England was still in religious turmoil and heresy was punishable by death.

Following their wedding at Bradgate, Sir William and the new Lady Cavendish set off for Northaw in Hertfordshire. It was probably the first time Bess would have seen the place, and sadly there is no surviving image of the manor house and no description. Thirty years later it was completely demolished and rebuilt. It was probably the first time she had met her stepchildren too. The eldest was twelve, only seven years younger than Bess, so she must have been very aware of the scrutiny from her new stepdaughters, not to mention from the servants who had previously been employed by Sir William's former wives.

Northaw's close proximity to London made it a prime location for a country retreat, and soon after her wedding Lady Bess Cavendish was presented at court. If the young king chose to speak to her she would have been able to ask about her young friend and former charge, Lady Jane Grey, who in early 1547 had been sent to join the household of the dowager queen Katherine Parr, widow of Henry VIII, then married to Thomas Seymour. The Greys had the help and support of Thomas Seymour, the boy king's uncle, in promoting their daughter as Edward's bride.

Bess had been fortunate in her household placements, and her experiences in the Zouche and Grey households stood her in good stead for her role as Lady Cavendish. Bess was a fast learner and revelled in the novelty of running her own household. Within a year she was keeping the books, paying bills and recording rents on leases. The financially prudent Sir William would not have allowed his wife to perform such tasks if she hadn't been capable.

Their first daughter was born ten months after their wedding. Sir William recorded the event: 'Frances, my ninth child and the first by the said woman (Elizabeth Hardwick), was born on Monday between the hours of 3 and 4 at afternoon, viz the 18th of June. Anno 2 RE 6.'[11] Because the baby was named after Lady Frances Grey, her namesake was the senior godmother and her thirteen-year-old son Henry Brandon was godfather. As soon as Bess was able to leave Northaw after giving birth, she joined her husband in London where they entertained in fine fashion. Bess's household accounts show large expenditures on servants and the necessities inherent in running two households. No doubt their presence was also required at the funeral service of Katherine Parr, who had died in childbirth. Lady Jane Grey had remained in Parr's royal household at Sudeley Castle, and in September 1548, at the age of eleven, she was the chief mourner at the dowager queen's funeral.[12]

In January 1549, the dowager queen's recently widowed husband Thomas Seymour was arrested and imprisoned in the Tower of London after the debacle in which he shot one of the king's spaniels. Rather surprisingly, it appears that Seymour had offered Lady Jane Grey assurances that he could arrange a marriage between her and Edward VI in exchange for a deposit of cash against the eventual sum of £2,000; with this in mind, Lady Jane became his ward and remained at Sudeley Castle. However, it was all to come to nothing as Thomas Seymour was found guilty of high treason and beheaded on 20 March 1549.

On 10 June 1549 Bess gave birth to a second child, a daughter they named Temperance. This was in honour of Princess Elizabeth, being Edward VI's nickname for the princess. The Countess of Warwick and Lady Jane Grey were godmothers, and the godfather was Francis Talbot, 5th Earl of Shrewsbury.[13] The choice of 'my lady Warwick' for godmother had to be significant. Her husband was now the most powerful man in the realm, and things were changing. Cavendish's role as Treasurer to the King's Chamber gave him regular access to the king, and he could see the boy had a weak constitution. Among the amounts paid to teachers, jesters and minstrels, Cavendish recorded payments to eight doctors and physicians who were part of the king's entourage.[14] An astute man, he knew that if the boy king died there would be political instability. According to Henry VIII's Act of Succession, the heirs to the throne after Edward were Mary and then Elizabeth, followed by their cousin once removed – Lady Jane Grey.

John Dudley, Earl of Warwick, the new Lord Protector, made no secret of the fact that he was backing Lady Jane Grey as a bride for Edward. If they were betrothed, Lady Jane could leapfrog over Mary and Elizabeth in the royal line, and children born to Jane and Edward would secure a peaceful, continuous lineage. The support of John Dudley would have greatly pleased Lady Frances Grey and her husband, yet neither Jane nor Edward seemed anxious to proceed. No decision was made, nor any announcement of a pending betrothal.

Bess was ambitious for herself and those she loved. She would have encouraged Jane and tried to show her the positive side of such an arrangement, but sadly there is no evidence that Jane could be swayed. She obviously didn't share Bess's motivation to rise through the ranks.

Meanwhile, Bess's husband Sir William Cavendish had other things on his mind. If Edward was to die without issue and Mary took the crown in accordance with their father's will, she would return England to Catholicism; there was a real danger of a counter-reformation. Even if civil war didn't break out, the country would be in chaos as she attempted to seize and restore all former Church lands, almost a third of all the land in England.

Cavendish was well aware that his own wealth was based on former Church lands, so he embarked on a form of sixteenth-century money laundering. He began to dispose of the former Church lands and properties he had acquired during the dissolution and instead bought secular lands and properties. The shrewd Cavendish wanted to establish a chain of secular buying and selling so there could be no doubt of his legal ownership.

The family of Bess's stepfather Ralph Leche had owned land and property in and around Bakewell, but as he was a younger son Ralph's share was relatively small. According to *Plantagenet Ancestry: A Study in Colonial and Medieval Families*, he is described as Ralph Leche of Chatsworth and Hardwick. From old legal documents we know that in the period 1533–38 Ralph Leche had fraudulently conveyed land deeds in Calver and Bakewell, but he quit the Calver property in 1541 and surrendered all his land in Holmsfield and Cawdwell in 1542. When he died in 1549 he owned property at Beeley in the manor of Chatsworth, which was later the subject of a court case between his widow and William Cavendish.

Bess's younger sister Alice was married to Francis Leche, Ralph's nephew and heir to the Leche lands, but in 1547 he found that she had been unfaithful to him. In a fit of malice he declared that 'rather than let bastards be his heirs' he would get rid of everything.[15] It wasn't just an idle threat – he sold his Chatsworth holdings to Thomas Agarde for £700.

Ralph and the rest of the Leche family were furious that Francis had let family land go for a pittance. They tried to rescind the deal, but Agarde refused. Francis presented his case to the Lord Protector, who ruled in favour of the Leche family, but there were complications. Having paid for the property, Thomas Agarde undoubtedly owned it; but now the Lord Protector ruled that 'we find that the bargain made by Leche should not disinherit the succession of that land, so all parties should attain their own.'[16]

Today a charge would have been put on the land, but in 1549 Agarde had what was called a damaged freehold, and no protection against further claims by the Leche family. Thomas Agarde died before the case was finalised, and it was left to his son to sort things out. He obviously didn't want to fight on, and on 31 December 1550 he sold the whole to Sir William and Dame Elizabeth Cavendish for the bargain price of £600.[17] The estate included 'the manors of Chatsworth and Cromford, and houses and land there, and in Calton, Edensor, Pilsley, Birchills, Bakewell, Baslow, Totley, Tideswell, Litton, Dore, Wheston, Abney, Chesterfield, Beeley, Matlock, Bonsall and Repton'.[18]

It was in the first months of 1550 that baby Temperance died. She would have been six or seven months old. Bess became pregnant again very quickly, and gave birth to a son in December 1550. Sir William wrote, 'Henry my eleventh child and my third by the same woman was born on Tuesday at 12 of the clock at night, the 17th day of December 1550.' The entry is followed by a list of most impressive godparents: seventeen-year-old Princess Elizabeth, Lord Protector John Dudley, and Henry Grey. These were three of the most important people in the land. Soon Bess was expecting her fourth child, and between two and three o'clock in the morning of 27 December 1551, William Cavendish was born. His godparents were Elizabeth, Marquess of Northampton, William Paulett, Earl of Winchester and Lord Treasurer, and William Herbert, Earl of Pembroke.[19]

Throughout 1550 and 1551, Sir William Cavendish continued selling parcels of land in the south and buying land in Derbyshire.

In May 1550, he bought the manor of Ashford-in-the-Water, due north of Bakewell, together with 8,000 acres of land. The perspicacious Cavendish was in an ideal position to purchase land from the Crown to further his ambitious plans to create a vast Derbyshire estate, but as he was not familiar with the county he would have undoubtedly discussed any plans with his young wife. It's also possible that the couple were 'tipped off' about land that could be purchased cheaply by Bess's mother Elizabeth Leche, who had local knowledge. It could have been Elizabeth who alerted them to the problems between her daughter Alice and Francis Leche, and subsequently enabled them to buy the Chatsworth estates so cheaply. Cavendish was too astute to ignore such an obvious source of information.

Things didn't always go smoothly, however. In 1551, Elizabeth Leche took her son-in-law to court over some land he had acquired at Beeley, held in the manor of Chatsworth. She claimed it had belonged to her late husband and was therefore legally hers.[20] The problem could have arisen because the precise boundaries were not drawn up in the deeds in this remote district where sheep outnumbered people 10,000 to 1.[21] This area was (and largely remains) a vast moor that could only be traversed by packhorse trails, so it would have been a long, tedious journey to Chatsworth. Miles away from any highway, locals and strangers alike got lost in this barren landscape which, according to Daniel Defoe, writing nearly 200 years later, 'stretched fifteen or sixteen miles together … a waste and howling wilderness over which when strangers travel they are obliged to take guides, or it would be next to impossible not to lose their way'.[22]

The first mention of Chatsworth is pre-Norman, when a Saxon chief named Chetal made it his homestead and called it Chetelsvorde. When the Cavendishes purchased the Chatsworth estate there was already a habitable manor house that had been owned by the Leche family. Small sums were spent on mending doors and locks to make the house secure, and Bess paid a master carpenter named Master Bissett 'for himself and his man for working at Chatsworth by the space of seventy-two days at eight pence the day for himself and five pence the day for his man'.

The old house was only intended to serve as a temporary base for the Cavendish family. They had ambitions to build a palatial new house and chose a perfect spot in the deer park which formed a sheltered valley above and parallel to the fast-flowing River Derwent. On 6 December 1551, William paid 20s to Roger Worde, a master mason, to design him a house. The professional architect did not exist in those days, but an experienced master mason would produce a design that would be altered by the owners and masons as the work progressed. The original Chatsworth House was a two-storey construction built of local stone around a central courtyard and rather resembled a medieval fortress with its turrets and battlements. The entrance was through an archway between turrets on one side, and the hall, buttery and kitchen ran along the opposite side.[23] Bess would later add another floor, which would house the state rooms and a long gallery.

In the meantime they inhabited the old house, and in 1552 Bess was writing to her steward Francis Whitfield that he should 'cause the floor in my bedchamber to be made even either with plaster, clay or lime, and all the windows where the glass is broken to be mended and all the chambers to be made as close and warm as you can'.

In April 1552, King Edward became sick with measles and smallpox but seemed to recover. The smallpox epidemic remained in London throughout that summer, and Parliament was dissolved, but William Cavendish was about to deliver a master stroke. He gave the king all his properties except those in Derbyshire and neighbouring counties, and in exchange he received a massive tranche of lands with mines and quarries, the bulk of which were situated in Derbyshire. It must have been a phenomenal deal for the Cavendishes. The document ends that the exchange is 'without fine and fee'.[24]

Fifteen days before Edward's death, Bess's household account book came to an abrupt end. Sir William no longer had any direct association with monastic land, and that summer he moved his family and all his goods and chattels north. Bess was five months pregnant, and with the prospect of a new arrival and the hot summer ahead, they had a good excuse to leave the capital and its coming dangers. By autumn the entire Cavendish household had been transferred from Northaw to Chatsworth.

5

A Problem of Succession

In February 1553, the young king Edward was again unwell. He was stricken with a severe respiratory infection, possibly acute pulmonary tuberculosis, for which there was no cure in the sixteenth century. There was no point in trying to arrange a marriage between the dying king and Lady Jane Grey, but the powerful nobles Henry Grey, Duke of Suffolk, and John Dudley, Duke of Northumberland, still planned to avert the course of Henry VIII's Act of Succession, under which the crown would pass to Princess Mary.

Until then, no woman had succeeded to the throne; typically, women had transmitted their claims to their male descendants. All Edward's ancestral families – York, Tudor and Lancaster – passed through the female line. Protestants also believed that female rule was against Scripture, but unfortunately all the living heirs of Henry VII, the patriarch of the Tudor dynasty, were female.[1]

A country having only heiresses was widely regarded as a disaster. It wasn't just Edward's half-sisters Mary and Elizabeth; there was also his cousin once removed Mary Stuart, Queen of Scots, granddaughter of Henry VIII's older sister Margaret. Mary Stuart was born in December 1542, and although Henry VIII had tried to organise a betrothal between his son Edward and Mary Stuart, it had been rejected in favour of a marriage contract between Mary Stuart and Francis, the dauphin of France.

The granddaughters of Henry VIII's younger sister Mary were considered preferable to Mary Stuart and the Scottish branch of the family. These included Edward's cousins once removed Margaret

Clifford, and Jane, Katherine and Mary Grey. All were in their teens and unmarried. In time any or all of these girls could produce sons, but time was in short supply.

With two formidable older sisters, Edward had grown up with 'a monstrous regiment of women'; he thus made the momentous decision to exclude all women from the succession. He clearly felt much resentment towards his sisters when he composed what was called 'The Device', leaving the crown to 'the Lady Jane's heirs male'.

How much of this idea came from John Dudley is unclear, but chroniclers consider that this decision was Edward's alone. If John Dudley had encouraged him he wouldn't necessarily have been acting against the interest of the country, but he may well have wanted to ensure that the future held a place for him. He realised that if Mary or Elizabeth were to take the crown, he would most certainly lose his high position and possibly even his head.

The first thing to do was to get the royal brood mares married and breeding, so with this in mind Margaret Clifford, daughter of Eleanor and Henry Clifford, Earl and Countess of Cumberland, was betrothed to John Dudley's brother Sir Andrew Dudley KG, one of the Chief Gentlemen of the King's Privy Chamber. He was at least thirty years older than Margaret, and the wedding, due to take place in June, didn't go ahead.

Jane and Katherine Grey were both betrothed at the same time as Margaret Clifford, and their weddings did go ahead. John Dudley's plan was to marry the fifteen-year-old Jane to his son Lord Guildford Dudley, and on 25 May 1553, in John Dudley's London home, the wedding took place. There's no doubt that Jane was bullied into this by her parents and was a very reluctant participant. Guildford, John Dudley's fourth son, was equally reluctant, but they were just pawns in a very high-powered game.[2]

It was a triple marriage ceremony. At the same time as Guildford and Jane married, Lady Jane's younger sister Lady Katherine Grey was married to fifteen-year-old Lord Henry Herbert, son and heir of the Earl of Pembroke. John Dudley's daughter Katherine, who had no claim to the throne, married Lord Hastings, son and heir of the Earl of Huntingdon, who, as a direct descendant of Edward IV's brother George, Duke of Clarence, did have a claim. The event was so rushed that the garments for the weddings had to be borrowed from the royal Master of the Wardrobe.[3]

Because Henry VIII's will was based on a parliamentary statute, the line of succession could only legally be changed with another. But Edward was dying. There was no time to call Parliament, and to change the succession without parliamentary authority was treason. Edward took matters into his own hands, and on 12 June he summoned the Chief Justice and the law officers to his bedside at Greenwich where he reminded them of their allegiance, and commanded them to make the necessary changes as outlined in the six paragraphs of the device he had written for the succession of June 1553. Instead of leaving the crown to 'The Lady Jane's heirs male', with the stroke of a pen Edward removed the 's' and added 'and her', thus leaving the crown to 'The Lady Jane and her heirs male'.

As they fleshed out the legal details they added the supposed justification that the Grey sisters were legitimate, of whole blood and married to English nobles while Mary and Elizabeth were bastards of the half blood and might marry abroad. Mary and Elizabeth's statutory rights were brushed aside on the grounds that, 'being illegitimate and not lawfully begotten', they were 'to all intents and purposes clearly disabled to ask, claim or challenge the said imperial crown of the realm'. Either of them could marry 'a stranger born out of this realm who might practice to have the laws and customs of his native country practiced within this realm to the utter subversion of the commonwealth'.[4]

Key figures were won over with promises of grants of land and office, and the letters patent was circulated broadly among the court and London elite for signature. The French ambassador offered military support if it should be needed and on 21 June the councillors and nobles countersigned the letters patent.

Fifteen-year-old King Edward VI died without issue on 6 July 1553 at Greenwich Palace.

The Nine-Day Coup

As the king lay dying, Mary Tudor was summoned to the council but instead set off for Kenninghall in Norfolk, a stronghold of the old religion. John Dudley's twenty-year-old son Robert made a desperate attempt to intercept her in order to convey her to a place of safety but he was unsuccessful. On 8 July news of the king's death reached her. The following day Mary proclaimed herself queen and despatched an authoritative letter to the Privy Council in London requiring them to endorse her claim. She began to assemble her supporters and moved south to the secure and formidable Framlingham Castle, the ancient fortress of the dukes of Norfolk, where she set up camp. First hundreds then thousands of men flocked to her standard. The Privy Council began to panic. If they had acted quicker and taken Mary prisoner, there would have been no rallying point and things might have been very different.

Hearing that her brother was close to death, Elizabeth had hedged her bets and stayed at Hatfield. She amassed a substantial force of her own but did not rush to the aid of Jane or Mary. She was simply doing what landowners had done since the age of knight service, mustering a small army in a time of crisis. Others were doing the same. But officially there were two queens, one Protestant and one Catholic. So where did people's loyalties lie?

Bess and her husband Sir William Cavendish openly endorsed the Protestant religion, but in the household accounts we find that over a period of years Cavendish also made regular visits and gave small gifts to Princess Mary while she was living in seclusion. The astute man was obviously careful to keep a foot in each camp, but like many in his circle he stood to gain most under Queen Jane. The Cavendish family, despite their deep friendship with the Greys, were not in London when Lady Jane was proclaimed queen. Later, the wily Sir William was to claim that he had mustered a fighting force of his own at Chatsworth to go to Mary's aid at a personal cost of 1,000 marks (£660).[5]

Lady Jane Is Proclaimed Queen

On 9 July, the Privy Council assembled at Syon House. From there they sent word to Lady Jane, ordering her to present herself. Jane told the messenger, Mary Sidney, that she felt too ill to meet the council, but Mary Sidney insisted and the two girls eventually took a barge to Syon House. Jane was greeted by two nobles who knelt, kissed her hand and referred to her as their sovereign lady. She was brought into the chamber of state, where her father-in-law John Dudley led her to the dais reserved for royalty. He then gave a lengthy speech, through which Jane finally learned of Edward's death and that his wish had been for her to take the throne after him. As they all knelt to her, Jane stood trembling and speechless. She swayed and fell, bursting into tears, but no attempt was made to help her stand, nor to stop her crying. Finally, she regained enough control to utter the words, 'I am insufficient to fill the role.' John Dudley and her parents admonished her, but she insisted.

The following morning Jane was dressed in the green and white of the Tudors, and to appear even grander she wore raised wooden shoes called chopines, giving her an extra 3 inches of height. Guildford, her husband, was adorned with equal splendour in white and gold.

Between three and four o'clock on the afternoon of 10 July 1553, a parade of barges took Jane and her attendants to the Tower. There was no celebration, no crowd lining the banks of the river to cheer. People were only just learning of Edward's death, and now here was a young, unwanted and unknown cousin claiming the throne. The Marquess of Winchester and Sir John Bridges, Lieutenant of the Tower, surrounded by civilian and military officials, greeted her at the Tower. Winchester knelt to present the keys to the fortress, and John Dudley immediately stepped forward to take them, making it very clear who would be the true power behind the throne.

Flags flew and guns rang out in salute as Lady Jane proceeded into the White Tower. Once inside, Jane was taken to the presence chamber, where she took her place under the state canopy. Winchester appeared, carrying some of the jewels and the Crown Imperial of the realm. Jane refused it. Winchester countered by saying he just wished her to put it on to see how it suited her, and finally she relented. Thus the reluctant queen was crowned. Jane stubbornly refused to declare her husband king. 'If the crown belongs to me, I would be content to make my husband a duke. But I will never consent to make him king,' she said. Guildford Dudley fled the room in tears. His scheming parents were livid that Jane dared to defy their wishes, but had every reason to believe that she would change her mind under pressure. After all, this was a patriarchal age, and no one believed that a woman could rule in her own right. Kingship was a man's role.

The Privy Council and leading judges declared Lady Jane Grey the new Queen of England, and that Sunday the sermon at St Paul's supported Jane as queen while declaring Elizabeth and Mary as bastards unfit for the throne. Jane was then forced to write letters demanding support from the gentry and known dissenters reminding them that 'under ordinances as the late king did establish in his life time, for the security and wealth of this realm, we are entered into our rightful possession of this Kingdom as by the last Will of our said dear cousin …'[6]

The people started to revolt, crying for Mary, daughter of Henry VIII and Katherine of Aragon, to be made queen. In an attempt to ease the fevered and dangerous atmosphere that was building up, Jane ordered the gates of the Tower to be locked and the keys brought to her. However, nobody seemed to know what to do. By 12 July, Mary and her supporters had assembled their military force at Framlingham Castle.[7]

In order to avoid unnecessary bloodshed, it was decided that two of Guilford Dudley's brothers – John, Earl of Warwick, and Lord Robert Dudley – would lead a troop of 600 men to meet Mary, who was heading an army marching on London. They soon gave up after hearing of the acceptance of Mary and the size of her army – an estimated 30,000. Henry Grey broke the news to his daughter Jane on 19 July, and then, to save their own necks, at around 6 p.m. on the eighth day at the cross in Cheapside, the Privy Council publicly proclaimed Mary the Queen of England. Jane sat under the canopy of state alone in the Tower. Having been the de facto monarch of England from 10 to 19 July 1553, Jane's status changed from queen to prisoner in the Tower of London. Her nine-day reign was not really a reign at all; it was the unravelling of a coup. Dudley's support collapsed, and Mary's grew.[8]

Jane was deposed on 19 July.[9] As members of the Grey and Dudley factions were rounded up, the Earl of Pembroke quickly annulled the marriage of his son and Katherine Grey to distance himself from any connection with Henry Grey. Many others did the same, but the Cavendishes did not desert their old friends in their time of trouble.

Elizabeth Supports Her Half-sister
Elizabeth wrote from Hatfield to congratulate Mary. The half-sisters who had been so callously discarded by their half-brother set aside their differences to unite in a show of Tudor unity. They met at Wanstead on 3 August, riding together to Aldgate where

they were greeted by cheering crowds. The half-sisters had much in common. Both had been declared bastards by their father, seen their mothers rejected, and had their places in the line of succession wiped out. Rejected and condemned, neither had known security or much happiness, but now Mary was being carried along on a wave of adulation as she made her state entry into the capital. She had the support of the majority of people no matter what their religious persuasion, because she was Henry VIII's daughter and the lawful heir. Religion was not an issue at this stage. The churches in which they worshipped were still the same as those where they had worshipped together twenty years before under the old religion. The jubilation of the crowds was no doubt bolstered by the knowledge that they had been spared the horrors of a civil war.[10]

Nevertheless, there was an undercurrent of uncertainty. In the sixteenth century it was considered to be against natural law for women to rule men. Knox took this one step further when he wrote *The First Blast of the Trumpet against the Monstrous Regiment of Women*, published in 1558. He declared that to promote any woman – 'those weak, frail, impatient, feeble and foolish creatures' – to any form of rule was the 'subversion of good order, of all equity and justice', as well as being contrary to God and repugnant to nature.[11] Others, although in general agreement, were inclined to accept that a woman ruler was a necessary evil that had to be endured from time to time.

The role of monarch was quintessentially male, and as a female Mary had only a 'woman's estate'. Her sovereignty was both conditional and temporary, lasting only until she took a mate; then her husband became king and took control while she became the consort. This was based on the claims of an heiress to noble estates and title. If the male line died out, the heiress could not take the title, but her husband could – along with her estates. Mary was in a similar position with regard to the crown.

This was a patriarchal age, and it was expected that wealthy, well-born women would marry; with this in mind, the fact that Mary was still single at thirty-seven was a mystery. In the normal course of events she would have been shipped off to some distant shore, the way her mother had been, to marry and bear the children of some foreign prince. Yet there seem to have been no such plans for Mary despite her mother recommending that she read Erasmus's *Introduction to a Christian Marriage*.[12]

Mary was in a unique position. She could marry an English nobleman, but she would then be marrying one of her subjects. This was unimportant for a king when choosing a wife; it would not change the social order. The king would still be king and his wife would be queen in a supportive role. But if Mary was to marry a subject, he would become king and she would have to transfer her power to him, thus raising him to a prominence greater than hers. When the Commons suggested that she should marry one of her subjects, she was so angry that she ignored convention and answered for herself, rather than allowing the Lord Chancellor to answer for her.

The alternative was to select a foreign bridegroom, a king or prince who in the social order stood above any home-grown aristocrat. But a prince in line for or already upon a foreign throne might see this only as a political advantage. Instead of putting down roots and working for the best interests of the country, he would simply subordinate the interests of England to those of his international dynasty.

This was a novel problem that the Privy Council could find no answer for, but Mary dismissed their intervention as an impertinence anyway. She haughtily informed them that the choice of a royal bridegroom was a matter for her to decide, and she did, weighing up all the practicalities and considering every available candidate on the marriage market. Her cousin Charles V suggested she marry his only son, Prince Philip of Spain.[13]

Philip had a son from a previous marriage and was heir apparent to vast territories in Continental Europe and the New World. As part of the marriage negotiations, a portrait of Philip by Titian was sent to her in September 1553.[14]

Mary's Coronation

The good relationship between Mary and Elizabeth continued, and seemed to breed a new optimism for the future as arrangements for Mary's coronation got underway. The nobility flocked to London to meet and greet their new sovereign, and there is no reason to believe that Sir William Cavendish was not among them. It's doubtful that Lady Bess was there, however, as she was in the later stages of pregnancy.

On the eve of the coronation, it was traditional for the monarch to create a group of Knights of the Bath. Noble families were honoured in this way, and fifteen youthful heads or heirs were thus created knights in the Order of the Bath, headed by the earls of Devonshire and Surrey. The traditional duties required the monarch to dub the newly formed knights, and according to ritual the knights were stripped and bathed, then knighted by the sovereign while still naked in the bath. Because the sovereign had always been male, this had never caused a problem. Now the sovereign was an unmarried woman, and female modesty decreed that the task be delegated. The task was performed by the Earl of Arundel, and the following day he created another, larger group of knights – the knights of the carpet, who remained fully clothed throughout. Mary felt that as a woman she could not exercise the chivalric or military aspects of kingship. Such symbolic functions done on the queen's behalf would in the future be carried out by her husband, making his role quite substantial.

At Mary's coronation on 1 October 1553, Elizabeth accompanied her sister to the Tower, and rode immediately behind her in the eve-of-coronation procession. Mary was the first woman to be crowned in her own right, but refused to be anointed with the holy oils consecrated by Edward's ministers, whose views she considered to be heretical. Instead, before the ceremony she wrote to the Bishop of Arras, who sent three lots of 'untainted' oil from Brussels. During the ceremony, Mary held two sceptres: the king's sceptre, and another bearing a dove that was traditionally given to the queen. This was the same sceptre that her mother Katherine of Aragon had held when she was crowned alongside her husband Henry VIII in 1509. Elizabeth sat with the newly crowned Queen Mary at her coronation banquet, and in an unexpected turn of events Lady Jane's younger sisters Katherine and Mary Grey became maids of honour to the queen.[15]

In November 1553, Lady Jane Grey, her pseudo-husband Guildford Dudley and his father John Dudley, Edward's former Lord Protector who had ruled for the boy king, were tried and convicted of high treason. Mary proclaimed herself to be merciful. Henry Grey, Lady Jane's father, and the rest of John Dudley's sons, including Robert Dudley, friend and later to be favourite of Elizabeth, were spared – temporarily.[16]

Another event for the Cavendishes came in November 1553, when Lady Bess Cavendish gave birth to their fifth child, a boy they named Charles. As she prepared for the birth, then nursed her newborn son, her thoughts must have been with Lady Jane, the manipulated girl whom she had first known as a bullied nine-year-old, and who was now facing a charge of treason. Jane's plight must have affected Bess deeply, and it's easy to imagine the horror she would have felt. Bess obviously had a soft spot for the girl, and kept a portrait of Lady Jane beside her bed for the remainder of her life.

The choice of godparents for baby Charles is very significant, and shows just how powerful and pragmatic the Cavendishes were. William and Bess would not have agonised over the principles of the different religious philosophies and values. They believed that people should be allowed to worship according to their beliefs and their convictions, and in this vein their son's godparents were not only very distinguished, but also of different religions. The proud father persuaded Queen Mary to be the baby's godmother, and his two godfathers were also rather surprising. The first was Bishop Stephen Gardiner, an ardent Catholic and great supporter of Mary and her mother Katherine of Aragon. During the reign of Edward VI he had spent many years in prison because he would not accept the terms of the reformed religion. The other godfather was Henry Grey, the bluff, larger-than-life friend of Sir William so recently engaged in trying to supplant the new queen with his own daughter Lady Jane. Added to this explosive mix was the fact that the service would have been performed in a Catholic church under Catholic rites. Altogether, this was a bold move that spoke of diplomacy, friendship, support and loyalty to the new queen.

From contemporary deeds and correspondence we know that between 1553 and 1556 Cavendish continued to improve and increase his Derbyshire estates, and building work was ongoing at the new Chatsworth House. The building, which contained thirteen bedchambers, was commenced with no expense spared, and one writer described it as 'splendid magnificence which must have been unequalled in Derbyshire and neighbouring counties'.[17]

An inventory taken in 1553 lists among the household furniture fifty-eight tapestries, and thirteen furnished bedchambers with matching coverings throughout. Bess and Sir William's bed is described as being gilt carved work with the arms of the couple, and a single valance of red cloth, inlaid with red silk and silver. Other beds, even more costly, had valances of cloth of gold embroidered with pearls. There were objects of gold and silver plate that amounted to 2,124 ounces, which if valued at the then current price of 6s per ounce, were worth £640.

The fields and hillsides were filled with sheep, and there were forty oxen for pulling the waggons that were used to transport all the moveable Cavendish possessions from their other properties to Chatsworth. It was therefore not a fair statement when Sir William described the property to his friend Sir John Thynne as 'my poor house'.[18]

The Return of Catholicism

Things changed between the royal sisters when Parliament took the first steps to legally restore Catholicism. Parliament also rehabilitated the memory of Mary's mother Katherine of Aragon; her marriage to Henry VIII was declared valid, and Mary was declared legitimate. It was probably due to this that hostilities recommenced between the two sisters and the old bitterness over their religious differences returned. The fact that Elizabeth was pretending to follow the Catholic religion without sacrificing her Protestant ethics didn't help. It obviously became impossible for them to remain in the same household, with the nineteen-year-old Princess Elizabeth living at court under Mary's somewhat reluctant protection. Mary began looking at ways of removing Elizabeth from the succession, and Elizabeth, though concerned that in her absence her enemies would try to poison Mary's mind against her, requested permission to leave. The queen gave her consent, and in December Elizabeth left the court to spend the Christmas period at her home Ashridge House near Great Berkhamsted, Hertfordshire.

Just a few months after Mary's coronation, the atmosphere had changed. Even though it had been expected, there was great resentment at the way the new queen had immediately tried to overturn the structure of the reformed Church. Mass was immediately restored in the Chapel Royal, and the Common Prayer service was used only for Edward's spartan obsequies. Within a short time Mary had issued a proclamation suspending the statutory penalties for attending Mass, and the Book of Common Prayer was outlawed. Edward's religious legislation was high on the list of matters for repeal at her first parliament on 5 October, and was carried by 270 votes in favour to 80 against. Not everybody was happy with this, of course; in fact, after her chaplain preached a Catholic service at St Paul's Cross, Mary was surrounded by a hostile mob.

The return of Catholicism went hand in hand with another radical development for the country when news arrived that Mary intended to marry Prince Philip II of Spain, son of Mary's protector Emperor Charles V. When compared to the English nobles, Philip of Spain certainly looked more promising. He was in his late twenties and already a widower, and as a direct descendant of John of Gaunt he had an impressive English lineage. But this couldn't hide the fact that he was a Spaniard, and Mary was also half Spanish through her mother Katherine of Aragon.

The queen had made her choice, and all that was left was for the Privy Council to implement her decision. Limits were placed on Philip's intrinsic powers as king consort in order to protect English interests against subordination to those of a foreign power, and in the absence of children his powers would lapse with Mary's death. But people were genuinely fearful that a Spanish king would also mean the Spanish Inquisition, which had been introduced to maintain Catholic orthodoxy in Spain. The idea that English Protestants could be subjected to the all-powerful, torture-mad Inquisition caused paranoia. Committed Protestants left England for Germany and the Low Countries to avoid persecution, and a small group of disaffected aristocrats planned simultaneous risings against the marriage across the south of England.

Wyatt's Rebellion, 1554
The plotters met in secret to formulate their plan to reverse Mary's religious policy, overthrow the government, block the Spanish marriage, dethrone Mary, marry Elizabeth to Edward Courtney, Earl of Devon (a descendent of King Edward IV), and put Elizabeth

on the English throne. According to a contemporary writer, 'at this time many bore such hatred against the Pope's power and the thought of a foreign yoke that Sir Thomas Wyatt and some Kentish men, within ten days of the marriage contracted betwixt Queen Mary and Philip of Spain, brake forward into open rebellion'.[19]

The revolt was named after Sir Thomas Wyatt the Younger, a senior courtier and son of the famous poet Sir Thomas Wyatt, who wrote two poems inspired by Anne Boleyn. The poet was besotted with Anne – it was rumoured that they were lovers before his rival Henry VIII claimed her for his wife – and now his son Thomas was prepared to fight for Anne's daughter. Thomas Wyatt was to raise an army in Kent, and there were to be a series of regional risings, including one by Jane's father Henry, Duke of Suffolk, who had returned to the Midlands to raise an army at Bradgate. In early January news of the plot leaked out. It was Edward Courtney himself who buckled under pressure, and understandably so. He was a young man and had already spent fifteen years of his life in prison, most of it in solitary confinement, simply because his father had displeased Henry VIII.

Realising that Courtney would not stand up to aggressive questioning, the conspirators met and agreed to bring their plans forward. On his way from Kent to Hertfordshire, Sir James Croft made a hasty detour via Ashridge House with a message from Wyatt to warn Elizabeth to move immediately to Castle Donnington, where she would be more protected from any attempts by Mary's men to take her into custody. It's unclear whether Elizabeth understood the severity of the situation, but apparently she was ill with nephritis, a painful kidney infection, and could not leave her bed.

Wyatt raised more than 6,000 foot soldiers and 500 mounted soldiers, and assumed that his fellow conspirators were doing the same in their areas. If they had then the rebellion might have succeeded, but the promised support from armies in the west, the Midlands and the Welsh borders failed to materialise. Wyatt made his move towards London on 25 January. A detachment was sent against them on 28 January, but some of Mary's troops lost their nerve and actually defected to Wyatt. Had other regional groups come to Wyatt's aid, things might have been different. On 3 February Wyatt and his rebels advanced on London but found the drawbridge on the southern end of London Bridge was up and the bridge was guarded with cannon. They moved downstream to the next bridge at Kingston and found it broken but not impassable. Panic broke out as Wyatt's army advanced from the west, but Wyatt's men seemed unsure what to do and split up, allowing Mary's troops, who outnumbered the rebels, an easy victory. Wyatt surrendered on 7 February and was taken to the Tower. The remaining leaders were rounded up, and this time Mary showed no mercy. Gallows sprang up all over London and Kent, and more than 300 men were executed, their bodies left swinging in the winter wind. The failure of Wyatt's Rebellion would lead directly to the execution of the ill-fated Lady Jane Grey;[20] possibly panicking at the prospect of a rebellion returning her to the throne, the government ordered Jane's execution. She was beheaded on 12 February 1554, along with her husband, Guildford.

Elizabeth Is Implicated in Wyatt's Rebellion and Becomes a Prisoner

Mary wrote to Elizabeth at Ashridge in firm but friendly terms, summoning her to court for her own safety. Elizabeth was not stupid enough to fall into such an obvious trap and declined, blaming ill health, the disturbed state of the countryside and the frozen winter highways.

On 8 February Mary sent a posse to bring Elizabeth to court, but because of her health the journey was delayed for four days. On Monday 12 February, the day of Jane's execution, they began their slow journey to London. Elizabeth rode in a horse-drawn litter, and every movement caused her great discomfort. Averaging 6 miles a day, Elizabeth's cavalcade eventually arrived in London on 23 February, the day that Lady Jane's father Henry was beheaded on Tower Hill for his involvement in Wyatt's Rebellion.[21]

Elizabeth was now a virtual prisoner, and was taken to Whitehall and placed in total isolation for two weeks before the government's interrogators got to work. She must have been aware that the Tower was filling up with many of the Wyatt conspirators, who were being questioned and likely tortured. Had Elizabeth's enemies been able to prove a positive chain of communication between Elizabeth and Wyatt before the rebellion this would have been enough to prove treason, but there was no evidence that she knew or approved of the objectives.

On 15 March, Wyatt stood trial at Westminster Hall. He denied conspiring to cause the queen's death or having had any contact with Elizabeth, but this just put more pressure on Elizabeth. The council charged Elizabeth with involvement in Wyatt's Rebellion on 17 March, and the following day she was taken to the Tower pending further investigations.

There's a story, possibly apocryphal, of Elizabeth's entry into the Tower. When she was told she would be entering through Traitor's Gate, she refused to get out of the boat. In fact, it's more likely that she landed at Tower Wharf and entered the Tower across the drawbridge to the west of the fortress. The way she entered would have been of less significance to Elizabeth than what confronted her once she had entered the Tower; there was still evidence of the scaffold used in the recent execution of Lady Jane Grey. Mary had shown Jane no mercy, so why would she treat her sister any differently?

There are stories that she had been taken to the Tower by moonlight so as not to draw attention and raise the sympathy of supporters, but her guards would have been well aware of this and, with consideration to the tide, would have made the journey in daylight. She was said to have been accommodated in the Bell Tower, which linked with the Beauchamp Tower where Robert Dudley was imprisoned. There are stories of their clandestine meetings. It is, however, more likely that she was accommodated in the generous set of accommodations known as the royal palace, which lay in the south-west corner of the inner ward of the Tower. This area had been rebuilt by her father Henry VIII to accommodate her mother Anne Boleyn on the eve of her wedding and coronation. Anne had also been lodged here three years later when she was brought to the Tower as a traitor and adulteress. It was from here that she had been taken to her execution. Was her daughter about to follow in her footsteps?

Despite being subjected to formal investigations to ascertain whether or not she was implicated in Wyatt's Rebellion, after two weeks there was still insufficient evidence against Elizabeth. Wyatt had been offered a pardon if he would implicate her, but he had refused. Elizabeth continued to protest her innocence, but the leaders of the revolt had used her as their figurehead and she must have been aware of this. Indeed, it was argued that they would not have presumed to use her in this way if she had not been in favour of the revolt. But Elizabeth still refused to implicate herself. Mary's supporters were anxious to convince Mary that she would never be secure while Elizabeth lived, but while Mary dithered the council bickered among themselves. There was insufficient evidence to proceed lawfully, but it was suggested that she should be sent to Pontefract Castle in Yorkshire. It was there that Richard II had met his mysterious end, and it was hinted that something similar could be arranged for Elizabeth.

This was probably said in the knowledge that Elizabeth would learn of it and decide to admit to her involvement. If this was the case, it didn't work; it did leave a lasting impression, though. On 19 May, after being held for eight weeks, Elizabeth was informed that she was being removed from the Tower and put under house arrest. She left the Tower by water, and public rejoicing broke out because people mistakenly thought she was at liberty. She wasn't. The barge arrived at Richmond Palace, a few miles downstream of Hampton Court Palace. A jealous Henry VIII had forced Cardinal Wolsey to take Richmond Palace in exchange for the opulent Hampton Court Palace, which the cardinal had made into the finest house in the land.

It was here at Richmond Palace that Elizabeth spent the night under the guard of Sir Henry Bedingfield, a staunch supporter of Queen Mary. In July 1553, he had been one of the first to rally to Mary's standard when she levied war against the recently crowned Queen Jane. His loyalty had earned him a place on Mary's council, and now he had orders to administer to the royal prisoner. He would have obeyed Mary's orders unquestioningly, and if those orders were to eliminate Elizabeth he would not have hesitated. This is why Elizabeth confided in her gentleman usher, 'This night, I think to die.'

She didn't, but for the next few months she lived in constant fear of assassination. Elizabeth didn't normally let her feelings show, but by constantly calling public attention to the likelihood of her assassination she was making it doubly difficult for Bedingfield and the government to act. From Richmond she was taken to Woodstock in Oxfordshire, which had been chosen as her place of imprisonment; the journey took a further four days.[22]

Woodstock was an ancient royal estate. The structure was mainly built in the reign of Henry II and modernised by Henry VII, but it was in need of an update. It also lacked security, not least because over half the warders and attendants were Elizabeth's servants. On a windowpane at Woodstock Elizabeth scratched the words, 'Much suspected, by me, nothing proved can be, Quoth Elizabeth, prisoner.'[23]

Elizabeth was in limbo. Until she was formally charged she remained a prisoner, yet she still insisted that she was innocent. She begged to be put on trial or to be allowed to speak to Mary or a delegation from the council, and eventually, in September 1554, she was given permission to approach the council in writing. Men like Bishop Gardiner and Simon Renard, Ambassador to Emperor Charles V, despised and mistrusted Elizabeth. They put pressure on Mary to execute Elizabeth to ensure her future safety, but Mary was reluctant to act. All three felt that Elizabeth was guilty, but Mary knew that the people of England would not stand for Elizabeth's execution unless there was solid evidence that she had been involved in the plot.

Many years later, when being pressed to name her successor, Elizabeth said that Wyatt's Rebellion had taught her that the second person in the realm was ever at the mercy of any person or group who chose to plot against the sovereign: 'I learned how to keep silent during the time of Queen Mary when had anything been proved against me, I should have lost my life.'[24]

Elizabeth would not have been unaware of what was happening in the outside world – her clandestine communication network would have made sure of that. She knew that the new queen was restoring Catholicism, and sweeping away all the changes made by Henry VIII and Edward VI. England was about to experience a counter-revolution, and there was no place in it for Elizabeth. Henry had removed his sister Margaret Tudor and her Stuart descendants from the line of succession. Edward had ignored their father's wishes and nominated Jane Grey as his successor, albeit unsuccessfully. If Mary was to do the same, Elizabeth could be removed from the royal lineage. Queen Mary could reinstate the Stuart line and nominate her namesake, the legitimate Catholic heir Mary Queen of Scots, as her successor. She had royal blood coursing through her veins, she was the queen's cousin once removed and, most important of all in Mary's eyes, she was Catholic.

6

Mary Marries Philip of Spain

Wyatt's Rebellion did nothing to prevent Mary from marrying Philip. Around the time that Elizabeth arrived at Woodstock, Mary began her slow journey west to meet her prospective husband, who landed at Southampton on 20 July 1554. It is widely believed that Philip was not impressed when he first saw Mary. The portrait he had been shown previously was flattering, and there was muttering that Mary was old enough to be his mother. This was not strictly true, but she was eleven years his senior, and in the 1520s she had been betrothed to his father for four years until the betrothal was broken off. She was delighted to have such a handsome young bridegroom, and the charming Philip was quite prepared to commit himself to the marriage.

It was obvious that the English people were not prepared to allow their country to be placed into Spanish hands, so in an attempt to moderate this last legal obstacle, a brief Act of Parliament was passed in April 1554. It declared that 'the regal power of this realm is in the Queen's majesty as fully and absolutely as ever it was in any of her most noble progenitors, kings of this realm'. Mary was now legally and unconditionally queen, and could bestow the title of king if and when she pleased. Under the terms of Queen Mary's Marriage Act, then, Philip was to be styled King of England, all official documents including Acts of Parliament were to be dated with both their names, and Parliament was to be called under the joint authority of the couple; however, all of this would hold for Mary's lifetime only. England would not be obliged to provide military support to Philip's father in any war, and Philip could not act without his wife's consent or appoint foreigners to office in England.[1] Philip was unhappy at the conditions imposed, but he was ready to agree for the sake of securing the marriage.[2]

Mary and Philip were married on 25 July at Winchester. It was St James' Day, an apt choice when St James was the patron saint of Spain. Philip's father handed over the kingdoms of Naples and Jerusalem from his ample store of titles, giving Mary and Philip one of the longest and most portentous royal titles ever seen in any English legal document. It was formally announced at their wedding that they were 'King and Queen of England, France, Naples, Jerusalem and Ireland, Defender of the Faith. Princes of Spain and Sicily, Archdukes of Austria, Dukes of Milan, Burgundy and Brabant, Counts of Habsburg, Flanders and Tyrol.'

In September 1554, Mary stopped menstruating. She gained weight, and felt nauseous in the mornings. For these reasons, almost the entirety of her court, including her doctors, believed her to be pregnant.[3] Parliament passed an Act making Philip regent in the event of Mary's death in childbirth.[4]

That Christmas at court there was much celebrating. Sir William, as a Privy Councillor, had to spend considerable time in London but had not renewed the lease on the London house, which they left at the time of the Lady Jane Grey affair.[5]

Both Bess and William shared an interest in the building work at Chatsworth, and in March 1555 Sir William wrote to his friend Sir John Thynne, who was building Longleat down in the West Country: 'Sir, I understand that you have a cunning plasterer at Longleat, which hath in your hall and in other places of your house made diverse pendants and other pretty things. If your business be at an end, or will be by next summer after this, I pray you that I might have him in Derbyshire, for my hall is yet unmade. And therefore now might he devise with my own carpenter how he should frame the same that it might serve for his work.' Sir William's hall was to remain unfinished until 1570.

Bess was eight months pregnant in March 1555 when Sir William wrote to Sir John Thynne with an urgent request, asking if he could lease his house in Brentford for a year. It was close enough to London for Sir William's work yet far enough out of town to be away from immediate danger and infection in an age when plague was rife. Sir John readily agreed, and three weeks later, on 31 March 1555, Bess gave birth to daughter Elizabeth. Lady Katherine Grey and the Marchioness of Northampton were her godparents.

Bess obviously stayed in close contact with the Grey family, and was probably one of the first to know that Lady Frances Grey, mother of Jane, Katherine and Mary, was planning to marry again less than a month after the execution of her husband Henry Grey. The Lady Frances was thirty-seven, and her young betrothed was her twenty-one-year-old former equerry, Adrian Stokes. What Bess thought about the match is not recorded, but Princess Elizabeth was appalled. She referred to Adrian Stokes as her cousin's horse keeper, due to the fact that he had recently been promoted to the post of Master of Horse. The hasty marriage was probably arranged due to the fact that Frances was pregnant, and she soon gave birth to a daughter they called Elizabeth.[6]

On 4 April 1555 the king and queen moved to Hampton Court Palace for Easter, and a few days later the queen was taken to her chamber where she was to remain until the birth of her child. She was confident that with her own sons and heirs to continue after her the Catholic future of England would be guaranteed, but there were whispers that her pregnancy was not progressing normally. It was even suggested that she was bewitched, and after it was revealed that Elizabeth had consulted her old tutor John Dee to cast the queen's horoscope, he was duly arrested. On 17 April, Elizabeth was released from house arrest at Woodstock and summoned to attend her sister at Hampton Court Palace where a close eye could be kept on her activities.

Elizabeth arrived at Hampton Court between 24 and 29 April to witness the pending birth.[7] The two half-sisters had never shown any family resemblance, but now the difference in their appearance was particularly marked. Mary was overweight and looked old and unwell, while Elizabeth, now twenty-two, had matured into an attractive young woman 'well formed with a good skin, although olive'.[8] False rumours quickly spread that the queen had been safely delivered of a son. Bells were rung, anthems sung and the news soon reached Europe.[9]

The next day it was reported that the news was false. There was no baby, but what had happened is unclear. Through May and June, the apparent delay in delivery fed gossip that Mary was not pregnant.[10] Mary's physicians were at last daring to doubt Mary's pregnancy, and were suggesting that it was due to physical or mental illness, although Mary was not prepared to admit this. She still insisted that she was pregnant, but Philip like many others now knew that she wasn't. The symptoms of her 'malady' included her body swelling and her breasts enlarging and giving milk, all of which could be misconstrued as pregnancy. Modern historians think Mary's phantom pregnancy was due to a large ovarian cyst, and this is also what led to her failing health and eventual death. Such things were not understood in the Tudor age, but when pregnancy was ruled out it had to be considered that she was terminally ill.[11]

While people fussed around the queen, Elizabeth asked to see the council. However, when she again refused to acknowledge her guilt in Wyatt's Rebellion she was threatened with a long imprisonment. The fear of assassination returned when she was summoned to the queen's apartment at 10 p.m. She was escorted by torchlight across the garden to the foot of the privy stairs, which led directly to Mary's bedchamber. Elizabeth knelt before her sister while Mary chided her for her refusal to admit her evident guilt. But with a year having passed since the rebellion, Elizabeth was sensing a changing mood. It would appear that Philip had been responsible for instigating this meeting, although he wasn't present.

Philip was now driven largely by self-interest and to some extent self-preservation. His interest in England had always been strategic rather than romantic; he had married Mary to gain English support for Spain against France. Any children of the marriage would make his position strong, but if Mary died childless, as seemed increasingly likely, the legitimate Catholic heir to the throne was the thirteen-year-old Mary Queen of Scots, who was betrothed to the dauphin of France. If Mary Queen of Scots became Queen of England, it would spell disaster for Spain. She would fuse England and Scotland before uniting them with France, making a vast Franco-British realm that would control the Channel and split the eastern and western halves of Spain's European empire.

He had to stop the Scottish queen from succeeding, and the most obvious way was to suggest an alternative: Princess Elizabeth. Previously Philip had only seen Elizabeth as an obstacle that might prevent the English succession of his own offspring. The idea to assassinate her may have originated with Philip, but now he saw how useful she could be as Mary's successor; all he had to do was convince his wife. Given that Mary believed in the legal and moral authority of husbands over wives, and the innate superiority of men, Philip did not envisage any problems.

Elizabeth, apparently restored to favour, remained with Mary throughout May and June.[12] This was partly due to sisterly compassion and partly because she was still theoretically a prisoner, but mainly because Philip had willed it. Elizabeth couldn't help but be moved by the way Mary waited month after month for the expected arrival. She saw her pain and mental anguish as several times a day she would spend time sitting on the floor with her knees drawn up to her chin in a stance that reflected both a physical and mental yearning for a child. Eventually, four months after she had taken to her chamber with pomp and publicity, it was obvious that there was no child and she could pretend no longer.

When she slipped away from Hampton Court Palace unannounced, the secrecy prompted the gossip. Many never doubted that the queen was in fact pregnant, but nevertheless turned nasty, suggesting that the foetus had been so badly deformed it looked like a pet monkey. It was said that there had then been a delay while a frantic search to find a normal replacement had been carried out, but that failed miserably because of the need for secrecy. The queen was understandably bitter, and decided that her false pregnancy was God's punishment for having tolerated heretics in her realm.

Philip had expected to rule as regent while the queen had been indisposed, and was not pleased to have been refused the authority to rule in his wife's place. He assumed that as the father of the heir to the throne his position would be strengthened, but that now seemed in question. Mary was thirty-eight, with a record of ill health and an overwhelming desire to have a child; she needed a husband in constant attendance to maximise her chances of conception. However, Philip had decided to cut his losses and leave to command his armies against France in Flanders.[13] He assured Mary that he would only be gone for a short while and set sail on 29 August – he would not return for two years. Mary was heartbroken and fell into a deep depression. The Venetian ambassador Giovanni Michiel was touched by the queen's grief; he wrote that she was 'extraordinarily in love' with her husband, and was disconsolate at his departure.[14]

In all, Philip was to spend only a year and a half in England during his four-year marriage. When he failed to return, Mary was left to wrestle with her insecurities. Her sorrow was compounded by stories of Philip's womanising, and she turned more and more to religion for consolation.

As well as a comfort, religion became Mary's obsession. She was determined to reinstate Catholicism, and showed no pity for those who were not prepared to denounce Protestantism. In early 1555 Mary's infamous burnings began, and she acquired the nickname Bloody Mary for this barbaric practice.[15] Those who were not prepared to bend with the prevailing wind began to escape abroad to avoid persecution, and as the crisis over religious differences accelerated throughout 1555 the trickle of exiles became a flood.

On 18 October 1555, Elizabeth eventually gained permission to return to her home at Hatfield House. Her old servants gathered around her, and some of the most interesting and remarkable women of the era found themselves drawn to Hatfield. In Elizabeth's company, conventional and unconventional views were expressed on religion, society and politics. Elizabeth never forgot the people who had helped her or suffered on her behalf during the traumatic time she had spent as a prisoner, and she showed her gratitude with positions and favours.

Mary couldn't hide away and spend her days in prayer and meditation. As queen she had to take up the reins of government, and she had to do it alone. On 21 October 1555 she opened her fourth parliament. How different things were from the previous year. Newly married and expecting a child, everything had looked promising back then. Now she was exposed as barren, and the mood of the government had changed.

The queen lacked confidence and authority, but to convey otherwise she concentrated on subjects closest to her heart; she declared the marriage of her parents valid and worked to abolish

Edward's religious laws.[16] Church doctrine was restored to the form it had taken in the Six Articles of 1539.[17]

She attempted to return former Church land and revenues to the Church, but understandably the commons were loath to surrender this valuable income as it would need to be replaced by the burden of higher taxation. They also saw this as moral pressure, the thin end of the wedge applied to force the similar surrender of their own gains from the Church and even the most pious were not prepared to submit to this. The former monastic lands remained in the hands of their influential new owners.[18]

Mary was on a mission, and she was out for revenge. By the end of 1554 the Heresy Acts were revived.[19] Numerous Protestants were executed, but around 800 rich Protestants chose exile instead.[20] Three weeks later Mary took things one step further with a bill to confiscate the estates of the exiles who had fled abroad to escape religious persecution at her hands. The use of the term 'exile' had infuriated Mary, who referred to them as 'those wretches, those heretics, those traitorous, execrable villains'. In her eyes they were enemies of the country and many had acquired their vast incomes through blasphemy and desecration. Formerly the law had allowed the seizure of moveable goods, but most of these were already out of the government's reach. What Mary wanted was to be allowed to confiscate their properties, their landed wealth.

As the crisis loomed, Parliament was at a loss as to what to do. Three days previously, on 3 December, they had been forced to pass the bill on ecclesiastical lands and revenues being passed back to the Church. The vote had been carried 193 to 126. Was the same thing going to happen again when they had to vote on the exiles bill? One man, Sir Anthony Kingston, was bold enough to retaliate, and locked the members inside. This rather unorthodox approach worked, and the bill was defeated. Kingston was sent to the Tower for two weeks, but three days after the bill was defeated Parliament was dissolved. Mary's campaign had come crashing down around her. Parliament was not prepared to back her personal vendettas, and for the first time in history there was no solidarity between the reigning monarch and her government. Royal authority had been broken. Unfortunately, Mary combined political obtuseness with a sense of her own righteousness.

The situation would have been at a stalemate if Henry Dudley, elder brother of the disgraced John Dudley, hadn't come up with a comprehensive scheme to overthrow Mary's government. His accomplice was Sir Anthony Kingston, the man who had forced the defeat of the exiles bill. Their plan was simple. Together they would march on London, marry Elizabeth to Edward Courtenay, the exiled Earl of Devon, and make them King and Queen of England. It was, in essence, a repeat of Wyatt's Rebellion, but again there was nothing that directly implicated Elizabeth.

To finance the operation the plotters appealed to the French King Henri II, but at the beginning of February 1556 Henri had signed the truce of Vaucelles with Mary's husband Philip of Spain. It was not a good time to destabilise Philip's position in England, so financial assistance was refused. Then news of the plot leaked out, and on 18 March the London plotters were arrested. Kingston died on his way to the Tower, but Dudley remained free in France. Arrests continued through April, and in May members of Elizabeth's household were rounded up and interrogated. Kat Ashley was again arrested, along with Elizabeth's Italian teacher Battista Castiglione and three others. As incriminating evidence against Elizabeth was too plentiful to ignore, the question of what to do with her became paramount. She was detained under house arrest as guards were put on the door while Mary wrote to her estranged husband Philip of Spain for advice.

Philip considered Elizabeth's evident guilt, her dabbling in treason and her desire to undermine Mary's desire to restore Catholicism, and weighed them up against his own dynastic self-interest. If Elizabeth was found guilty she would be executed, and that would mean Mary Queen of Scots, future Dauphiness of France, as Mary's successor. Despite the recently signed treaty, France and Spain were still enemies and Philip had no desire to strengthen their hold on Britain. In Philip's mind there was only one answer.

He wrote back to Mary instructing her to drop all enquiries into Elizabeth's guilt. He also instructed her to make it known that any of Elizabeth's servants who were implicated in the plot had used their mistress's name without authority. Mary promptly obeyed, sending two of her most trusted councillors to assure Elizabeth that despite her servants' confessions the queen did not believe that her sister was implicated in any way. Furthermore, they said the queen did not believe that her sister would undertake anything against her sovereign, and in testimony of her good opinion Mary sent Elizabeth a diamond. In obeying Philip's instruction, Mary had lied through her teeth and Elizabeth knew it. She felt nothing but contempt for her sister. But Mary had a small victory when she insisted that Elizabeth underwent a form of house arrest. It was not in the same league as her incarceration at Woodstock, but Sir Thomas Pope and Robert Gage were put in charge of both her person and her household for the next six months.

There was also the matter of Elizabeth's marriage, and Philip had chosen her bridegroom – his friend Emmanuel Philibert, Duke of Savoy. Being abroad, Philip could not convince Elizabeth to accept the betrothal but he put enormous pressure on his wife to do this for him. When Elizabeth told Mary emphatically that she had no interest in marrying Emmanuel Philibert, Mary threatened Elizabeth with a parliamentary declaration of her bastardy and an acknowledgement of Mary Queen of Scots as her heir. Nonetheless, Elizabeth refused to comply and parliamentary consent looked unlikely.[21]

The politics of Europe in the early 1550s was dominated by the rivalry between the house of Austria, personified by the Emperor Charles V, and the house of Valois under Henri II, King of France. Charles V handed Spain and the Netherlands to his son Philip in 1556, and the struggle narrowed to a rivalry between Spain and France.

In January 1557 Henri II broke the truce of Vaucelles and resumed war with the Habsburgs, and in March Philip had to return to England to lobby for support in the war. Both England and Scotland were like pawns in this rivalry; England because Mary I was married to Philip of Spain, and Scotland because Mary Queen of Scots was betrothed to Henri's son Francis.

The relationship between Mary and Philip might have been over, but they must have slept together at some point because Mary soon fancied herself pregnant once more. She must have been totally besotted by Philip, and desperate for the marriage to work. She readily agreed to the pressure he put on Elizabeth to marry Emmanuel Philibert, who was now Philip's chief general in the north. Elizabeth was told that if she accepted Emmanuel Philibert she would have immediate assurance of her place as Mary's successor, but it would come courtesy of the King of Spain and with strings attached. She had no desire to be indebted to Spain for anything, and she had seen how Mary had lost the affection of her people after marrying a foreigner. Elizabeth was shrewd and used delaying tactics. She was confident that if she waited long enough, her position as Mary's heir would come to her anyway as laid down in her father's will. It would happen with or without Philip's support.

Despite the dire financial state of the country, Mary was determined to help her adored husband raise funds for his war with France. She promised him the support of the English navy, and after a clash of opinions with her Privy Councillors, 6,000 foot soldiers and 600 cavalry were pledged to stave off a French attack on the Spanish-occupied Netherlands. In order to send financial aid to Philip, Queen Mary despatched privy seals across the country asking the powerful landowners of each county to loan her £100. In Derbyshire, Sir William Cavendish is reported as refusing to comply.[22]

Probably many others refused as well, because when Mary's request failed to raise sufficient funds she forced a minting of new coins for general supply. As the newly minted coins flooded the market, they could not be supported by the Treasury and the groat was considerably devalued. This caused great concern among London merchants but enabled Mary to raise 150,000 ducats for Philip. His visit lasted just three months. He left on 5 July, and for Philip it had certainly been worth a brief reconciliation with his wife.

The Cavendish Downfall

Bess returned to Chatsworth to give birth to her seventh child, Mary, born in January 1556. She could have continued to live the life of a country lady, surrounded by her family, having babies, overseeing the completion of Chatsworth and dealing with the administration of the estate, but Sir William's health was causing concern. On 9 July he wrote to Sir John Thynes at Longleat, cancelling his intended visit as 'I am fallen into my old disease and sickness, and am so ill that I shall not be able to ride'.[23]

Although he would never fully recover, Sir William was at work in London at the time of Philip's arrival in England. Meanwhile at Chatsworth, on 2 March 1557, Bess gave birth to her eighth child, Lucretia, named for a classic heroine whose chastity and liberality were famed. Both Lucretia's birth and Sir William's presence in London coincided with another event that was about to change the lives and fortunes of the Cavendishes.

Driven as they were by a desire to acquire money for Philip, Mary's home policies were desperately unpopular with her mediators and counsellors. She felt she was surrounded by malevolent Protestant advisers, and, determined to get rid of them, she demanded an audit of every department in her administration. Many of the men who had acquired major offices under her predecessors had purchased their positions and been appointed on very low salaries. Their low wages were expected to be offset by the sale of favours, which in effect amounted to an indirect tax. This was an accepted part of life in the Tudor court, but Mary saw it as an area where she could claw back money.

Among those who came under scrutiny was Sir William Cavendish, and his Privy Chamber accounts for his entire period of office from February 1546 until 1557 were examined.[24]

The Lord Treasurer William Paulett had the task of sorting out payments and receipts, a time-consuming and laborious task when many of Sir William's private and official business accounts were mixed up. He had been doing nothing different to other similarly placed officials, but the audit revealed significant errors. The total claimed by Sir William during the period in question exceeded the amount that could be accounted for by £6,000. The discrepancies would have to be explained and made good.

The obvious questions were asked. How had he been able to build up his estates? He had paid £600 for Chatsworth through short-term borrowing and swaps. He had made deals at bargain prices, sometimes in return for favours, but the question remained: how was he able to afford to buy bargain properties at the time they appeared when he had no financial means?

How had the Cavendishes acquired all the lavish assets listed in the 1553 inventory?[25] All the precious commodities that furnished Chatsworth had to be accounted for. Were they bought, or were they the spoils of his work during the dissolution? There were no records.

Perhaps they were gifts resulting from favours bestowed by Sir William. He had purchased his post as Treasurer for £1,000, and according to the custom of the times it was quite acceptable – expected, in fact – that he would earn this sum back through the perquisites of the office. It could have been down to careless bookkeeping, although there is no indication of this in any other aspect of Sir William's life – nor is there any reason to believe that he set out to deliberately embezzle.

Errors in bookkeeping might be at least partly to blame. Sir William claimed that there were some major issues of allowable expenditure which had not been entered in the accounts, and he blamed such discrepancies on his assistant Thomas Knot, who had served under Sir William's predecessor Sir Bryan Tuke. Sir William had inherited him along with the job, and as he told the court, he found no reason to question his honesty or ability. Thomas Knot kept the books, and some of the accounts that survive today at Kew Public Record Office are in Knot's handwriting, which would confirm this. Even more significant, as soon as the audit began Knot vanished and could not be traced, leaving Sir William to 'carry the can' alone. Being reliant on the dubious bookkeeping of a dishonest clerk who was probably lining his own pockets made it doubly difficult to get to the bottom of the problem.[26] Sir William further claimed that due to his recent illness his personal accounts, prepared by the errant Thomas Knot, were found to be short of an amount in excess of £1,231.

Sir William ended his statement with a personal plea to the queen, but whether she ever received it is doubtful. She never responded, and in midsummer 1557 he was summoned to appear before the Star Chamber to answer the charges against him. Bess immediately left Chatsworth to go to her husband, leaving five-month-old Lucretia in the care of a wet nurse. She set off on 20 August with a small group and travelled fast, taking just three days and nights when the journey normally took four. Her urgency must reflect the mental and physical state that Sir William was in. His letter to the queen had spoken of his innocent children, who were utterly undone, and how they were 'like to spend our days in no small penurie'.[27]

Not only did Sir William want his wife by his side, he wanted her to use her assiduous bookkeeping skills to help sort out the many ledgers that the court demanded. Over the next few weeks, with Sir William's secretary Robert Bestnay, they submitted nine books of updated accounts, together with a letter explaining that Sir William was too ill to attend his court hearing on 10 October before the Star Chamber. This was not an exaggeration; on 7 October a priest said Mass in the house, which would this indicate that Sir William had asked for the last rites. On the day before the hearing, the books were returned with a letter stating that there was no hint that peculation was suspected. However, having taken into account all the extra allowances he had claimed, the deficit over the previous eleven years up to October 1556 still amounted to £5,237 5s ¼d.

Sir William's health deteriorated further, and on 25 October 1557 he died. Bess made the final entry in the pocketbook in which Sir William had entered the details of their marriage and the births of each of their children:

Sir William Cavendish Knight, my most dear and well-loved husband, departed this present life of Monday, being the 25th day of October, betwixt the hours of 8 and 9 of the same day, at night in the year of Our Lord God 1557 on whose soul I most humbly beseech the Lord to have mercy, and to rid me and his poor children of our great misery.[28]

In the sixteenth century it was customary for a widow to enter into a Month's Mind, a period of intense mourning and lamentation. Bess was now thirty, mother of six children under eight years old, chatelaine of her own great house with its staff of dependent servants and facing bankruptcy. It was fortuitous that Sir William had left everything to Bess for her lifetime, only entailing the land and house at Chatsworth to their eldest son after her death. This meant there was nothing upon which to base a wardship, so at least

Bess could avoid the crippling consequences her family had suffered when she was a child.

Sir William was interred in the family tomb at the church of Saint Botolph without Aldersgate in London, and although the children were sent back to Chatsworth, Bess remained in London. Despite her husband's statement of appeal, his debt was still over £5,000 and it didn't die with him.

Massive debts owed to the state were not unusual, and a means of getting the money back was the subject of legislation by Parliament in February 1558 when it was proposed to confiscate Cavendish lands to recover the debts. Bess was faced with a seemingly impossible situation, and the obvious answer was to allow her properties to be confiscated without making any attempt to find an alternative. But an enforced sale to pay back the Exchequer would only recoup part of the property's value and someone would get Bess's beloved Chatsworth at a real bargain. That thought alone was probably enough to spur Bess on, yet as a lone woman with no official position, few permitted rights and no strong male relative to take up her case, how was she going to fight the legal action? Few if any non-royal women of that era are known to have fought Parliament, but Bess was preparing to fight back.

Things looked bleak but not hopeless. To keep what she already had and bring up her young family in the face of such difficulties required financial acumen beyond the ability of many, but the figures didn't stack up. The income from the Cavendish estates both owned and leased was £500 a year, a substantial enough sum if she didn't have the debt to the Exchequer to consider. If she was to pay back half of her entire income each year it would not only leave her with inadequate funds to maintain her estates but would take a minimum of twenty-six years to pay back the capital sum alone. With this in mind, Bess appealed to the network of her late husband's powerful friends, writing to many for help. One letter was written to her friend Sir John Thynne of Longleat:[29]

> Sir, I am now driven to crave your help. I have deferred the time of my sending to you for that I well hope till now... that I should have had no occasion to have troubled you. But now there is a bill in the Parliament House against me. It is a general bill and doth

touch many and if it pass it will not only undo me and my poor children, but a great number of others. It has been twice read in the Lord's House but it shall be brought up again of Monday or Tuesday, so that it is thought that it will be Wednesday or Thu ere it is brought into the Lord's House.

If it should please you to be here at this time, I should think myself most bounded to you, and although I be in no ways able to recompense you during my life, I will never be forgetful.

The time is so short that I would not thus boldy have sent for you unless you might have had more time to have prepared yourself in, but that Master March willed me in any ways to entreat you to come, which is more than becometh me, all things considered.

I trust I shall have a great many friends and if you will take the pains to come I shall have many more by your means ... And so I take my leave praying you to bear with my rude letter, in considering what a trouble is able to do. Your poor friend for ever, E. Cavendish.[30]

For a recently widowed lady to be in contact with men outside her family for any reason, let alone business matters, would be considered unfeminine and immodest, but that did not trouble Bess. In another appeal, she admitted to feeling 'great fear' at the immensity of the task she had taken on, but she knew it wasn't just Cavendish property that was at stake. Many of their peers were also affected, and this is what Bess was gambling on in her next letter when she wrote, 'The bill is so evil liked of the house and I trust through the help of you and others, true made my friends, it shall take small effect and not do me any hurt ... for there are few in the house that they or their friends should not smart if the Act should pass.'[31] She probably touched a nerve, because when the petition was presented in court in February 1558, despite Bess having gone against the queen, all the men she had approached came to her aid and voted against the decision. The bill was duly opposed, and lay in abeyance for some years. Bess was still indebted to the state, but there were no immediate plans to seize her properties to pay the debt. It was a well-won victory for Bess, but she was exhausted both physically and mentally.

It was no longer necessary for Bess to remain in London, so she returned to her family at Chatsworth. There is no further mention of baby Lucretia, so it is assumed the baby died, making this a time of double mourning for Bess. Many years later Bess made a tapestry of the classical heroine Lucretia, probably in memory of her daughter. It is still at Hardwick.

In London, Queen Mary was also in mourning for her absent husband. She was still convinced that she was pregnant, but this time she was sure that her child would live and she would die. It seems likely that she summoned her sister Elizabeth to be with her during her labour, just as she had been two years previously. Elizabeth duly arrived at her London base, Somerset House, on 25 February but left on 5 March to return to the country. Mary made her will as the ninth month approached on 20 March, convinced that the crown would go to 'the heirs, issue and fruit of my body'. She also stipulated that Philip would be appointed guardian and regent for the child. Money was left for the work she had begun but not had time to complete, and finally she commanded all her subjects to obey Philip. That summer, there were widespread rumours that the queen was suffering from a fatal dropsy.

The Cavendish account book had stopped on 13 October 1557, exactly twelve days before Sir William's death. It began again on 13 June 1558, by which time Bess was back in London, renting the Brentford house from Sir John Thynne for a year. A few days later she had the children brought down to join her.[32]

Though the legislation she had so feared was no longer an immediate threat, the huge debt still loomed over her head. Bess had an idea, however, and planned to work on it. Forgiveness of Sir William's debt was in the sovereign's power, so Bess intended to ask for clemency. William had ministered to the queen to the best of his ability, but his obligation and relationship had gone even further. After all, Sir William had befriended the lonely princess when she had been exiled. Over a period of years, he had paid visits to Princess Mary and given her small gifts. When she was attempting to reclaim her crown from Lady Jane Grey, he had mustered a fighting force of his own at Chatsworth to go to Mary's aid at a personal cost of 1,000 marks.[33] When Bess had given birth to her fifth child, Charles, in November 1553, Queen Mary had been his godmother. Surely all this counted for something; surely the queen must feel some obligation to her former minister who had been the victim of someone else's misdemeanours. But Bess had waited too long. Queen Mary was a desperately sick woman. She had only brief periods of respite from pain in which to make decisions, and any official business was totally beyond her.

Undeterred, Bess made plans to appeal to the queen-in-waiting, Princess Elizabeth, who was just a couple of hours ride north of Brentford at Hatfield House. When Bess closed the London house to return to Chatsworth on 25 September, it would not have been out of her way to go via Hatfield and pay her respects. It would have been a good time to make contact, and confirm her support before Elizabeth was swamped by courtiers defecting from Mary's court. After all, in December 1550 the seventeen-year-old Princess Elizabeth had been godparent to Bess's son Henry, so they were not strangers.

There is no record of what happened to Bess in the two months between leaving Brentford on 25 September and returning there on 25 November. Bess may have returned to Chatsworth or stayed at Hatfield House. Its highly probable that she met up with her friend Sir William St Loe, who was a member of Elizabeth's household. His father, Sir John St Loe, was a neighbour of her friend Sir John Thynne, and very much a member of the Protestant set to which Sir William Cavendish had belonged along with Dudley and Henry Grey. William St Loe had spent time in the Tower before being transferred to the Fleet Prison for his part in Wyatt's Rebellion. He was lucky not to have lost his life, and on his release Elizabeth immediately acknowledged her debt to William St Loe by naming him captain of her personal guard.

If Bess did return to Chatsworth, it's probable that William St Loe kept her informed of events in the capital as Mary's health gradually declined. She had bouts of insomnia, depression, loss of vision, headaches and weakness.[34] In early October she became dangerously ill. Her doctors sent regular bulletins to Philip, but he was busy arranging the funeral of his father Charles V and made no attempt to visit his dying wife.[35]

On 28 October, Mary added a codicil to her will confronting the fact that 'God hath hitherto sent me no fruit nor heir of my body' and in the absence of her own issue and heir she would be succeeded by 'my next heir and successor by the laws of this realm'. No one was mentioned by name, but in case of trouble, Elizabeth was advised to take up residence at Brocket Hall. It was only 2½ miles north of Hatfield Old Palace, but it had better defences and could withstand any possible attack. This must have been a stressful time for St Loe, who was responsible for Elizabeth's safety at all times.

Sometime between 5 and 6 a.m. on 17 November 1558, forty-two-year-old Queen Mary died, leaving a will that is a pathetic testament to disillusion and obsession. There was no child, no heir to continue her lineage. Mary acknowledged that Philip would have no further part in the government of England, but she beseeched him to take England under his wing. When Philip heard of Mary's death he wrote that he felt a 'reasonable regret'. Pole, who died the same day, described her life as 'like a flickering light, buffeted by raging winds for its utter extinction, but always kept burning by innocence and lively faith'.[36]

Mary is remembered more for her failures than her successes, yet she deserves more than our pity; she deserves our respect. Against all the odds, she had claimed her throne, married the man of her choice and turned the religious wheel round by making England a Catholic country again. She was a woman in a man's world. She had proved that a woman could be queen and rule a country, and as such had set a template for Elizabeth to follow. It was her role as a wife and mother that had let her down. Elizabeth would have watched the way Mary handled the task of being queen and she would have learnt from her sister's mistakes. It was a lesson that would stand her in good stead as the next Queen of England, but Mary had not nominated her successor, and there was tough competition from across the Channel in the shape of Mary's cousin, Mary Queen of Scots.

7

Who Will Be Queen of England?

The Stuart family ruled Scotland for nearly 340 years, although their early ancestors were not of royal blood. The family name was originally Steward, the etymology of which suggests a servant role. They were stewards to the ruling family of Brittany, and later great stewards to the kings of Scotland. Walter Stewart, 6th High Steward of Scotland, married Marjorie Bruce, daughter of Robert I (Robert the Bruce, 1274–1329). Walter fathered Robert II, who after a fifty-year wait became King of the Scots and thus founded the Steward/Stewart royal line in 1371. Robert II was a handsome, charming man who had two wives, many mistresses and numerous children. The number of children that he produced is unclear, but in 1390 he was succeeded by his legitimate son Robert III. In 1406, James I took the throne and ruled for thirty-one years. He was followed by James II (1437–60), James III (1460–88) and James IV.

Many of the early Stewart kings came to the throne in their childhood, and because of the lack of adult succession this not only weakened the power of the Crown but allowed powerful chieftains and nobles to grasp power for themselves. It also encouraged predatory advances from England, resulting in endless wars. But King Henry VII of England was a wise king, and in an attempt to forge friendship between the two countries and stop the never-ending wars he married his eldest daughter, Margaret Tudor, to James IV of Scotland, who became king in 1488. It didn't work. When Margaret's brother Henry became King Henry VIII of

England there was still much trouble, and at the Battle of Flodden Field James IV lost his life at the hands of the English.

The crown of Scotland went to his baby son James V, and the country was ruled by regents until James became of age and obtained power in 1528. Henry VIII tried to mirror the action of his father, and suggested his own daughter Mary Tudor as a bride for James, but James saw it as his uncle's attempt to envelope Scotland and shunned the suggestion. Henry VIII was angry that his suggestion had been rejected.[1]

James was more interested in Catherine de Medici and her staggering wealth, but this suggestion was viewed very unfavourably by the Pope. Eventually James V's prolonged search for a wealthy bride resulted in a marriage with Madeleine, the sixteen-year-old daughter of Francis I, King of France. Madeleine arrived in Scotland in May 1537 and died two months later. In January 1538, a marriage contract was drawn up between the recently widowed James V and the recently widowed Mary of Guise, who was twenty-two years old. Mary had a three-year-old son named Francis, the new Duke of Longueville, by her first marriage so was clearly capable of bearing children. This was particularly appealing to sixteenth-century monarchs; as covered above, Henry VIII was also interested in a marriage with Mary of Guise.

Accompanied by a fleet of ships and 2,000 lords and barons sent from Scotland to escort her, Mary of Guise landed at Crail in Fife on 10 June 1538, just over a year after the landing of Princess Madeleine.[2] The marriage was definitely one of convenience, and James, who was rumoured to have a mistress at Tantallon, was said to 'set not much store by the queen'.[3]

From the letters Mary sent to her mother in France, she appears to have been terribly homesick and desperately missed her little boy, whom she had been forced to leave behind. Among the letters, Francis sent her lengths of string to show how he was growing. [4] In May 1540 Mary gave birth to James, the longed-for heir, and in April 1541 she produced another son, but he lived for only two days. Within a week, little James was also dead and Scotland was once again without an heir. The royal couple must have been devastated, but Mary assured the king that they were both young enough to have more children.[5]

When Henry demanded a conference in York in September 1541 to plan a way to plunder the Catholic Church, James refused to discuss such a plan or attend the conference. This infuriated Henry, and by the summer of 1542 English forces were being mobilised in the north in an act of suzerainty.

Mary of Guise was again pregnant, and against his better judgement James was forced to assemble his own troops. On 24 November, these forces encountered the English near the River Esk at Solway Moss. The weather was bitter, the conditions appalling and as the Scottish troops were being driven back many were drowned by the incoming tide. Some 1,200 Scots were captured, among them many of the leading nobles. Those who were not captured by the English quarrelled among themselves, showing their strongest loyalty was to themselves rather than to the troubled monarchy. King James, in a state of mental anguish, rode to Edinburgh where he made an inventory of his jewels and treasure, then rode to Hallyards in Fife, the seat of the Treasurer, Sir William Kirkcaldy of Grange. From there he rode to Linlithgow, where he spent time with his wife, then in her final month of pregnancy. He took the defeat of his country personally, and the humiliation and worry brought on a nervous collapse. He was taken to the palace at Falklands, where he oscillated between loud fulmination and silent melancholy.

When the news was received that the queen had given birth to a daughter, the king's servants thought he might pull himself together. The much-needed heir was born on 8 December 1542, the Feast of the Immaculate Concept of the Virgin Mary, but James received the news without emotion. In the sixteenth century, for a country to have a child heiress at its head was widely regarded as disastrous, and all lamented that the realm was without a male to succeed.[6]

Only a generation after the Battle of Flodden Field, in which his father James IV was fatally wounded, James V had been defeated at the Battle of Solway Moss. Within a week he was dead. The 'puir wee lass', as he called his new baby daughter on his deathbed, became Queen of Scotland, and the eighth Stewart ruler.

The infant Mary was baptised by tradition in the Church of St Michael at the gates of the palace of Linlithgow. She was described as a weak child, not likely to survive, but rumours of her ill health were probably fuelled by the previous deaths of her two baby brothers. Chapuys, the Imperial ambassador in London, wrote to the Queen of Hungary on 23 December that both mother and baby were ill and despaired of by their physician.[7]

The situation would have been disastrous if the baby had died, but because Mary continued to live the country was facing the prospect of a long minority. The country was divided, but if Scotland was to survive as an independent nation then the office of governor, the most powerful position in the realm, had to be filled immediately. This was no simple matter. Due to the numerous progeny of Robert II, the first Stewart king, and the intermarriages common to all Scottish noble families of this period, there was a vast number of rival Stewart families, and by the 1540s these ambitious relatives surrounded the crown, eager to secure their hereditary claims. A fierce controversy arose.

On 9 September 1543, Mary was crowned Queen of Scotland at Stirling Castle as the eighth Stewart ruler. Almost immediately negotiations began concerning her marriage. A union between the infant Queen Mary and Prince Edward, son of Henry VIII of England, seemed a strong choice which could put an end to the hostilities between the two countries, but when Catherine de Medici, wife of the future King Henri II of France, gave birth to a son in 1544, this was considered a better alliance for Mary. This infuriated Henry VIII, who sent his armies north in what has become known as the 'rough wooing'. They made constant forays into Scotland, laying siege to castles, savagely attacking abbeys and setting the city of Edinburgh on fire, making it necessary to move the little queen from one castle to another for her own safety.

Early in 1548, a contract was signed consenting to the marriage of Queen Mary of Scotland to Francis of Valois, the Dauphin of France, on condition that the French would provide armies in the defence of Scotland when necessary. On 7 August 1548, the five-year-old queen was taken to France; she would spend the next thirteen years there. The formal betrothal of Mary and Francis took place on 19 April 1558, and the wedding itself was solemnised with pomp and ceremony on 24 April in the cathedral of Notre-Dame, Paris. From then on, their official titles were to be king-dauphin and queen-dauphiness.

Seven months later, on 17 November, Queen Mary of England was at St James's Palace in London when she died. She had been reluctant to name her half-sister Elizabeth as her successor, but, bowing to the inevitable, she had sent Jane Dormer, one of her most trusted women, to Elizabeth at Hatfield with a number of her jewels to ask for Elizabeth's assurance that she would be good to Mary's servants, pay her debts and maintain the Catholic faith in England.

On hearing of Queen Mary's death, King Henri of France was anxious to redress the balance of power and formally declared his daughter-in-law Mary Stuart, Queen-Dauphiness of France, to be Queen of England, Ireland and Scotland. Mary was granddaughter of Henry VIII's sister Margaret and daughter of Mary of Guise, and the Guise family was one of the most powerful, ambitious Catholic families in France. For them, Mary Stuart was the obvious choice as successor to the English throne as Elizabeth was the daughter of 'the king's whore' and a living symbol of the war of faith that divided Europe. The Venetian ambassador commented, 'They have made the Queen-Dauphiness go into mourning for the late Queen of England.' No one was in any doubt as to where these instructions had come from.[8]

Elizabeth Becomes Queen of England

Despite the assumption – in France at least – that Mary Queen of Scots would be Mary Tudor's successor, in England the announcement of Queen Mary's death was swiftly followed by the proclamation that twenty-five-year-old Elizabeth was queen. Fearful of being tricked by a premature rumour of her sister's death, Elizabeth had instructed Sir Nicholas Throckmorton to ride post-haste to Hatfield with Mary's black enamel betrothal ring from Philip as soon as the queen died. Elizabeth and her entourage were expecting the news, and according to legend, a delegation of the late queen's councillors left London for Hatfield and found Elizabeth walking in Hatfield Park. They knelt before her under an oak tree and she purportedly fell to her knees and uttered the words of Psalm 118: '*A Deo factum est; Et mirabile in occulis nostris* (It is the Lord's doing; it is marvellous in our eyes).'

From mid-afternoon the bells of all the London churches were rung, tables were set up in the streets for people to eat, drink and make merry, and bonfires were lit in celebration of the new monarchy. Few regretted Mary's passing; with her death they received a young, beautiful queen with two English parents. The Spanish yoke had been lifted.

Elizabeth had put her time as a potential successor to good use. She was prepared for her takeover of power, and three days later made her first public speech in the Great Hall at Hatfield. Elizabeth had appointed William Cecil as her Principal Secretary. Astute, hardworking and dependable, Cecil had known Elizabeth for years. He was an academic who had adapted to the cut-throat world of court and council, and knew the business of government inside-out. Elizabeth paid much attention to Cecil's advice, and he would prove to be one of the men upon whom she would rely for most of her reign. More immediately, Elizabeth had instructed Cecil to prepare an agenda for the following day's council meeting when she was to announce a significant cull.

She favoured those who had shown her loyalty and opposed the Catholicism of Mary's reign. Elizabeth showed her gratitude to those who had actively supported her and gone to prison for their part in Wyatt's Revolt, rewarding them with titles and favours. These included Sir Nicholas Throckmorton, a cousin of Katherine Parr, who became Chief Butler and Chamberlain of the Exchequer before becoming ambassador to France. Thomas Parry, her former adviser, became Treasurer of the Household. The post of Lord Chamberlain went to her mother's cousin Lord William Howard of Effingham, and Sir Edward Rogers was made Vice-Chamberlain. Nicholas Bacon, brother-in-law of William Cecil, became Lord Keeper of the Great Seal. Sir James Croft was made Captain of Berwick Castle, and John Harington became one of her favourite courtiers. His wife Isabel, who had also been sent to the Tower, was a former maid of honour, and Elizabeth was godmother to their son Jack. When granting Jack a favour, Elizabeth wrote, 'I do this because thy father was ready to serve and love us in trouble and thrall.'[9]

Sir William St Loe, who had served Elizabeth faithfully at Hatfield House, was officially made Captain of the Queen's Guard. Being accountable for her safety at all times meant almost constant attendance at court. He was also responsible for handling £10,000 advances annually from the Treasurer to pay the Lieutenant of the Tower, the gentleman porters, yeoman warders and all other officials and guards who were housed in the Tower of London.[10] A few weeks later he was given a life annuity of 100 marks a year and several lucrative sinecures. These included Chief Butler of England and Chief Butler of Wales, plus all profits from the office. This was indeed a plum job. He was responsible for stocking the queen's cellars with fine wine, and organising deputies who imposed duty on imported wines, rather like early Customs and Excise officers.

Another rewarding sinecure was Master of Horse, and this position was given to Lord Robert Dudley, who had also been imprisoned for his involvement in the Wyatt's Revolt. The position of Master of Horse carried enhanced prestige under a female sovereign because its holder was closest to the queen outside the confines of the palace. He would be by her side when she rode in procession and when she hunted.

Also on the agenda were positions in the royal court or the chamber, which was the name given to the household above stairs. These posts were highly sought after and dealt with the public ceremony of the court as opposed to the personal body service of the lodgings. Each post was valued for the access to the queen it provided, and because this was a female monarch almost all the body servants of the privy and bedchamber had to be female.

The essential shape of both Elizabeth's council and court was decided, with key appointments agreed and the essential process of fusing the old and new councillors begun, but in France the king-dauphin and queen-dauphiness assumed the royal arms of England in addition to those of France and Scotland. This was a rather premature, pretentious act, instigated by the French king to aggravate a delicate situation, and the English state papers show a definite preoccupation with the subject. The French considered Mary's claims to be no more than just, and French writers eagerly commented on the dauphiness's English connection and celebrated her accession to the triple crown in enthusiastic verse: 'Without murder and war, France and Scotland will be with England united.' The match was described as the union of the white lily of France and the white rose of the House of York – an allusion to Mary's Tudor descent.[11]

Unperturbed, Elizabeth left Hatfield on 23 November, but it was not until 28 November, ten days after her accession, that she entered the city of London. At the head of the procession rode her escort of lords and gentlemen; then came the royal party, with Elizabeth dressed in royal purple velvet. Musicians played, trumpets sounded and guns fired royal salutes. There was a general feeling of optimism in the air. The dour days of Queen Mary, with her fractious government, internal dissensions and bad housekeeping, were over. The council ordered all incoming consignments of rich fabrics to be held in readiness 'towards the furniture of her coronation', because Elizabeth intended that no expense would be spared for her coronation procession no matter what state the Treasury was in. Everyone that took part was given one set of clothes; the queen had at least three sets, and the total cost for material alone was in excess of £16,000.

The destination of the royal procession on 28 November was the Tower of London, where Elizabeth had been taken as a prisoner under suspicion of treason and in grave danger just four years before. This time, the twenty-six-year-old was entering in triumph. She remained in the Tower for six days, and then on 5 December left by water to be rowed upstream towards Westminster. Instead of entering the royal palace complex, however, she went to her old home, Somerset House, where she remained until 23 December before moving to Whitehall.

It was an exciting time to be in London. Bess had opened up the house at Bentford by 26 November, and soon sent for the children to join her. In December, hearing of the death of Sir John St Loe, a former friend of Sir William Cavendish, Bess took the opportunity to call on Sir William St Loe to offer her condolences on the death of his father, and to congratulate him in person on his new position in the royal court. William St Loe's inheritance, plus the lands, properties and positions that he had earned in his own right, made the forty-year-old a very rich and successful man, which may have appealed to the thirty-one-year-old widow.[12]

It was decided that Queen Mary's funeral should be a lavish, traditional and Catholic affair. On 10 December her body began its leisurely journey to its final resting place, and after she lay for three days before the altar at St James's Palace the funeral procession made its way to Westminster Abbey. Religious persecution during Mary's reign had led to 300 burnings, 100 deaths in custody and 800 fleeing into exile. Would the tables now be turned, and Catholics persecuted? With the spotlight on religion, it was reported that Elizabeth continued to go to Mass privately at Somerset House, but it was believed that she conformed only outwardly. At heart she was a Protestant, as was her confidant William Cecil, and they thought that true religion was between man and his maker. Many of her contemporaries believed that for a Protestant to take part in a Catholic service was hypocrisy, even apostasy.

For Elizabeth, the move to Whitehall meant that on Sundays, at least, she had to worship in all the publicity of the Chapel Royal. All eyes were on the young queen as she processed with her ladies to hear Mass on Christmas Day. The officiating bishop vested himself for the Mass all in the old form. Elizabeth watched and waited until the gospel was said, then when she should have descended to the altar to make her offering she turned, and, accompanied by her lords and ladies, withdrew to her own chambers. Elizabeth was showing her heterodoxy.

The day for the coronation ceremony was to be 15 January 1559, a date chosen as propitious by the astrologer Dr John Dee.[13] Not only was Dee an astrologer, he was also a serious mathematician and scholar who had taught Elizabeth and her half-brother Edward. This interest in the occult was something that Elizabeth shared with many in her circle, including Bess, who consulted an astrologer to predict the date and time of her wedding to Sir William Cavendish. Dee claimed that the configuration of the heavens on Sunday 15 January presaged a long and successful reign, but the French Catholic seer Michel Nostradamus had predicted imminent catastrophe for Protestant England.

On Thursday 12 January 1559, following an old tradition, the uncrowned monarch travelled by royal barge from Whitehall to take possession of the Tower, the symbolic heart of London. On the Saturday Elizabeth left the Tower for the traditional procession to Westminster, and the next day she was crowned Queen of England. There was a chill in the air and there were flurries of snow, but all the bells of London were pealing joyously and the water conduits ran with wine for several hours. Far from acting like a distant icon, the new queen interacted with her subjects, acknowledging their good wishes and answering their loyal shouts. After a service in Westminster Abbey on the Sunday, a state banquet was held at Westminster Hall; as Chief Butler of England, it was Sir William St Loe who ceremonially offered the first cup of wine to the new sovereign.

In her account books, Bess records a payment for her children to watch the procession from a prime vantage point in the processional stand. There was no mention of her own viewing arrangements, most probably because she was given privileged seating in the abbey as an invited guest. It also very probable that this was arranged by Sir William St Loe. There was obviously a growing attraction between the couple.[14]

On 25 January, Elizabeth was wearing her parliamentary robes for the opening of her first parliament. Sir Nicholas Bacon, the Lord Keeper, read the opening speech, which was measured and authoritative. Bacon told the assembled lords that their main task was to consider the 'well-making of laws for the according and uniting of the people of this realm into a uniform order of religion'. They were to avoid 'all sophistical, captious and frivolous arguments and quiddities ... comlier for scholars than councillors'. They were not to insult each other with terms like 'heretic, schismatic and papist'. Elizabeth wanted religion to be debated in a way that avoided extremes. She had inherited a Catholic country, but in those early months confronting Catholicism was difficult and dangerous.

At Christmas she had shown her disapproval of the old religion, but at Easter she enthusiastically participated in the new. Instead of the Latin Mass, the English communion service was used, and instead of a stone altar there was a wooden communion table covered in a black cloth. Instead of the chalice being reserved for the officiating priest, the laity also communicated, led by the queen, who received communion kneeling at the altar.

Elizabeth established a religious framework around which a new ceremonial religion, with its surviving hodgepodge of rituals and routines, could grow. On 12 May 1559 the new English service began in the Queen's Chapel, and a month later the book of Common Prayer became obligatory, and all the while Elizabeth was giving her enthusiastic and open endorsement of the changes. There were pockets of resistance, but that was to be expected; overall the transition was open, seamless, swift and unopposed.

Mary Queen of Scots Leaves France

Across the channel, the French remained so confident of the Mary Stuart's right to be Queen of England that, at the wedding of Princess Claude at the beginning of the year, the king-dauphin and queen-dauphiness bore the arms of England quartered with those of France. At the state entry to the town of Chatelherault a canopy of crimson damask with the arms of England, Scotland and France was carried over Mary's head, and the arms of England were engraved on the queen-dauphiness's silver plate.[15]

Then, on 30 June 1559, King Henri was seriously injured in a jousting competition; he died of his injuries on 10 July. Elizabeth ordered solemn and splendid obsequies at St Paul's, and Sir William St Loe was one of the four attendant knights appointed along with four peers to be official mourners at the ceremony.

The fifteen-year-old Francis was crowned King of France on 18 September 1559, and his sixteen-year-old wife Mary Queen of Scots also became Queen Mary of France. A great seal was struck bearing the royal figures of Mary and Francis, dated 1559 and with an inscription referring to Francis and Mary as king and queen of the French, Scottish, English and Irish. When peace was declared between England, France and Scotland the following year, Elizabeth was prepared to accept that the use of the English arms was not due to any ambitious desire on Mary's part, rather a decision made and instigated by her father-in-law. However, when the practice continued after Henri's death, it was felt prudent to point out that because she was not the rightful heir to the English throne, she had no entitlement.

On 5 December 1560, just fifteen months after being crowned King of France, Francis died; he left young Mary a widow at just three days shy of eighteen. Francis was succeeded by his younger brother Charles, with his mother Catherine de Medici acting as regent. She became increasingly hostile towards the widowed queen, whose position at the French court was now less secure. Mary decided to return to Scotland, and on 14 August 1561 Mary and her small group of courtiers set sail from Calais. If the winds were favourable, she would be in Scotland within a week.[16] It is claimed that on leaving her friends and family in France, Mary stood gazing tearfully back at the shoreline, repeatedly whispering, 'Adieu France, adieu.'[17]

The small group arrived at Leigh and made their way to the royal palace of Holyrood House in Edinburgh. Mary intended to claim her Scottish kingdom, but was she also intending to claim England? Elizabeth never acknowledged Mary as heir presumptive to the throne, but that made little difference; Mary's proximity in the royal bloodline was enough without any legal endorsement. However, Henry VIII's will formally remained in place, and by those terms the next claimant after Elizabeth was her cousin Lady Katherine Grey, younger sister of Lady Jane, who had been queen for nine days. Katherine Grey represented the Protestants and Mary Queen of Scots the Catholics, and Elizabeth couldn't stand either of them.

8

Love Affairs and Poison

In July 1559, six months after Elizabeth had become queen, Sir William St Loe and Lady Bess Cavendish had announced their betrothal. The queen had approved the marriage, and appointed 27 August for the ceremony. This would indicate that the queen was present, but no records exist to verify this or show where the wedding took place.

Bess had clearly felt affection for her late husband, the father of her children, but Sir William Cavendish had been twenty years her senior and had suffered from ill health for the last three or four years of his life. Those last few years had not been good for Bess. She had lost two babies and nursed Sir William through his deteriorating health. The trauma of his death had been exacerbated by the crippling debt he had left, but she had fought the court and been allowed to defer payment. Finding the money was causing her a lot of anxiety, and despite having no formal training she had taken on the management of the Cavendish estate.

When St Loe entered her life, Bess could forget her problems for short periods and just be a woman. At forty, St Loe was only nine years older than Bess, physically fit and madly in love with her. His surviving letters show this affection when he addresses her as 'his sweet love', and 'my own sweet Bess ... more dearer to me than I am to myself'. She obviously possessed great charm and charisma, as well as a natural beauty that is obvious in her earlier portraits. One that hangs in the long gallery at Hardwick, after the style of Hans Eworth, is incorrectly labelled Maria Regina but has been authenticated as Bess. It can be dated to the early 1560s by the clothes, and could have been painted to mark the occasion of her betrothal and marriage to St Loe.

He may have been besotted by Bess, but any man marrying her would automatically be responsible for her six children, all under twelve years of age, with two stepdaughters for whom a dowry must be found, and land and property encumbered by crippling debts. Most men would fight shy of taking on such a responsibility, but St Loe was unperturbed. He had two daughters from a previous marriage and welcomed Bess's large and extended family.

A wedding invitation that St Loe sent to Bess's old friend Sir John Thynne still exists:

> Saving your promise ... and not forgetting your friendship, these lines are to satisfy you that the day of my marriage is by my Mistress appointed upon Sunday this sennight (27 August). At which time both her ladyship and myself (hope) to see you there. She hath with terrible threatenings commanded me not to forget making of her hearty commendations unto you and to my lady your wife, unto whom I pray you let me be also commended ... from Somerset this Tuesday 15th August. William Seyntlo.[1]

The wedding may have taken place in Somerset, but by late September Bess and St Loe were back in London for St Loe's official duties. Inevitably, his attendance at court meant long absences from Bess; when he tried to get leave from the queen his requests were often denied, and when he was with Bess the queen often complained and called him back again. The wily queen found a solution, though, when she appointed Bess a lady of the Privy Chamber. This is believed to have been a wedding present from the queen, and although it was a great honour, there was obviously an ulterior motive. As the queen's bodyguard, St Loe's presence was much in demand at court and on official visits. On many occasions he complained of being apart from Bess, so her appointment meant they both needed to spend long periods at court. Bess spent the whole of the winter of 1559/60 in London with St Loe while the industrious major-domo James Crompe looked after Chatsworth.

Bess's mother was also there, looking after the children, and they had a tutor with the rather appropriate name of Master Ledger.[2]

At thirty-one, Bess was one of the older women waiting on the queen. In the hierarchy, maids of honour were the young, unmarried or lowest-ranking ladies waiting on the queen. Next in precedence came ladies-in-waiting, then ladies of the Privy Chamber, and finally, the most senior women, the ladies of the Bedchamber. Only the most senior ladies were chosen for this role, as attending to the queen's most personal needs gave them a special place in the household. These positions were much sought after, and when any of the queen's attendants retired from service the Chamberlain was besieged with requests from high-ranking families who wanted the position for their wives or daughters. Bribes were frequently offered for such positions.

The service was not arduous. Duties included bathing and dressing the queen and organising her toilet. The queen's ladies were there when the queen was relaxed and stripped of her emblems of rank. They would gossip and tell stories, laugh, sing, play games and tell secrets They would take care of the queen's jewels and clothes, although any menial tasks were performed by the household servants. Although the queen discouraged her ladies from asking favours or talking politics, when the queen was relaxed she was at her most approachable, and no doubt Bess used her position to her advantage. She was also a good listener, and Elizabeth needed an impartial sounding board. In Bess she had found a friend, and she unburdened all her secrets.

Robert Dudley Affair

The queen was besotted with her childhood friend Lord Robert Dudley, whom she had made Master of Horse, a prestigious position that demanded much personal attendance on the queen. As well as being responsible for organising her public appearances and progresses, the holder was closest to the queen outside the confines of the palace, riding and hunting with her. This position suited Robert Dudley perfectly – not only was he a skilled horseman, but he was also a great athlete.

Robert Dudley's brother Guildford Dudley had been married to Lady Jane Grey, and because Robert supported his brother and his father in their attempt to install Lady Jane on the throne, he had been imprisoned in the Tower of London. He had been kept in the Beauchamp Tower, close to the Bell Tower, where Elizabeth was a prisoner after Wyatt's Revolt, and according to legend they had seen a lot of each other during that time.

Although Elizabeth valued the wisdom of older men in her team of advisers, in her leisure time she preferred to surround herself with young people. She encouraged extravagant fashions, a lively, joyous atmosphere and the latest dances from the Continent for her personal entertainment. Robert Dudley had a flair for the spectacular, and shared the queen's love of drama and music. He regularly organised the queen's personal entertainment, and the fact that she preferred his company to any other didn't go unnoticed in her court.

The queen lavished titles, properties and money on Robert Dudley, who was known from then on as the Earl of Leicester and a Knight of the Garter. In physique and features he was surprisingly similar to Thomas Seymour, who had possibly seduced the teenage Elizabeth while living in the household of the dowager queen Katherine Parr. He was also similar in temperament, possessing great charm and magnetism. Elizabeth was in love. It was clear to see the sexual tension between them, and rumours were rife that Elizabeth and Dudley were lovers. The problem was that Robert Dudley was also married. In 1550, the wedding of eighteen-year-old Robert Dudley and Amy Robsart, the daughter of a Norfolk squire, had been celebrated in great style, and was attended by Elizabeth and her brother Edward. Robert, being a fifth son, had no claim on his father's land and titles, but Amy was an heiress. It's doubtful that it was a love match, but the marriage was financially advantageous.

'He does what he likes,' the scandalised Spanish ambassador reported. 'It is even said that her Majesty visits him day and night. They go so far as to say that his wife has a malady in one of her breasts, and the queen is only waiting for her to die, to marry Sir Robert.'[3]

Double standards were everywhere. When a king's roving eye fell on a shapely young woman at court the result was invariably another royal bastard, and no doubt some dividends in land and office for the young woman's family. For an able young man to catch the eye of the unmarried Elizabeth was shocking, particularly because that man was married.

These facts were not lost on Kat Ashley, Elizabeth's former governess and now the chief gentlewoman of her Privy Chamber. Kat was Elizabeth's closest personal attendant. She implored Elizabeth to stop the affair. She went down on bended knee asking her mistress to see sense, saying that such a relationship would only cause heartache. When Elizabeth tried to reason with her, Kat declared that rather than see her mistress make such a mistake she wished she had strangled her in her cradle.

In her privileged position, Bess would have been very aware of exactly what was happening. She may have tried to reason with Elizabeth, whose subjects wanted her to marry and produce an heir, but there was only one man that the queen wanted and he was married.

Bess, the Chief Overseer of Chatsworth

Bess returned to Chatsworth in April 1560, but because his duty to the queen took precedence over everything else St Loe remained in London. His visits to Chatsworth were short and infrequent, but he agreed to finance the continuation of the work there and named Bess 'the chief overseer of my works'.[4]

Construction had been suspended during the crisis period prior to and after the death of Sir William Cavendish, but now Bess lost no time in resuming work. The wages at Chatsworth for the autumn of 1559 include payments for chopping wood, threshing, hewing, winnowing and other agrarian activities, but on 13 April 1560 the accounts show that rebuilding work had begun again. Glaziers and slaters were at work repairing the old house, and men were paid to dig shallow pits to extract coal and limestone. The coal would fire the limekilns to make plaster for the new house, or 'the newe byledng' (new building) as it was written in the account book.

The weekly average wage bill had jumped to over 30s with payments to joiners, sawyers, plasterers and glaziers. Bess wrote to ask her old friend Sir John Thynne if he would loan her his plasterer as she was ready to begin 'flowering her hall'. In a momentary mental slip, the letter is signed Elizabeth Cavendish. When she realised her mistake, she put a line through the Cavendish and wrote Seyntlo above.[5]

When Bess was not at Chatsworth James Crompe was left in charge, assisted by another loyal family servant, Francis Whitfield. Bess sent frequent instructions on how the work should be done and even sent bundles of garden seed so that her aunt Marcella Linaker, who was living at Chatsworth, could make a garden beside the new house.

Bess Is Poisoned

St Loe decided that in order to give Bess the security that his estates provided he would make an indenture whereby he and Bess held his lands jointly. His family were not happy, particularly his brother Edward, who had assumed he would be Sir William St Loe's heir.

Bess continued to spend much time in London in her capacity as a lady of the Privy Chamber. When not at the court Sir William and Bess stayed at the London house of John Mann in Red Cross Street, and it was there that an almost fatal incident took place in early 1560. Sir William St Loe's mother Dame Margaret and brother Edward visited to pay their respects, but the visit was not a success. Edward St Loe was a thoroughly bad sort. He had married a Mrs Scutt after the sudden death of her husband, but she too died two months after the marriage, leaving Edward St Loe considerably better off. However, Edward St Loe considered that his father had been grossly unfair in leaving most of his estate to his eldest son, Sir William, and this caused a heated row between the two brothers. During the visit, Bess became ill and poison was suspected. In a subsequent letter Dame Margaret wrote that she was convinced that Bess would have died had a remedy not been to hand.[6] Poisoning was a constant worry for Elizabethans, and emetics were kept handy to act as a remedy.

The poison was thought to have been intended for both Sir William and Bess, but for some unknown reason Sir William avoided it. Perhaps the poison was concealed in a garment he didn't touch, or a meal he didn't consume. What didn't seem in doubt was the fact that it had been planted by Edward St Loe. Once he was assured that Bess was alright, Sir William began making enquiries among his brother's known associates and tracked down one Hugh Draper, keeper of a Bristol inn about 12 miles away from Sutton Court, where Edward St Loe lived. Draper was arrested, charged with 'necromancy against my Lady Sentlo', and committed to the Tower on 21 March. Bearing in mind that Sir William was a popular man and friend of Edward Warner, the Lieutenant of the Tower, it wouldn't have been a pleasant incarceration for Hugh Draper.

Hugh Draper was an astronomer and carved an astrological calendar as a device for casting horoscopes on the walls of his cell in the Salt Tower. Over it he carved the words 'Hugh Draper of Bristowe made thys sphere the 30 daye of May anno 1561.' The device still survives and is pointed out to visitors as one of the most interesting graffiti in the Tower.[7]

Four others were accused of conspiring with Hugh Draper, but, rather curiously, Edward St Loe, the man who had no doubt orchestrated the poisoning, seems to have escaped any punishment. Sir William was not prepared to give up, however, and began collecting evidence to sue his villainous brother privately. He ordered him to leave Sutton Court and issued a writ against him alleging that he had acted contrary to the trust and confidence implicit in his position as Steward of Sutton Court, and contrary to the natural duty that one brother owes another. He was charged with lying and embezzlement, forgery of signatures and false accounting, taking the profits of the estate as his own and using menacing and threatening behaviour toward tenants in order to defraud.[8]

Edward was unrepentant. He refused to leave Sutton Court, and he did not reply to the charges that he had lied and embezzled. Instead, he claimed that Bess had used unnatural means – like those she used to recover from poison – to persuade Sir William to put her name on his estate documents. As mentioned before, Sir William St Loe had made an indenture whereby he and Bess held his lands jointly in order to give Bess the security that his estates provided. Edward wasn't just hinting at witchcraft – he was making a positive statement, a very dangerous allegation if taken seriously. As the case continued, with accusations and counter-accusations, the judge was perplexed and unsure how to proceed; it was one brother's word against the word of another. In the end, an unsatisfactory compromise was reached.

William now became concerned about Bess and how she would be treated in the event of his sudden death. A man normally left everything to the eldest male relative, so as things stood Edward could inherit all the St Loe estate and income, and it was obvious he would not deal kindly with his brother's widow. This prompted William St Loe to make a new will, cutting out his brother entirely and leaving everything to Bess. Furthermore, there was a clause stating that following her death his estates and incomes would go to her heirs forever.[9]

Sir William St Loe had been on a mission. He had spent time with Bess at Chatsworth before riding down to Somerset, where he had remained for a week to collect evidence against his foolish brother. When he returned to court, the queen was not pleased and received him with much coolness. He wrote to Bess, 'The queen has found great fault with my long absence, saying she would talk with me further and that she would well chide me ... I answered that when her majesty understood the cause she would not be offended whereup she said, "Very well, very well." However the queen had not offered me her hand to kiss as was her usual custom; it was her way of demonstrating her displeasure.'

Elizabeth Falls Critically Ill

There is no doubt that the poison incident with Bess would have been much talked about at court, and a few weeks later Cecil wrote a memorandum about the necessity for caution against any attempt to poison the queen:

> We think it very convenient that your Majesty's apparel and especially all manner of things that touch any part of your Majesty's body be circumspectly looked at. And no person be permitted to come near but those who have the trust and charge thereof ... No manner of perfume either in apparel or sleeves, gloves or suchlike... be presented by a stranger or other person ... that no foreign meat or dishes being dressed out of court, be brought to your food without knowledge of from whom it cometh. May it please your majesty to take advise of your physician for receiving twice weekly some preservative.[10]

A few months later, on 8 September, things took a dramatic turn at court; however, poisoning was not the issue. The body of

Leicester's wife, Amy Robsart, was found at the foot of the stairs at their home of Cumnor Place near Oxford. She had a broken neck and murder was suspected. Her death was generally felt to be too providential, and many pointed the finger at Leicester, feeling he had killing his wife so that he would be free to marry the queen. Although this was never proved, understandably the subject caused a major scandal. The queen banished Leicester to his house at Kew and ordered a full enquiry, but that didn't stop the malicious rumours. A verdict of accidental death was reached and he was allowed to return to court, but he would never be free of the suspicion that he had deliberately killed his wife – more than this, Elizabeth was suspected of collusion. There was little she could do but order the court into deep mourning for a month.[11]

Sir Nicholas Throckmorton, Elizabeth's powerful adviser who had operated behind the scenes in an unofficial capacity for many years, was now her ambassador in France. He informed Cecil that what they were saying about Elizabeth's conduct in Paris made him ashamed to write. Cecil lost no time in informing Elizabeth that he would resign if she should take Leicester as her consort.

Although Leicester was now free to marry, such a marriage would have torn apart the kingdom. Elizabeth allowed her advisers to persuade her not to marry Leicester, but she refused to give him up. He was her trusted friend, and remained so throughout the 1560s. Leicester proposed to the queen many times, but Elizabeth knew how unpopular such a marriage would be. With her unmarried status she was able to negotiate many lucrative deals abroad, shrewdly yet discreetly tendering herself and the throne of England, like dangling a carrot before a stubborn donkey. She was a canny operator and doyen of empty promises, but remained unmarried and with no direct heir to the throne.

It was just four years into Elizabeth's reign when, on 10 October 1562, the anxiety over succession again peaked. Queen Elizabeth was at Hampton Court Palace when she became unwell. She had smallpox, which in the 1500s killed many and could cause blindness and scarring in those who survived. Treatment was primitive. Smallpox was a major killer, and as Elizabeth lost consciousness things looked bleak. The childless queen had not named her successor, and with no obvious heir the situation was widely regarded as disastrous.

The nobles met privately in each other's houses for heated discussions while Elizabeth's life hung in the balance, but no agreement could be reached as to who would succeed Elizabeth. There was the ever-present danger of a squabble between cousins over the crown sliding into open war.

Mary Queen of Scots was back in Scotland and had the support of the Catholics at home and abroad, so the newly restored Protestant faith – and with it the peace and the stability of England – was in danger. This could all be avoided if Katherine Grey, younger sister of the late Lady Jane, was nominated as Elizabeth's successor – but there was one very major problem.

Katherine and her younger sister Mary had both been given positions at court by their cousin Queen Mary I on the death of their sister Jane, and they had retained these positions under Queen Elizabeth, but she showed open hostility to the two girls. In October 1559, it had been reported that Queen Mary's former husband, Philip II of Spain, was considering an alliance between his heir and Katherine Grey. The English ambassador in Madrid, in correspondence with William Cecil, added that Katherine would probably be glad to leave the English court as she was not in the queen's good books.[12]

The Katherine Grey Affair

In the summer of 1558, eighteen-year-old Katherine Grey had attracted the attention of nineteen-year-old Edward Seymour, son of Edward Seymour, Duke of Somerset and former Lord Protector of King Edward. Katherine was a friend of Edward Seymour's sister Jane (probably named after her aunt, the unfortunate nine-day queen), who agreed to pass messages between the lovers but was told by her brother to 'break with the Lady Katherine touching marriage'. This may have been because the political landscape was stormy enough without the Protestant heir being involved in a dangerous romance when there were negotiations in progress to marry her to Philip of Spain's heir. Equally, it might have been because in the eyes of the law Katherine was still married to Lord Henry Herbert, son and heir of the Earl of Pembroke, from when John Dudley arranged the triple marriage ceremony on 25 May 1553 for his son Guildford Dudley and Jane Grey prior to her being elected queen.[13]

The growing rumours of a love affair between Edward and Katherine brought considerable risks, and Queen Elizabeth's secretary William Cecil advised Edward to cool his ardour for Katherine. Cecil was not a man to be ignored, but in withdrawing his affections Edward distressed Katherine, who had heard that he was flirting with a girl named Frances Mewtas. Katherine sent him a furious letter, and he wrote back immediately swearing his love and his desire to marry her. He then approached Katherine's mother, Lady Frances Grey, who was then Lady Frances Stokes, having married her groom, Adrian Stokes. She readily gave her consent for them to marry, but the next obstacle was gaining the queen's permission.[14]

As Katherine was a potential claimant to Elizabeth's throne, the law stated that it was a penal offence for her to marry without the sovereign's consent, so Lady Frances agreed to write and petition the queen for her permission. Soon afterwards, though, before she could write the letter, she went into premature labour and died in October 1559 while giving birth to a stillborn son.

As son of the late Protector Somerset, Edward Seymour was a suitable candidate. He had a good position and was allied to powerful friends, so it was suggested that he should acquire as much support as possible from the Privy Council before approaching the queen. In November 1560, Edward Seymour gave Katherine Grey a pointed diamond ring and, in the most foolhardy move possible, promised to marry her in secret at his London home, Hertford House, the next time the queen left London. They didn't have to wait long. The queen and her court left the Palace of Westminster at the end of November for a hunting trip, and Katherine claimed she had toothache. Her friend Jane, who was consumptive and often ill, also claimed she was too sick to travel, so the two were excused. As soon as the royal procession left, the two girls slipped out the back door and down the orchard steps that led to the river. The tide was out, so they walked along the sands to the earl's house at Cannon Row where they expected to be met by Hertford and a clergyman, but there was no clergyman. Undeterred, Jane went to find another, who left after performing the short wedding service with just Jane Seymour as their witness. Time was precious as maids of honour had to account for any absence to the Chamberlain, but the wedding was consummated before the two girls returned to the palace.

For a time it was all very romantic, with secret trysts between the newlyweds, but three months after the secret marriage Jane Seymour died, making it more difficult for the couple to meet. Then, in April, the queen ordered Hertford to accompany William Cecil's son on a subsidised tour of Europe to finish his education. Katherine kept her position at court, and under other circumstances their marriage should have been secure and blessed, but it was still a secret. When she found she was pregnant, she kept her secret despite the growing gossip among the court matrons. Then, in early August, at the same time that Mary Queen of Scots was making her way back to Scotland, Katherine sought out her mother's old friend and confidant Bess, who now held the privilege of a lady of the Privy Chamber. Bess valued her friendship with the Grey family, and treasured the piece of jewellery set with an agate given to her by Lady Frances when she was in her service, so initially she was pleased to see Katherine.

Katherine soon confided in Bess that she had secretly married the Earl of Hertford the previous autumn and was now pregnant. Distraught and frightened, she begged Bess to help her break the news to the queen. It's reported that Bess broke into 'a passion of weeping'.[15] It's very possible that the two ladies cried together at the hopelessness of the situation; it was not a good position for either of them to be in. As heir presumptive to the crown, Katherine Grey needed permission to marry and she had not gained this. The fact that Bess was now aware of the situation made her an accessory to the fact. She could be sentenced under the 1536 Royal Marriage Act, because it was treason for anyone of royal blood to marry without the queen's consent – the sentence could be life.

Katherine's condition could not be ignored, but Bess told her to go to bed while she thought about it, no doubt intending to discuss it with her husband. However, Katherine began to panic and decided to approach Robert Dudley, Earl of Leicester. Through her sister Jane's marriage to Guildford Dudley, Robert was her brother-in-law once removed. Not only was he her kinsman, but he was a family friend and had the queen's ear. If she could gain his support and beg him to mediate for her then she might gain the queen's sympathy – or so she thought. Robert Dudley was a dismayed as Bess had been, and sent the girl away while he spoke to the queen.

Elizabeth reacted in predictable fashion. The furious queen ordered Katherine to be taken to the Tower under armed guard. Messengers were sent to France demanding Edward Seymour's immediate return, and on 17 August, the day after Katherine's arrival at the Tower, the queen wrote to Sir Edward Warner, Lieutenant of the Tower:

> ... how many knew of the love between her and Edward Seymour from the beginning. And let her know she shall have no manner of favours lest she shall show the truth ... for it doth now appear that sundry persons have dealt therein ... You shall also send to Alderman Lodge, secretly, for Sentlow, and shall put her in awe of divers matters confessed by the Lady Katherine, and so also deal with her that she may confess to you all her knowledge in the same matters. It is certain that there hath been great practises and purposes, and since the death of Lady Jane, she [Lady Sentlow] hath been most privy [with Lady Katherine]. and as you shall see occasion so you may keep Sentlow 2 or 3 nights more or less, and let her be restored to lodges or kept still with you as you shall think.[16]

Elizabeth was not willing to accept that Bess, with her close connections to the Grey family, had no inkling of what was going on, yet no evidence of her complicity ever came to light. Despite her position as one of Elizabeth's ladies of the Privy Chamber, Bess was not immune from the dangers that lurked at court. In August 1561 she was questioned by her husband's close friend Sir Edward Warner, who would, in the circumstances, go easy on her. There is no record of this interview, and Bess is not listed as a prisoner in the Tower, so although the experience could have been traumatic she was presumably cleared of any suspicion of collusion. She was released and her involvement is not referred to again in state papers, although some reports state that she was detained for weeks. This may have arisen from the fact that Bess stayed in London after her questioning, probably to give support to Katherine whom Bess had known from the age of seven when she went into service in the Grey household at Bradgate Manor.

Bess may have been with Katherine on 24 September 1561 when she gave birth to her son, Edward Seymour, Viscount Beaucham, while still in custody in the Tower. Under the will of Henry VIII, he would follow his mother in the line of succession as heir to Elizabeth, so at last England had a protestant male heir to inherit the English throne. The queen's inquisitors found no evidence of any plot against Elizabeth, but the queen was not happy. She was bent on having the marriage between Edward Seymour and Katherine Grey declared invalid, and the child declared a bastard. In February 1562, a commission headed by Archbishop Parker was set up to investigate the marriage. They found that no banns had been read, that the priest who conducted the service could not be located, that no one gave the lady to the earl, that their only witness (Edward's sister Jane Seymour) was dead and that there was no certificate of marriage.

Bess used her time in London arranging the marriage of her thirteen-year-old daughter Frances Cavendish to fifteen-year-old Henry Pierrepont, son of Sir George Pierrepont of Holme Pierrepont, Nottingham. Sir George was far from well, and, in the fear that his death would place his son and estate in wardship, was looking for another way to retain his huge wealth. He was anxious to draw up a marriage contract, but Bess must have returned to Chatsworth because he refused an invitation to go there on account of the pain and discomfort such a journey would cause him. It was arranged for Frances to go to serve as a gentlewoman in the Pierrepont household, just as Bess had done with Lady Zouche at the same age. This was to give all parties the opportunity to see if they got on, with the marriage formalised the following year. The two were subsequently married in 1562.

Bess remained in London because her suit with the Exchequer concerning the £5,000 deficit in Sir William Cavendish's accounts was finally brought to court. St Loe appealed to the queen to look leniently on the matter, and in consideration of the esteem in which she held the couple, she did. She agreed to cancel the debt on payment of a fine of £1,000, to be paid to the Exchequer. Sir William St Loe willingly paid the fine. For Bess, the burden and worry of the debt was finally removed and her beloved Chatsworth was out of danger.[17]

In May 1562, the Archbishop of Canterbury, who had carefully examined all the evidence in the Grey/Seymour case, pronounced that there was no marriage between Lady Katherine and Edward Seymour. Instead the couple were found guilty of fornication. Edward Seymour was fined £15,000 for 'seducing a virgin of the blood royal', they were both sentenced to imprisonment during Her Majesty's pleasure, and the baby Edward, Lord Beauchamp, was officially declared illegitimate.

Who Will Succeed Elizabeth?

Against this background, in October 1562, Queen Elizabeth had contracted smallpox. Fearing that she would die, she asked that Robert Dudley be made Protector of the Realm and in an uncharacteristic show of affection declared that she 'loved him dearly, and had long done so, but called God to witness that nothing unseemly had ever passed between them'.[18]

As to naming her successor, that was another matter. Unlike her father Henry VIII, who had given the question of succession serious consideration, for the duration of her reign the ever-vigilant Elizabeth had the attitude that 'so long as I live, there shall be no other queen in England'. The lack of a decision meant that she could play one party against another, encouraging their hopes in exchange for favours or dashing them over favours refused. It was a dangerous game which she played for over forty years.

A powerful faction headed by Thomas Howard, 4th Duke of Norfolk, was in favour of Katherine Grey, who would keep England a Protestant country, but the Privy Council were loath to name Katherine as Elizabeth's heir when the commission had reached the verdict that the Grey/Seymour marriage was a sham and their son and heir illegitimate. Added to this was the argument that it was also highly possible that Lady Katherine's claim to the throne had been invalidated by her father's treason.

The Privy Council were equally loath to name the Catholic representative, Mary Queen of Scots, as Elizabeth's successor. Because of the barbaric way Mary Tudor had tried to reinstate Catholicism, it was doubtful that England was ready to return to the papal fold. However this did not prevent the Catholic community at home and abroad from constantly plotting to put Mary on the English throne and return England to Catholicism. One such ardent Catholic was Lady Margaret (Meg) Douglas, Countess of Lennox, granddaughter of Henry VII, half-sister of James V of Scotland, first cousin of Queen Elizabeth, and aunt of Mary Queen of Scots.

Meg should have been a strong candidate for the English throne through her mother, Margaret Tudor, Dowager Queen of Scotland, but she bore the stigma of illegitimacy. It was claimed that after the death of King James IV of Scotland her mother had secretly married Lord Stuart of Annerdale, and he was still alive when she married Archibald Douglas, 6th Earl of Angus. Furthermore, it was claimed that at the time of the marriage Archibald Douglas had another wife still alive, so this was a case of double bigamy. The illegality of the marriage made their daughter Lady Margaret (Meg) Douglas illegitimate, something that was always held against her by the Scottish Parliament.[19]

Meg had spent her childhood at the English court as a close friend and companion of her cousin Mary Tudor. Meg fell in love with Thomas Howard, brother of the Duke of Norfolk and uncle of Henry VIII's second wife Anne Boleyn, and while Anne was in favour their courtship was viewed favourably. Once Anne was in disgrace, though, Meg and Thomas were sent to the Tower. Thomas would die there.

In 1544, Meg married Matthew Stuart, 4th Earl of Lennox. A man of ambition with descent from James II, Lennox had a claim to the Scottish throne. He had already attempted to overthrow the Regent of Scotland during the minority of Mary Queen of Scots, and having been pronounced guilty of treason saw his Scottish estates confiscated by the Scottish Parliament. But Meg was a favourite of her uncle Henry VIII, and the Lennox fortunes thrived in England and up through the reign of Edward VI. During Queen Mary's five-year reign, Meg had rooms in Westminster Palace to serve her cousin and lifelong friend, who told the ambassador

Simon Renard that Meg Lennox was better suited to succeed her to the throne than her half-sister Elizabeth. Many Catholics also wanted this, but, fearing a repeat of the wretched fate of Jane Grey, it had been considered prudent for the crown to go to Mary's half-sister Elizabeth.

Meg was the chief mourner at Queen Mary's funeral in December 1558, but because she refused to denounce her faith and remained a staunch Catholic all her life, she was not acceptable at Queen Elizabeth's court. She spent more time at her home at Temple Newsam on the outskirts of Leeds in Yorkshire. It was known to be a centre for Roman Catholic intrigue and a thorn in the flesh of her cousin Elizabeth.

As a staunch Catholic, Meg Lennox was constantly persecuted, harassed and heavily fined, but she was a determined lady with royal blood coursing through her veins. She had been denied the fruits of majesty, but was adamant that her children would not be forced to deny theirs. Sadly, despite giving birth to eight children, only two of her sons survived to adulthood. In 1562, as her cousin Elizabeth lay critically ill, Meg was working on an ambitious plan to marry her eldest son Henry, Lord Darnley and Douglas (earlier spelling Dowglas), to his cousin Mary Queen of Scots. As Elizabeth's most direct heir, the twenty-year-old Scottish queen would unite the crowns of England and Scotland, but she needed a suitable husband by her side. In Meg's eyes there could be no one more suitable than her own seventeen-year-old son. He was in the line of succession as a great-grandson of Henry VII, so Mary and Henry could rule together; her son could be King of England and Scotland.

The country was in total disharmony, and although the Countess of Lennox had slightly more success, all the noble plans and schemes came to nothing when, against all expectations, the queen recovered and the potential catastrophe was averted. She vowed that 'death possessed every joint of me', and from then on she painted her face white to cover up the unsightly scars caused by the smallpox. The Privy Council and the country as a whole gave a collective sigh of relief, and rejoiced. The Royal Mint struck gold coins to celebrate the queen's recovery, but the issues with succession could not go unchecked.

When Parliament assembled in January 1563, Elizabeth was petitioned to name a successor; she ignored the appeal. When she discovered that Meg Lennox and her husband had been making plans to marry their eldest son, Henry, to Mary Queen of Scots to strengthen her claim to the English throne, she summoned them to London. The earl was placed in the Tower and his wife was placed in the custody of Sir Richard and Lady Sackville at Sheen. The earl became ill, probably suffering from typhus (often known as jail fever), and Meg wrote many letters to William Cecil, Lord Burghley, asking for her husband to be allowed to join her at Sheen.

Her cousin Lady Katherine and Edward Seymour were still held in captivity at the Tower. Many people were sympathetic to their plight, including Sir Edward Warner, Lieutenant of the Tower, who allowed Edward Seymour to visit his wife. Her accommodation was exceedingly comfortable. She had a suite of rooms with eight or nine servants and a child's nurse, but Sir Edward's kindness was exposed when Katherine announced she was about to have a second child. Elizabeth promptly had Sir Edward Warner dismissed from his prestigious post and locked up in his own prison for the lack of security that had allowed Katherine and Edward to enjoy their conjugal rights. Their second son, Thomas Seymour, was born in the Tower on 10 February 1563, and he too was declared illegitimate, despite the fact that the parents continued to proclaim themselves married.

In the summer of 1563 there was an explosion in cases of the plague in London. People were dying at a rate of 400 a week in the capital, and in all an estimated 21,000 people died of the plague that year. For their safety, Edward Seymour and his son Lord Beauchamp were sent under house arrest to his mother's home at Hanworth, but Katherine and the baby Thomas were allowed no liberty. Katherine refused to eat, and sent piteous letters to friends and family, who hoped that as the years passed and the drama of the affair receded the queen might be ready to forgive. She may have done, if Katherine's younger sister Mary hadn't decided to follow the same path by marrying Thomas Keys in secret. Her husband was imprisoned, and Mary spent years in miserable detention.

Eventually, in 1563, the Earl and Countess of Lennox were released. Although ruined financially, they were allowed to go to their home in Yorkshire. Because they were not taken back into royal favour they were even more determined to advance their son's marriage to Mary Queen of Scots, so while Meg stayed at home with her younger son Charles, the earl and Henry Darnley went to Scotland to meet Mary. Although Darnley was three years younger than the Scottish queen, he was tall, good-looking and utterly charming. Mary was besotted.

Bess Is Widowed for the Third Time

Meanwhile, Bess was spending more and more time at Chatsworth. In 1564, her third son, Charles, had joined his two older brothers at Eton. Her eldest daughter, Frances, had married Henry Pierrepont in 1562 and was living at Holme Pierrepont, the family seat at Nottingham, so just her two daughters Elizabeth and Mary were at home. The building and refurbishing program at Chatsworth that she had embarked on four years earlier had finally come to an end, and that summer and autumn the lives of Bess and Sir William St Loe moved at a more leisurely pace. St Loe returned to court after an extended stay that autumn, but Bess remained at Chatsworth until December for the twelve nights of celebrations over Christmas.

Around February 1565 she received a letter from her brother James Hardwick asking if she could advance him a loan in return for the security of his coal mine at Heath or some land he owned. James was ill and in serious debt. When her mother wrote to ask her to help she wrote, '... It is very good land ... I think it is very good for you daughter and it is worth much to my comfort that you should have it before any other.'[20]

Her mother's message made Bess decide to return to Derbyshire to discuss things, but she could only have been there a few days when a message arrived that St Loe was critically ill in London.[21] She set off immediately on a return dash to London, but her husband was already dead, probably even before she received the message. To her horror, she discovered that her husband's detestable brother Edward had been with him on the day of his death and several days prior. He then produced an indenture signed by Sir William before his death, agreeing that Edward St Loe had a legal right to Sutton Court. Bess knew that her husband would never have signed such an agreement, particularly without consulting her first. Sir William's will was laudably brief, with no ambiguity. It read:

> In consideration of the natural affection, mutual love and assured good will which I have ever perceived and found in my most entirely beloved wife, Dame Elizabeth St Lowe, I do give and bequeath unto her, the said Elizabeth, all and all manner of my leases, farms, plate jewels, hangings, implements of house-hold, debts, good and chattels, whatsoever, to have, hold, use and enjoy to her own proper use, and behalf. Which said Elizabeth my wife I do ordain and make my sole and whole Executrix of this my last Will and Testament.[22]

Not only did Edward St Loe's claim seem highly questionable, bearing in mind his attempt to poison Bess and the mysterious deaths of his former wife Bridget and her earlier husband John Scutt, Sir William's death looked extremely suspicious. But just as in the other cases, there was nothing to prove that the shifty Edward St Loe had killed his brother. Bess would have done all she could to find proof, but she found nothing. Lacking any evidence, she had to drop the charge. In February 1565, Sir William St Loe was buried at the church of Great St Helen's at Bishopsgate, alongside his father.[23]

On the same day, Bess learnt that Margaret Norton, the younger daughter of Sir William's first marriage, was contesting the will in which he had left everything to Bess and her heirs; no doubt she was urged on by Edward St Loe. She claimed that it was unnatural for a father to leave his own children 'not one groat' and was demanding that justice be done on her behalf. People said that Bess had cruelly robbed Margaret and her sister Mary of their inheritance, and questioned why a rich and generous man would leave nothing to his daughters. The probable answer would be that he had already blessed them with suitable dowries and believed they were adequately provided for within their marriages.

After seven years of happy marriage, Bess was alone again – and just like last time, she was being forced to fight for her rights.

9

Mary Queen of Scots, Darnley and Bothwell

Nineteen-year-old Mary Queen of Scots, the Dowager Queen of France, was back in Scotland in the autumn of 1561, and once more the courts of Europe were speculating on who she would marry. She was not short of suitors. Tall and slender, she had inherited her height, carriage, athletic build and fine features from her mother and the Guise side of her family. With a flawless complexion, amber eyes and a profusion of red-gold hair, she possessed style, grace and a personal magnetism that brought men under her spell. She had inherited the latter from her father, along with cyclical high spirits and poor health.[1]

Her bloodline ensured that she was next in line to the English throne whether she wanted to be or not, and when Queen Elizabeth was critically ill in October 1562 Mary's supporters were preparing her for succession. Then Elizabeth recovered, and the situation continued very much as before, with Elizabeth refusing to name her successor. It was around this time that Mary met Henry, Lord Darnley, the son of the Earl and Countess of Lennox. Like Mary herself, as a grandchild of Margaret Tudor he was in line for the English throne. At twenty years of age Darnley was three years younger than the Scottish queen, and an idle fop too; but he was good-looking and extremely tall. Mary was over 6 feet, and he was one of the few men she had met who was taller. Elizabeth had described him as a long lad, while Sir James Melville had described his appearance as beardless and lady-faced.[2] Mary, however, told

Melville that he was 'the properest and best proportioned long man that ever she had seen'.[3]

His appearance and his proximity to the English throne endeared him to Mary, and on 29 July 1565 they were married at Holyrood. Darnley was given the title of king, and Mary was happy to have him beside her and his signature as King Henry alongside hers on all official documents.[4] But Darnley was not interested in the process of government, although he continued to demand the crown matrimonial, giving him equal if not superior power to Mary.

Meg must have been ecstatic at her son's success, but her jubilation was soon dampened. When Queen Elizabeth heard of the marriage she was furious. Unable to vent her wrath on the absent Earl of Lennox, who was out of her jurisdiction in Scotland, she summoned her cousin Meg to London. She hadn't exactly committed treason, but it was viewed in the same light. Matthew, Earl of Lennox, was stripped of his English properties, and on 22 June Meg, Countess of Lennox, was imprisoned in the lieutenant's lodgings at the Tower of London, where she had been consigned thirty-five years earlier by Henry VIII.[5]

Mary and Darnley should have been a good match, but they weren't. He was handsome, vain but effeminate and called 'an agreeable nincompoop'. He spent his time in pleasurable pursuits and was known to indulge in 'unnatural' practices with his company of gentlemen, who were willing to satisfy his warped appetite and vicious habits. Not only did this disgust many of the Scottish lords, but Darnley antagonised them to such an extent that James Stuart, later Earl of Moray, and many of the others withdrew from the court, considering him unworthy of the high honour Mary had bestowed on him.

Sadly, by the time Mary's eyes had been opened to his flaws she was pregnant. The prospect of motherhood, much desired for dynastic reasons, didn't compensate. Perhaps if her aunt Meg (who was now her mother-in-law) had been around things could have been different; the Spanish diplomat Guzman de Silva is reported as saying, 'If only Margaret had been in Scotland … Her son would not have been led astray, nor would these disputes have taken place, as she is prudent and brave, and the son respects her more than he does his father.'[6]

Mary had no one to turn to, no one to confide in, and in near desperation, she unburdened her problems to her secretary David Riccio. In Darnley's warped mind Riccio was replacing him, so he conspired with a handful of nobles to assassinate the man, who was stabbed to death in front of Mary. She became convinced that her own life and that of her unborn child was in danger, so was taken to the safety of Edinburgh Castle, where, on 19 June 1566, she gave birth to her son James. It was a prolonged, difficult birth and he was born with a fine membrane or caul stretched over his face.[7]

This boy should have brought much rejoicing because Scotland had an heir, but the country was in turmoil. Meg, still imprisoned in the Tower of London, would have been unaware of the immense friction and hostility in the Scottish royal household. She was not around to witness the birth or baptism of her grandson, but she must have been ecstatic. Her eldest son was king consort, and her grandson would be King James VI of Scotland in his own right. As Mary was the nearest relative to the childless Elizabeth and theoretically her heir, the ambitious Meg saw no reason to doubt that one day her grandson, the only male in an otherwise female line, would unite the kingdoms of Scotland and England.

Queen Elizabeth must have heard of James's birth with envy, and it was suggested that she should send Cecil to Scotland to attend the christening.[8] The Scottish queen had a kingdom, a husband and a son to continue the line, although the royal marriage was only functioning for the sake of outward appearances.

Mary's illegitimate half-brother James Stuart, later Earl of Moray, had become her chief adviser, and it was with him and a small group of noblemen, including James, Earl of Bothwell, her Lieutenant on the Borders, that Mary began discussions regarding her husband's scandalous behaviour. Divorce was mentioned, among other things. Then, on 9 February 1567, Darnley was staying at a house in Kirk o' Field, recovering from a 'great fever of the pox' – probably syphilis – when the building was blown up. Burning the enemy's house over his head was a comparatively common sixteenth-century practice, but Darnley didn't die in the fire. He had obviously tried to escape, and his strangled body was found in a nearby garden. As Sheriff of Edinburgh, it was Bothwell's duty to attend the scene of the crime; popular opinion held that he had left it only a few hours earlier.

At Holyrood, Mary was woken with the news of her husband's death; her reaction was said to be one of horror and shock. She behaved with perfect correctness, ordered the court into mourning and embarked on the traditional forty days of mourning. The extent of Mary's own complicity was and remains intensely controversial, but the preponderant view has been that she is likely to have been an accomplice in Bothwell's designs.[9]

It was widely believed that the principal people of Scotland were implicated in the act because they were dissatisfied with Darnley as king. Ambition and intrigue among sixteenth-century Scottish nobility was rife, and human decency was often set aside when convenient. Villainous acts were common and presented a problem to the young queen, who lacked the knowledge and experience to deal with dangerous men. Unlike Queen Elizabeth, who had built up a council of wise, trustworthy ministers, Mary's long absence from Scotland meant she had not. The men who could advise her were heavily involved in the plot and were hardly likely to counsel a course alien to their own interests. A few years earlier, the mysterious death of Amy Robsart, wife of Queen Elizabeth's favourite Robert Dudley, had brought a similar reaction in England. The main difference was that Elizabeth had good advisers and rode out the storm. Mary's lack of loyal advisers meant that she didn't.

Darnley's father, the Earl of Lennox, wanted vengeance for the slaying of his son and named Bothwell as the culprit. A trial was arranged, but on the appointed day the Earl of Lennox with just six followers shrank from appearing when faced by 4,000 of Bothwell's adherents swarming the city. Although the due processes were observed in a mock trial, the absence of the earl as accuser meant that Bothwell was inevitably acquitted; however, the outward appearance of justice was enough. When news of Darnley's death reached Elizabeth, in pity she released his mother Meg from the Tower, but the Countess of Lennox was inconsolable. Her dreams had been shattered.

Despite the fact that he suffered from the pennilessness common to the contemporary noble, Bothwell, like many of his class, was keenly interested in royal favour and the acquisition of royal castles – and his next move was far more ambitious. He planned to convince the nobles that the inexperienced queen needed a husband and that he was the best person to fill the role. He felt that once he had the approval of the nobles he would have no problem getting the queen to select him for the now vacant position of king.

With this in mind, at the end of the sitting of Parliament on 19 April 1567 Bothwell entertained twenty-eight nobles, the leading peers temporal and spiritual of Scotland, with a dinner at a tavern on Cannongate, Edinburgh, kept by an innkeeper called Ainslie. This event became known as Ainslie's Supper. There Bothwell managed to persuade the dignitaries that the only way to remedy Scotland's sad state of public affairs was to have a strong leader, and a masterful consort to share the strains of the government of Scotland with the queen. He obviously convinced the nobles, and the following day eight bishops, nine earls and seven barons signed the Ainslie Tavern Bond, recommending Bothwell as the best suited and most appropriate husband for Queen Mary of Scotland. They also pledged to assist in defending such a marriage.[10]

It was subsequently alleged that on 19 April 1567 Mary had signed a warrant authorising the lords to sign the bond, but Mary denied this. She refused to accept Bothwell's proposal, despite the fact that her chief advisers were pleading with her to take 'this man of resolution well adapted to rule, who has ever been the queen's most trusty and obedient adherent'. This direct request and the signatures on the Ainslie Tavern Bond threw the queen into a state of confusion. She was prepared to accept that she needed help, but she was lethargic and indecisive, unable to see where her best interests lay. Should she rely upon her ministers, or take a husband who would help shoulder the responsibility? If she chose the latter option, she certainly didn't consider Bothwell to be the best suited man to be her consort – and why wasn't anyone taking into account the fact that Bothwell had married Jean Gordon on 24 February 1566?[11]

On 21 April 1567, Mary spent the day with her ten-month-old son at Stirling Castle. It would be the last time she saw him. The following night she slept at the palace of Linlithgow, where she had been born, and the following morning the queen and her small troupe resumed their journey to Edinburgh. Some 6 miles from their destination, Bothwell suddenly appeared with 800 men, telling the queen that danger threatened in Edinburgh and for her own safety he was taking her to Dunbar. Accepting this as true, she allowed herself to be conducted about 40 miles across the heart of Scotland and by midnight, the queen was securely within Dunbar Castle, the gates firmly closed behind her.

When the threatened danger in Edinburgh never materialised, the people realised that their queen had been abducted. Bothwell obviously felt that an abduction would put an end to further lengthy discussions about a possible marriage, but at this stage Mary still saw Bothwell as her supporter among the nobles. She was probably unaware that his plan was not just formal abduction but rape. These were the depths to which Bothwell was prepared to sink for the fulfilment of his ambitions. Bothwell effectively ensnared the queen by the act of physical rape. However, Mary may not have been totally innocent. She is reported as having said that she would follow Bothwell to the end of the world in her petticoat.[12]

Bothwell's appearance was far from pleasing if Buchanan's report that 'he is hideously ugly, like an ape in purple' can be believed. Leslie, another of Mary's supporters, described him as having 'great bodily strength and beauty, although vicious and dissolute in his habits.[13] The only known portrait of him is a miniature by an unknown artist in the Scottish National Portrait Gallery, and his mummified corpse measured 5 feet 6 inches. Yet Bothwell's relationship with women was well known, and he had several mistresses, including the dominating courtesan Janet Beaton, the Lady of Buccleuch, made famous as Sir Walter Scott's Lady of Branxholm, who could 'bond to her bidding the viewless forms of air'. It was said that the queen had consented to the murder of Darnley as a result of the witchcraft of Janet Beaton.

All strata of society, including the lawless nobles, were immensely preoccupied with superstition and witchcraft, which had long played its part in the fabric of Scottish society. Bothwell had acquired an interest in the black arts while in France, and is said to have studied sorcery and magic in Paris. Rumours persisted about Bothwell and witchcraft, and he was often accused of having enchanted Mary, using magic to secure her affections. Today we would probably accuse him of drugging her, or even date raping her, but in 1567 placards in the streets broadcast how he had used witchcraft to 'breed Bothwell's greatness with the Mary'.

The forces of aristocratic reaction were coalescing against Bothwell's meteoric rise, and on 1 May 1567 a party of dissidents met at Stirling, vowing in yet another communal bond that they would set their queen at liberty. These same weak, fickle individuals had only recently signed the Ainslie Tavern Bond, promising to back Bothwell.

But Bothwell was a determined man. His marriage contract to Jean Gordon, made on 24 February 1566, was formally annulled and on 7 May 1567 she was given judgement against her husband by the Catholic Archbishop Hamilton on the grounds of adultery.[14] The deposition at the time of his divorce named his mistress Bessie Crawford, a blacksmith's daughter, but this was likely a smokescreen to deflect from the abduction. On 15 May, just a week after Bothwell's divorce and three months after Darnley's death, Mary and Bothwell were married at Holyrood. A superstition holds that it is unlucky to marry in May, and records do show a decline in marriages during that month. In Scotland there's a saying: 'Marry in May and regret it for aye.' It was certainly an inauspicious occasion for Mary; in stark contrast to her two previous weddings, this time there was no extravagant reception. There was no plethora of gifts, no rejoicing, no expensive trousseau. Mary wore a yellow gown relined with white taffeta, an old black dress decorated with gold braid and a refurbished black taffeta petticoat. Bothwell received no great presents. Mary gave him a genet fur, recycled from her mother's cloak. The wedding ceremony took place in the Council Hall of Holyrood, and the short Protestant ceremony was followed by a dour wedding breakfast eaten in silence.

For Mary, married life held no personal happiness. Two days after the wedding she and Bothwell were heard screaming at each other and Mary called for a knife that she might kill herself. The next day she threatened to drown herself.[15] It was reported that not one day passed without the queen shedding abundant tears at Bothwell's unkindness. He delighted in humiliating her in public. He was rude, jealous and violent. It was common knowledge that

Bothwell loved his former wife a great deal more than he loved the queen, but his ambitions knew no bounds.

None of Mary's advisers were able to speak to her without him being present, and if his intention was the break her then he almost succeeded. Mary wrote of her own helplessness and broken spirit and her inability to deal with the situation. Her exhaustion and despair weren't helped by Bothwell's tendency to search for violent solutions to problems. A seasoned soldier, he showed signs of a certain administrative ability but his personal qualities negated his usefulness in any delicate situation. He was violent, rash and boastful, which made him the last person capable of uniting the disunited Scottish nobility. Many were suspicious of his motives, which made the whole situation worse.

Bothwell's actions during his five weeks as consort were positively ruinous for the country, leaving his fellow nobles seething in open revolt. Their concerns may have originated in some secret feud among the lords, or from long-hidden grievances, but it now seemed convenient to bring in a new dimension of morality. Bothwell's many enemies decided that his past crimes, which included seizure and violation of the queen, had to be accounted for. More than this, the country took the speedy marriage as proof that the couple had been jointly involved in Darnley's murder. Mary was denounced as 'the Scottish Whore'.

With the county on the verge of revolution, on 6 June 1567 Mary and Bothwell sought sanctuary at Borthwick Castle, a stark, twin-towered fifteenth-century fortress in a valley watered by the River Esk, about 12 miles south-east of Edinburgh. Built as a stronghold capable of withstanding attack from the invading English, originally it had a moat, drawbridge and portcullis around its 100-foot-high walls. Mary had previously stayed there in 1563 during a progress, but this time her stay was far from peaceful as Borthwick was quickly surrounded. Deciding that Borthwick was ill placed to withstand a siege, Bothwell escaped, leaving Mary behind. The besiegers called up to her to abandon her husband and accompany them back to Edinburgh. She refused, and according to the statesman William Drury in a letter he wrote to London, they shouted insults too evil and unseemly to be told to 'this poor princess'.[16]

That night, following Bothwell's example, disguised as a boy Mary escaped the castle. She met Bothwell at the nearby Black Castle at Cakemuir and together they made their way to Dunbar. It was from Dunbar that, on 15 June 1567, Mary and Bothwell went to meet the opposing army at Carberry Hill, about 8 miles east of Edinburgh. Neither army seemed sure as to how to proceed, the queen lacking troops and the nobles lacking authority. They once again asked the queen to abandon Bothwell and return with them to Edinburgh, where she would be restored to her throne and they would be her loyal subjects. Mary was furious. She reminded them that they were the same lords who had signed the bond endorsing her marriage to Bothwell, and it was through their efforts that Bothwell was now in the position he was. Despite all his faults, he had shown himself loyal to her, which was more than these fickle lords had.

Things had reached a stalemate. Bothwell wanted to return to Dunbar Castle, which stood in a strong, virtually impregnable position by the sea. There they could rally more troops in support of their queen. But Mary saw the ensuing battle as needless bloodshed. She was prepared to trust her rebel lords in order to avoid this, and, having agreed a safe passage for Bothwell, on 15 June she accompanied them back to Edinburgh. All her life Mary had been greeted publicly with enthusiasm and adulation, but now there were cries of 'Kill Her! Drown her! Burn the whore!' She had freely surrendered to the Scottish nobles, but now she was a humiliated captive. To the people of Scotland she was no longer their queen; she was an adulteress who four weeks earlier had become the willing bride of a murderer.[17]

In Edinburgh the queen was not taken to her own residences of Holyrood or Edinburgh Castle but to the house of the Laird of Craigmillar, Provost of Edinburgh. In a horrified daze, she allowed tears of shock and humiliation to pour down her cheeks. This queen, who had fascinated half of Europe, appeared now a demented creature, shrieking out that she had been betrayed. The people of the city were shocked into pity at the queen's wretched state, their disapproval of her moral conduct replaced by sympathy. The confederate lords were aware of this and decided that it was in their own interests to remove her to a more isolated, secure prison as fast as possible. She was taken north to Kinross-shire, where late at night they reached the vast waters of Lochleven (near Fort William and Glencoe). Here, occupying almost the whole of one of the four islands in the middle of the loch, lay the dour castle of Sir William Douglas.

Mary was rowed across the bleak waters of the loch, and once on the island was escorted to the laird's room, which had not even been prepared for the royal visitor. Mary became ill, her sickness aggravated by pregnancy, despair and exhaustion. Many thought she would die. On 16 June, the warrant for the queen's imprisonment was signed by nine lords; three of these fickle men had signed the Ainslie bond just eight weeks before.

Bothwell was officially called to answer for murdering Darnley, kidnapping the queen and forcing her to agree to marry him. Ignoring the statutory three weeks' notice to appear, Bothwell was immediately declared an outlaw and a rebel, with his titles, offices and dignities forfeit. He managed to avoid capture and make his way to Orkney; others who had been implicated in Darnley's murder were not so fortunate. Despite all their efforts throughout the summer of 1567, though, the Scottish lords could find no evidence that the queen was involved. If they had any proof or damning evidence against her, this would have been the time to use it – but they didn't. She was told that if she agreed to denounce and divorce Bothwell she would be restored to freedom and liberty. She refused. She had no wish to compromise the legitimacy of her unborn child, and she was suspicious of the lords. She had good reason to be. If they had truly wanted to re-establish her they would have done so after she surrendered to them at Carberry Hill. Instead they had stripped her of all dignity and reduced her to the status of a prisoner.[18]

The brutal attitude and hostility of the Scots towards their sovereign shocked Queen Elizabeth, who sent Throckmorton to Scotland to give an account of the situation. He reported that he was genuinely convinced that Mary's life and that of her infant son James was in danger. Elizabeth, ever watchful to see what advantage could be obtained from the situation for England, suggested to no avail that the little boy should be brought to England to be raised by his paternal grandmother, Meg, Countess of Lennox. The French apparently suggested that the little boy should be brought up in France, but nothing came of that suggestion either. The infant prince James was kept at Stirling Castle under the governorship of the Earl of Mar.

The propaganda of the nobles ensured the continued alienation of the Scottish people from their woeful queen, who miscarried in July. In this weak state she was asked to sign letters for the resignation of her crown, and, outraged at such a request, she refused. She was threatened, and with no allies she was convinced her life was in danger. On a tiny island in the middle of an enormous loch, the icy waters could claim any victim silently without the circumstances of their death ever being properly known. It was while Mary was in this state of terror and despair that Throckmorton managed to smuggle a note to her in the scabbard of his sword, telling her to sign to save her life. He assured her that something so clearly signed under duress could never afterwards be held against her. He was wrong. Signing such a document without advisers, surrounded by soldiers and traitors while being held prisoner on an isolated island, must surely have been illegal and highly immoral, but that is how Mary Queen of Scots signed away the crown she had inherited twenty-four years previously in favour of her infant son.[19]

On 22 August 1567, Mary's bastard half-brother, James Stuart, Earl of Moray, was appointed regent to rule Scotland during his nephew's childhood. His new status gave him the opportunity to take possession of Mary's rich hoard of jewellery, although Mary accused him of stealing them. Some of the jewels should have been permanently held with the crown of Scotland, but others were her own private property, given to her by King Henri of France or her first husband Francis. Regardless, Moray gave some to his wife and sold the majority.

On 8 December 1567, Mary Stuart reached her twenty-fifth birthday; it was not a time to celebrate. By the winter of 1567, the lords needed to provide some justification for Mary's continued imprisonment at Lochleven. For the first time, they mentioned certain documents which implicated Mary in the crime of murdering Darnley. Despite the fact that these were never produced, and only mentioned a year after the event, the blame was shifted from Bothwell to Mary in what was a bad omen for Mary's future. She wrote to Moray asking for a hearing and even offering to lay down her queenly rank. When he refused her request, she wrote as many appeals for help as she could smuggle out of the island. One was to her mother-in-law Catherine de Medici, begging her to send French soldiers to help her and stating that 'it is by force alone I can be delivered'; another was to Queen Elizabeth. After ten months of captivity, she was desperate.

Among Mary's admirers at Lochleven was the debonair young George Douglas, younger brother of the laird. Mary no doubt appreciated his adoration, and probably encouraged it, because George Douglas, Willy Douglas and a few others whom she had won over by her kindness and captivated with her charm were planning her escape. However, things got worse when the Laird of Markyston, a notorious wizard, predicted that Mary would escape by the beginning of May and made a bet on it. As a result, her guard was increased.

The key element of any escape from the island was obviously crossing the loch, and the first attempt involved Mary disguising herself as a washerwoman and escaping by boat with a bundle of laundry. This was thwarted when the boatman recognised her and she was returned to the castle. Having suborned the boatman, George Douglas's next idea was to carry the queen off in a box. This was dismissed in favour of disguising Mary in their next attempt, which took place on the evening of 2 May. All the boats were lined up on the shore, and Willy Douglas pegged all but one to the shore, and the escape was underway. In her room while the others ate, Mary put on a hood like those worn by country women. Willy dexterously removed the laird's keys, and as Mary approached the locked main gate he opened it and she walked straight through. He relocked the gate and threw the keys into the loch as they hurried to the waiting boat.[20]

On the far shore they were met by the faithful George Douglas and John Beaton with fast horses. They met Lord Seton, the Laird of Riccarton and their followers, crossed the sea at Queensferry and were at Niddry by midnight. Mary Stuart was at liberty after ten and a half months of captivity at Lochleven, Having escaped her bonds, Mary feared to remain anywhere too long and headed to Dumbarton, west of Glasgow, where she hoped to draw her subjects back to her and enlist French help. If all else failed, France could be reached from Dumbarton if the situation became desperate. In her desire to be restored to her throne she was even prepared to negotiate with Moray, but he refused. In the hopes of drawing him out, Mary's followers, estimated to have now risen to 6,000, skirted Glasgow where on 12 May, at the village of Langside, Moray and his army were encountered. It has been hinted that pre-arranged treachery was to blame, because squabbling broke out among Mary's men, and half of them broke away. Rather than attacking Moray's men, the royalists were more inclined to exchange blows among themselves, handing the queen a colossal defeat. Over 100 of the queen's party were slain and over 300 were taken prisoner, giving Mary no alternative but to ride at speed away from the scene of defeat before she too was recaptured.[21]

Dumbarton was cut off by hostile troops so Mary fled south for Dumfries, a journey of about 60 miles through rough country where conditions were primitive in the extreme. She wrote to her uncle in France, 'I have endured injuries, calumnies, imprisonment, famine, cold, heat, flight, not knowing whither, 92 miles across the country without stopping or alighting, and then I have had to sleep upon the ground and drink sour milk and eat oatmeal without bread and have three nights like the owls.'[22]

At Terregles, Mary made the decision to seek an English refuge. Her supporters advised against it, warning her that Anglo-Scottish dealings in the past had been unproductive and destructive. England was a Protestant country where Mary had no party, no money, no estates, no relatives and of which she had no knowledge. Perhaps ten months in prison had given Mary a false image of England, and dreams of friendship and alliance with Queen Elizabeth, because despite their warnings and entreaties Mary stood by her decision.

At Dundrennan she wrote to Elizabeth, whose permission she needed before entering the country; however, seeing no reason to delay, she went straight down to the little port at the mouth of the Abbey Burn. In borrowed linen, with her glorious red-gold hair cut short and her face hidden by a hood, there was little chance that the lady who had been born a queen would be recognised as she climbed on board a common fishing boat. At three o'clock in the afternoon of 16 May 1568, in this humble fashion, Mary Stuart, Queen of Scotland and Dowager Queen of France, left her native country forever.[23]

According to tradition, during the four-hour sea journey Mary had a sudden premonition of the fate that awaited her in England and ordered the boatman to take her instead to France. She had taken this same sea route from the western shore of Scotland past Wales and Cornwall as a child. She had lived in France for thirteen years. In France she had the inalienable estates and incomes of a queen dowager of the country, and with the support of her brother-in-law Charles IX and her Guise relations she could rally support.[24]

But the change of heart was made too late. The winds and tide were against her, and the little boat sailed remorselessly towards England. As she stepped ashore at Workington, Cumberland, at seven o'clock in the evening of 16 May she stumbled – something that was considered a bad omen. Even Shakespeare referred to it in his *Henry VI*: 'Men that stumble at the threshold are well foretold that danger lurks within.'

Mary rested at Workington and was taken inland to Cockermouth the following day. Her hurried escape in disguise had left her without a change of clothes, and her appearance was reported as 'very mean'. From the time of her arrival in Workington she wrote regularly to Elizabeth, outlining her need for help in regaining her Scottish throne and her trust in her cousin to provide that help. At this stage she still had confidence that her decision to come to England was the right one, but Elizabeth and her English court were of the opposite opinion. How were they to treat the royal fugitive? She was not a captive and had arrived of her own free will, yet she posed a whole series of problems which could not be ignored.

It was unwise for a Protestant queen to take arms against Scotland on behalf of her Catholic cousin, but if England didn't then France might, and they would enthusiastically seize the opportunity to land on English soil. For the same reason they could not allow Mary free passage through England to France. If the Scottish queen was to be received at the English court, this might be a focus for the English Catholics to rise up in support of Mary as Queen of England. Ten years earlier, as the Dauphiness of France, she had claimed to be the rightful queen of England rather than heiress-presumptive to the throne.

For Elizabeth and her advisers, the best course of action seemed to be to send Mary back to Scotland rather than let her lose in

England or France. After all, subjects should not be allowed to rebel against their queen. Cautious inquiries would have to be made to discover under what terms the Scots would accept Mary back, and in the meantime she had to be detained – not exactly a prisoner, but not exactly free. The unresolved matter of Darnley's death and the scandal she had caused marrying the chief suspect was a convenient excuse to delay matters. Elizabeth couldn't really help Mary without putting herself in jeopardy, and she wouldn't hand her over to the Scottish rebels because she was an anointed queen and her near kin.

From Cockermouth Mary was moved north to Carlisle, where she was taken to Carlisle Castle, that vital bastion on the turbulent frontline of Anglo-Scottish warfare dating back to the Roman era. It was certainly a safe refuge for Mary, as only twenty-eight years earlier, in 1540, Henry VIII had adapted the castle for artillery. On 28 May 1568, Mary was visited by Sir Francis Knollys on instructions from Queen Elizabeth. Knollys was a chivalrous and loyal courtier with strong Protestant convictions. Mary nicknamed him the schoolmaster, because as she spoke only French and Latin, during the next few weeks he taught her to write and speak English.

Knollys reported to Elizabeth that Carlisle Castle was far from luxurious, particularly for a lady of high rank who had been surrounded by luxury all her life. The English queen seemed unperturbed. In her opinion, Mary had arrived in England with nothing so she should be grateful for what she had. Knollys also reported that there were heavy iron gratings across Mary's windows and guards in the antechambers outside her rooms. Whenever she was outside she was guarded heavily, and it soon became obvious Carlisle Castle was Mary's prison.

In the six weeks she was at Carlisle she wrote twenty letters to Queen Elizabeth, but when Elizabeth didn't respond Mary wrote to Catherine de Medici, Charles IX, the Duke of Anjou and her uncle the cardinal. Some of these letters asked for money. She was in desperate need of the income from her French estates to provide for herself and her household, having arrived in England without a penny. In a letter despatched to Elizabeth on 30 May, she made it clear that if Elizabeth did not help her, she would seek help from France and make arrangements to go there as soon as possible.

Elizabeth was not prepared to let this happen, particularly as she had received information from Moray in Edinburgh in the form of the 'privy letter', which contained translated copies (the originals were written in French) of an unspecified number of the queen's writings which would denounce her.

With such matters being discussed and intrigues being spun between London and Edinburgh, it was decided to move Mary from Carlisle, which was considered dangerously near to the Scottish border, but the move was complicated by the fact that Mary was not officially a prisoner. When the suggestion of a move to Bolton Castle, the bleak, solitary fortress overlooking Wensleydale in the North Riding of Yorkshire, was first mentioned to her, she asked whether she was to go as a captive or of her own free will. At this stage she had no reason to regard herself as anything but a temporary guest, and she made the comment that since she was in Elizabeth's hands the English queen might dispose of her as she willed.[25]

The arrival of the kingdom-less Mary put Elizabeth in an unenviable position. The unmarried Queen Elizabeth sat precariously on the throne of England, and Mary Queen of Scots was still her most obvious and likely heir, with huge support from the Catholic community at home and abroad. What was Elizabeth to do with a fellow queen who lacked a kingdom and was in a strong position to take hers? Elizabeth was torn between protecting her own throne and wanting to be seen as a champion of the rights of a fellow queen.

She decided that Mary was to be detained in England, but she refused to grant her cousin an audience. In June messages revealed that Moray had acquired some letters he claimed had been written by Mary to Bothwell, that verified her involvement in Darnley's murder. When Mary heard of this, and the fact that the letters were to be used against her, she was reduced to tears of frustration and implored Elizabeth to ignore the letters as they were 'falsely invented'.

Unperturbed, Elizabeth appointed commissioners to investigate whether Mary was involved in Darnley's murder. One of them was the 4th Duke of Norfolk. It was suggested by John Lesley, Bishop of Ross and Mary's special ambassador to England, that Norfolk should marry Mary and restore her to her Scottish kingdom, but when they tried to push this suggestion Mary replied, 'I'll not be rushed into any further bridal yoke.'

On 13 July 1568, when the time came to leave Carlisle, an angry Mary began to weep. When this achieved nothing, she allowed herself to be moved quite placidly on the condition that she should be allowed to dispatch messages to her supporters in Scotland. The 50-mile journey from Carlisle Castle to Bolton Castle took two days, with an overnight stay at Lowerther Castle and a night at Wharton, so the royal captive arrived at Bolton on 15 July 1568. Here she was placed under the joint guardianship of Sir Francis Knollys and Henry Scrope, 9th Baron Scrope of Bolton, the senior English official on the western side of the Scottish border. On arrival Knollys pronounced that she was 'void of displeasant countenance'.[26]

Bolton Castle was not a cold, damp fortress. It was warm and comfortable, and its living quarters had one of the first central heating systems anywhere in Britain. Mary was given Henry Scrope's own apartment in the south-western tower, while tapestries, rugs and furniture were borrowed from nearby Barnard Castle to make her stay as comfortable as possible.

Elizabeth now promised to restore Mary to her Scottish throne if she stood trial and renounced her claim to the crown of England during the lifetime of Elizabeth and her lawful issue. The fact that the English court had no right to try the Queen of Scotland for a crime said to be committed in Scotland seemed less important than the fact that Mary believed herself to be on the eve of liberty, so she agreed. With a trial pending, Moray now had every incentive to paint Mary as the villain, with the incriminating letters between Mary and Bothwell being central to the case. Taken from a silver casket in her rooms after her arrest, the letters, which became known as the casket letters, if genuine, contained undeniable evidence of her guilt in Darnley's murder. The letters grew in importance and, rather surprisingly, in number until they numbered sixteen. Mary was not allowed to see them but was horrified to hear that letters supposedly written by her were being used against her. She ended one of her letters to Elizabeth with the plea to excuse her bad writing as the letters, so falsely invented, had made her ill.[27]

It was decided at a conference in York that the trial should take the form of examination of the evidence. Mary agreed, seeing the trial as a mere formality because she had been assured by Elizabeth that she would be set free afterwards.

This was a period when Mary made no attempt to escape. She saw no reason to try because she expected so much from Elizabeth and the pending conference at York, which began in October. Win or lose, she believed that the result could not fail to restore her to her rightful place on the Scottish throne. Moray was equally determined that Mary would be seen to be guilty and would never sit on the Scottish throne again. The debatable casket letters were produced, and those allowed to see them expressed the view that they were not all they seemed. This argument was counteracted by the comment that so many letters could hardly be counterfeited.

As she waited for the trial, Mary became increasingly frustrated at her isolation at Bolton so it was arranged for her to spend two days as the guest of Sir Christopher Metcalfe, High Sheriff of Yorkshire, at Nappa Hall, one of the few surviving medieval fortified houses in the Yorkshire Dales, built in 1459 by Thomas Metcalfe. At this stage, Mary didn't feel that she was under arrest; she thought she could leave Bolton of her own free will whenever she wished. However, her understanding changed after an abortive attempt to leave made her realise that she couldn't. The Scottish queen got as far as Leyburn Shawl, now known as Queen's Gap, before being forcibly taken back to Bolton Castle, where security was tightened. Elizabeth's advisers pressed the queen to execute Mary, but she refused – the situation was too similar to that which she had experienced when her name had been linked to plots against her sister Mary. 'I stood in danger of my life, my sister was so incensed against me,' she had said.[28]

During her six months of enforced confinement at Bolton Castle Mary's very presence posed a danger to Elizabeth and the English court, so she had little say in the matter of her own future. While in England she was theoretically a prisoner, and the decision was made to move her to more secure accommodation in the centre of England, equidistant from London, Scotland and the dangerously Catholic northern counties. When Mary realised this, she resorted to tears and rage, and told Sir Francis Knollys that she would rather be bound hand and foot than be moved against her will. Her weeping protests were to no avail.[29]

10

Bess the Jailor

Under normal circumstances Bess would have shown a keen interest in what was happening with Mary Queen of Scots, but as well as grieving for her late husband, Sir William St Loe, she had other things on her mind. Edward St Loe was refusing to pay Bess the rents from his brother's former properties at Sutton Court, and in retaliation she declined to make payments against the backdated sums that Sir William had agreed to pay to Edward. The case was brought to court within two months of Sir William's death, and the whole thing must have brought Bess very low as it dragged on for two years. The judge finally ruled that Edward's wife Margaret St Loe would have a lifetime interest in the manor of Sutton Court, with the property reverting back to Bess, or Bess's heirs, after Margaret's death. This rather reassuring twist ensured that Edward St Loe didn't arrange an early death for his second wife. Edward St Loe was sent to serve the Queen's Majesty in the remote northern area of Ireland for a minimum of two years, so at last Bess could relax.

She was now thirty-eight years old, and in August 1566 she returned to court and her old position serving in the queen's bedchamber with her friends Frances Cobham, Blanche Parry and Dorothy Stafford.

That winter it was rumoured that she was to marry Henry Cobham, brother-in-law of her friend Frances. Her name was also linked with Lord Darcy and her old friend Sir John Thynne. January 1567 saw the passing of Bess's neighbour Gertrude Talbot, daughter of the Earl of Rutland and wife of George Talbot, 6th Earl of Shrewsbury. Shrewsbury had been godfather to Bess's daughter Temperance back in 1549, so Bess would no doubt have written to Shrewsbury offering her condolences. A few months later, George started paying court to Bess.

George Talbot was premier earl in command of the armies of the north, Lord Lieutenant of Yorkshire, Derbyshire and Nottinghamshire, Chamberlain of the Exchequer and one of the richest men in England. His wealth was securely founded on ancestral estates, and on the profitable mines and industries of Sheffield, whose castle was his principal seat. He also owned vast expanses of land in Derbyshire, Nottinghamshire, Shropshire, Staffordshire and Yorkshire, with castles and manor houses including Sheffield Manor (and Castle), Wingfield Manor, Worksop Manor, Buxton Hall, Welbeck Abbey and Rufford Abbey, together with leases from the Crown, among which were Tutbury Castle and Abbey in Staffordshire. There were also at least four properties in London to add to this impressive list.

No details survive of the courtship between George and Bess, but a portrait of George Talbot in his prime shows a commanding figure with a serious expression. They were of the same age, had much in common and from the start their relationship looked very promising. They married in 1567 in an effective triple ceremony. Bess married the earl and officially became the Countess of Shrewsbury; her eldest son and heir, Henry Cavendish, then aged seventeen, married the earl's eight-year-old daughter Grace Talbot; and the earl's second son, sixteen-year-old Gilbert Talbot, married Bess's youngest daughter, twelve-year-old Mary Cavendish.[1]

This was not unusual in influential families. It was an effective way to ensure a powerful dynasty, and Bess was determined to form one of the strongest in the land. The Greys and Seymours were powerful families, and one person who would have been sadly missed at the wedding celebrations would have been Bess's friend Katherine Grey. She had spent seven years imprisoned with her baby sons, and had been moved between five prisons before dying in captivity on 27 January 1568. She was twenty-seven at the time, and probably died of anorexia because she had refused to eat properly for over a year in the hope that her cousin the queen would take pity on her. She didn't. Only after Katherine's death was

Edward Seymour finally allowed out of the Tower with his sons and permitted to reappear at court, but he still faced ruinous fines.

As a three-time widow Bess had her own considerable wealth, land and property, but as a married woman this was all taken by her husband. A married woman had to give up all her financial independence, and in marrying Bess, Shrewsbury gained control of her combined lands. However, Bess had a clause written into their marriage settlement stipulating that in exchange for giving all her land, property and wealth to Shrewsbury, one-third of his unsettled income would go to Bess on his death. She also made some stipulations about keeping Chatsworth House and a few other properties over which she wanted to exercise a measure of personal control, and Bess's eldest son Henry Cavendish, as the Cavendish heir, would automatically inherit Chatsworth House on her death. That was no problem, and the earl readily agreed. Marriage in the high society of sixteenth-century England was very much a business arrangement. The combined wealth of the Cavendish and Shrewsbury families from landholdings, mineral rights and farming was enormous. Their portfolio of properties was extensive, but everything was administered by the Earl of Shrewsbury, and despite being one of the wealthiest men in England he was known to say of his vast wealth that 'the riches they talk of are in other men's purses'.[2]

The marriage was off to a good start, and in surviving correspondence from Shrewsbury to Bess he addresses her affectionately as 'my none' (my own), 'my own sweetheart' and 'my own dear heart'. The couple did not attend court during the first few months of their marriage, but in the autumn they sent the queen a gift of some venison with Bess's nephew Anthony Wingfield, son of her half-sister Elizabeth Wingfield. His audience with the queen lasted an hour, and at the end of the conversation she had asked him when Lady Shrewsbury intended to come to court. When he said he didn't know, she said, 'I am assured that if she have her own will she would not be long before she would see me. I have been glad to see my Lady St Loe, but am I now more desirous to see my Lady Shrewsbury. I hope my Lady hath known my good opinion of her ... I assure you there is no Lady in this land that I better love and like.'[3]

In autumn 1568, Shrewsbury was summoned to London by Queen Elizabeth. The English court had moved to Hampton Court, and on 6 December 1568 Shrewsbury sent a letter to Bess from there. He wrote how he had his interview with the queen in the gardens as 'she would not tell me within about the custody of the Scotes Quene ... what she shall do yet is not resolved of'. In a further letter to his wife, dated 13 December, he wrote, 'Now it is sarten the Scotes Quene comes to Tutbury to my charge. In what order I can't ascertain.'

The Earl and Countess of Shrewsbury qualified as suitable custodians of the Scottish queen on several counts. He was a staunch Protestant and loyal to his queen, with a wife who was equally trustworthy. As the council wrote to the Archbishop of Canterbury on 29 September 1567, 'she has long served with credit in our court'.[4]

Queen Elizabeth had informed the earl that he had been chosen as Mary's custodian in consequence of his approved loyalty and faithfulness, and the ancient blood from which he was descended. Queen Elizabeth was not averse to flattery when necessary – it was cheap and effective. The earl was undoubtedly pleased that he had been chosen for the duty of custodian to the Scottish queen, yet Tutbury Castle was not a residence in a fit state to receive a queen. It was an old motte-and-bailey castle built after the Norman conquest by John of Gaunt. Patched up and altered over the centuries, the castle had in parts fallen into ruin. The roofs leaked and the walls were crumbling, with 'only indifferent repairs', as a Dutch surveyor reported in 1559.[5]

The ancient structure was built beside a marsh from which malevolent fumes arose. The middens stank, and the draughts and winds whistled through the chambers. It was used only occasionally as a hunting lodge, so furniture was sparse, but Queen Elizabeth paid no heed to this. Her main concern was that it was remote and fortified. Despite Shrewsbury's concerns and his request for a more suitable place to be found for the Scottish queen, he was met with a wall of silence and secrecy. Over the next month he repeatedly wrote asking for news and instructions, yet heard nothing. Bess only received her letter from Leicester instructing her to prepare Tutbury on 20 January, six days before Mary's cavalcade set off from Bolton.

Bess replied immediately:

> My Lord, I was much grieved ... to have in readiness within
> Tutbury Castle, the house being unready in many respects for
> the receiving of the Scottish queen coming suddenly. I have
> caused workmen to make forthwith in readiness all such things
> ... most needful to be done before her coming. And God willing,
> I shall cause three or four lodgings to be furnished with hangings
> and other necessities. And rather than I should not with true
> and faithful heart answer the trust reposed by the Queen's
> Majesty, I will lack furniture of lodgings for myself ... Tutbury
> this 21 January 1569. Elizabeth Shrewsbury.[6]

Despite the weather being wet and raw, and the journey through
the north of England being frightful, Queen Elizabeth refused to
consider any delay. Mary was accompanied by six ladies-in-waiting,
a very large number of servants and two companies of English
troops. Knollys was put in charge of the arrangements, but in the
midst of all the turmoil involved in the removal he received word
that his wife was critically ill. He begged Queen Elizabeth to allow
him to go to her bedside, but the queen showed no compassion
and refused. Lady Knollys died, and even then Lord Knollys was
refused permission to return home to bury her, so it was a mournful
cavalcade that trudged south over moors white with winter snow.
The rutted tracks were frost hardened and extremely hazardous.
Mary and her ladies were cold and exhausted when they reached
Ripon, where they stayed overnight.

They broke their journey again at Pontefract Castle, but before
reaching Rotherham Lady Agnes Livingston became so ill that
she was unable to continue the journey. Two days later Mary
collapsed, and the cortege had to be halted while she recovered.
They were on the Yorkshire–Derbyshire border by the city of
Sheffield, where George Talbot owned Sheffield Castle and Sheffield
Manor. They may have planned to stay there temporarily, but
during this state of limbo a message arrived stating that Sheffield
Castle was uninhabitable. The weary procession continued south,
but on reaching Chesterfield Mary begged to be allowed to rest to
try to relieve the pain in her side. It was Bess's relation Sir Godfrey

Foljambe who received her at Walton Hall on the outskirts of the town, providing food and accommodation for Mary and all her attendants.

The following day they were forced to reluctantly continue their journey, as Mary had recovered enough to sustain her for the next few miles to South Wingfield Manor. This was one of Shrewsbury's Derbyshire houses, but their stay was brief. Queen Elizabeth was adamant that Mary must make the last stage of the journey to Tutbury Castle. The royal party reached Tutbury Castle after eight tedious days on the road. There was no great excitement, only relief when the weary royal party eventually arrived at their final destination. Mary immediately took to her bed. This unhealthy abode is where Mary felt her true imprisonment began.[7]

On 3 February, just a year after their marriage, the Earl and Countess of Shrewsbury became the custodians of Mary Queen of Scots. The Scottish queen had become a captive under house arrest, with strict instructions that 'being a queen of our blood, treat her with the reverence and honour mete of a person of state and calling and for her degree. To be accorded all the ceremony due to her position nor by this removing have her state amended but ensuring that she does not escape or meet anyone likely to help her escape.'

Tutbury Castle stands on a hill on the Derbyshire–Staffordshire border and commands extensive views in all directions, but Mary was not impressed. She disliked the place at first sight, and described it as 'a walled enclosure sitting squarely on top of a hill in the middle of a plain, as a result of which it is exposed to all the winds and injuries of heaven. The ramparts of earth are on a level with the highest point of the building so that the sun never shines upon it for which reason it is so damp that you can't put any piece of furniture in that part without it being in four days completely covered with mould.'[8]

The place had no drains, which meant that a large stretch of marshy ground below the castle gave off malevolent fumes and noxious smells that were hazardous to health. The castle was large enough to be more like a fortified town than a fortress, but Mary complained bitterly that the rooms allocated to her and her household were too small, crowded and uncomfortable. Her household was supposed to consist of thirty people but had risen to sixty at this stage, so we can sympathise with the Shrewsburys who, without notice or consideration, had to provide accommodation for this influx of people. It's a situation we can only equate to running a hotel. A household of sixty people was probably not a huge number for one who had lived as a queen all her life, but it was certainly a large enough number to ensure that, despite being classed as a prisoner, her life was undoubtedly comfortable. With four officers in the pantry and three officers in the kitchen, including a master cook and a pottager, she was certainly not on a basic bread-and-water diet.

Even though she was given a suite of three rooms, a great chamber, an inner chamber and an outer chamber for her own personal use, Mary complained that her only privacy was in 'two paltry holes with windows facing the dark surrounding walls'. The effects that Bess had sent from Sheffield – 'beds and bolsters of tyke filled with feathers, chairs and footstools upholstered in crimson satin and cloth of gold, plus twelve small carpets of "Turkey making"' – obviously didn't make the rooms any more habitable for the bad-tempered queen in exile.

The first thing she did on leaving her bed was to write a long letter to Queen Elizabeth complaining that the ancient structure was 'damp and admitted every draught and wind which whistled into every corner of my chamber'. The letter ended with an apology for her poor writing as 'this damp and uninhabited house has given me a cold and a headache'.

Queen Elizabeth's response was to send nineteen tapestries, chairs, carpets, linen sheets and wool blankets for bedding from stores in the Tower of London. Mary also requested three or four hundredweight of feathers 'to amend old and thin beds and bolsters'.[9]

Meanwhile Shrewsbury was also complaining to Queen Elizabeth. In desperation, he wrote that as Mary's jailer he had received no money to provide for her and needed an immediate grant of £500 since he was destitute. That comment might seem laughable when we know that Shrewsbury was one of the richest landowners in England, but he obviously saw the situation as a business arrangement like any other. The honour of being appointed jailer to a spoilt royal captive was performed out of loyalty to the queen, but the honour was outweighed by practical considerations and obligations. Shrewsbury was obviously keen to make that plain from the start, but needless to say the extra burden of organising the household fell on Bess's capable shoulders, and neither she nor Shrewsbury could expect any financial reward for their unstinting service.

With Mary's retinue of sixty people plus women and grooms of the chamber, the living accommodation was very crowded and the expense of keeping and feeding so many people very high. Eight dishes per meal were allowed for the queen's gentlemen and five dishes for the ladies. In 1580 the annual cost of fuel, wine and spices at South Wingfield came to more that £1,000, a huge percentage of this being spent on 2,520 gallons of wine provided for the household to drink and for Mary to bathe in. Bathing in those days had a medicinal purpose, and the alcohol in the wine acted as a disinfectant to kill parasites on the body.

Throughout the whole period of her imprisonment Mary steadfastly refused to make any financial contribution, although as the widow of Francis II she had a dowager's pension of £12,000 per annum which she continued to use to finance her plans for escape. After each plot security had to be stepped up, with a corresponding rise in costs to be met by Shrewsbury.

Queen Elizabeth paid Shrewsbury £52 a week, which was certainly not enough. He was allowed 6d a day each for twenty-four guards but employed double that number at his own cost. He also spent £1,000 on pewter and plate, and during the course of Mary's imprisonment constantly complained of rising prices, servants' keep and inadequate subsidies. Shrewsbury's seventeenth-century biographer Johnston estimated that it was costing him £30 a day or £10,000 a year to keep Mary and her household.

Despite each complaining about the other, at their first meeting on that cold February day Mary and her new captors got on quite satisfactorily, despite Mary making her position very clear from the start. A prisoner she might be, but first and foremost she was a queen, and she had no intention of letting people forget that. She insisted on having a cloth of state, the rich tapestry canopy with the embroidered motto 'En ma fin est mon commencement', arranged as a backdrop over and behind her chair/throne. This signified her royal estate, and she attached much importance to this.[10]

In late February 1569, Nicholas White journeyed to Tutbury in order to report to Cecil on the circumstances surrounding the incarceration of the Scottish queen. He, like many men before him, found Mary dangerously fascinating although he feared to be seduced by this famous 'basilisk' – a serpent that could kill by its breath or glance. White reported that 'she hath withal an alluring grace, a pretty Scotch accent, and a searching wit, clouded with mildness. Fame might move some to relieve her, and glory joined with gain might stir others to adventure much for her sake.' He was secretly in awe of her and could see how her mesmeric charms were inducement enough for men to risk life and limb to free her from captivity. Was he covering up his own feelings by stating that men would do this for fame, glory and gain? White's words were actually prophetic.

One man who didn't seem to be influenced by Mary's charms was Shrewsbury. It's said that he treated her with unfailing courtesy and consideration, aware that one day she might be Queen of England. No doubt Bess shared his sentiment. If Mary became queen she would reward those who had helped her, so the Shrewsburys showed her every courtesy and consideration.

In the early days of her captivity Mary had a very good relationship with Bess. They spent many hours together, sharing needlework projects. Despite their twenty-year age difference, Bess and Mary were both gifted needlewomen and spent time together embroidering in Bess's own chamber. Keeping Queen Elizabeth informed of events, in March 1569 Shrewsbury wrote, 'The queen continueth daily resort into my wife's chamber where she sits working with the needle. They talk together of indifferent trifling matters, without any sign of secret dealing or practice.'[11]

Normally the extended Shrewsbury household would move to another of their properties after two months, using houses on a system of rotation to allow the properties to be cleansed for health reasons. Mary Queen of Scots' retinue and the extended Shrewsbury household was estimated to total around 200, so by March a move was urgently required. The sudden arrival of so many extra people and their horses not only put an unrealistic pressure on toilet facilities, but also on supplies of wood, corn, hay and other locally sourced commodities. Then Mary's health became a matter of concern. She was in the habit of fainting and complained of a constant pain in her side. She then developed a fever. In March 1569 Shrewsbury wrote again to Queen Elizabeth informing her that Mary was suffering from 'grief of the spleen', and the unhealthy conditions at Tutbury were endangering her health further.[12]

Elizabeth was not convinced. She replied that there were too many unauthorised persons living there and the number must be cut. Shrewsbury assured the queen that the matter would be sorted but more immediate action was needed. She was not swayed and more correspondence followed as the situation got worse. Eventually Elizabeth agreed that Mary could be moved to another of the Shrewsbury properties, South Wingfield Manor.

South Wingfield was called Winfeld by the Anglo-Saxons, a name that almost certainly derives from the quantity of win or gorse that grew wild in the locality. The site commands far-reaching views, but the approach to the manor is almost precipitous on all sides except where it's protected by a sunken ditch and heavy defences rendered in the Middle Ages. With its two quadrangles, its design is in accordance with the requirements of a fortress. On the left after passing through the entrance from the south to the north quadrangle is the 72-foot High Tower. Adjoining this and stretching along the left-hand side is the site of the suite of apartments said to have been occupied by Mary Queen of Scots. These apartments have now disappeared, with only the clinging fireplaces, tottering chimneys and vacant windows to bear sad but silent testament to their former use. There are no buildings on the right of the quadrangle, but it is conjectured that this is where the chapel stood. The whole of the north side was occupied by the state apartments, a great banqueting hall off which were the state apartments and ballroom. Under the bedrooms further to the west and communicating directly with the banqueting hall were the buttery and kitchens, and underneath the whole was the crypt. Whether this was a storeroom and wine cellar (as its position close to the banqueting hall and kitchens would suggest), or a chapel or soldier's hall has puzzled historians for years. The small gardens, accessed via a staircase in the keep, were situated on the north side of the building and protected by a deep sunken ditch. To Mary and her supporters it must have appeared every bit as fortified as a prison.

Getting Queen Elizabeth's permission to move the chronically sick Mary from Tutbury Castle to South Wingfield Manor was comparatively easy when compared to the actual transfer, which took place on 20 April 1569. It was a major operation transporting the Scottish queen and her miniature court the 26 miles, financed by Shrewsbury and assured of security by the assistance of the local justices of the county. But the move did not help Mary's condition, and two doctors sent from London said it was aggravated by unsanitary conditions, the result of which caused 'windy matter to ascend to the head'.[13]

Shrewsbury was not impressed. He was emphatic that her ill health was not caused by the unsanitary condition of his manors, but by 'the continual festering and unclean order of her own folke, together with the noisome smells from her horses, dogs and other pet animals kept on the premises'. As well as having ten horses in the adjoining stables, in her apartments she had a greyhound, several small dogs, caged birds and other birds including barbary fowls and turtle doves.

Mary's health continued to decline, not helped when she heard news from Scotland, which continued to be a hotbed of warring factions. Mary's letters and presents to her baby son James were stopped by Elizabeth, and Mary became so depressed that she'd sit weeping uncontrollably, making her whole face swell up. In desperation, Shrewsbury, who himself was not well, arranged for the household to be moved yet again so that South Wingfield could be cleaned and sweetened. This time the move was to Bess's Chatsworth House, beautifully situated in parkland by the River Derwent in the heart of Derbyshire.

By 12 May 1569 Mary Stuart was critically ill, and according to contemporary accounts the 'quences howsholde' now included a doctor named Mr Burgon, a surgeon named Mr Jarvys and a Catholic priest named Sir John Morton to administer to her spiritual needs. It's not clear whether she instigated this, or whether Shrewsbury realised it. He probably considered that it was best to turn a blind eye, although he did worry about the reactions of

Queen Elizabeth and Parliament if they were to hear of this blatant act of heresy.

Throughout her illness, Mary remained in comparative isolation while her supporters conspired to procure her release. There were frequent plots to free Mary, and Shrewsbury's servants were regularly questioned about smuggling out her letters. To ensure that they would not be bribed into helping Mary, he paid his servants an extra £400 per year to secure their loyalty. When it was later discovered that Mary was participating fully in escape plans, she was unrepentant. She remained adamant that since her imprisonment was illegal she was perfectly entitled to try to achieve her liberty. However, she was wary of any scheme in which she became a pawn for a major power, and strongly objected to any hare-brained, half-hearted schemes.

It was during the summer of 1569 that Mary became engrossed in a frequent and affectionate correspondence with Thomas Howard, 4th Duke of Norfolk. Whether or not she ever met him is debateable, although it is possible that they met at Bolton Castle during Mary's forced stay the previous year. Norfolk's sister was Lady Margaret Scrope, custodian of Bolton Castle. His influential family and his solid qualities commended him. At thirty-three, widower and experienced administrator Norfolk came of ancient lineage and was the only duke in England. Many Catholics were prepared to support this alliance, and when the Bishop of Ross, Mary's official envoy, informed her that an annulment of her marriage to Bothwell was now possible, she began to consider Norfolk as a potential bridegroom. Mary saw marriage to an English duke as a necessary and honourable exit from her captive state, yet she was suspicious of marriage. She had believed Bothwell to be the choice of her nobles, and he had turned out to be their bane.

It was not surprising that she should greet the first approaches over the Norfolk match with considerable doubt despite believing that this was what Elizabeth wanted. Mary wrote to him, affectionately calling him 'my Norfolk', and he responded by sending her a diamond which she told him she would wear round her neck – 'unseen until I give it again to the owner of it and me both'. She sent him a miniature of herself set in gold with the message, 'You

COUNTESS OF
SHROESBURY

Above: Bess of Hardwick, from *Bess of Hardwick and Her Circle* by Maud Stepney Rawson (1910; hereafter BHC).

Below: Ault Hucknall Church, where some fragments of the painted glass memorial window to John Hardwick have been incorporated into a nineteenth-century window. (Author's collection)

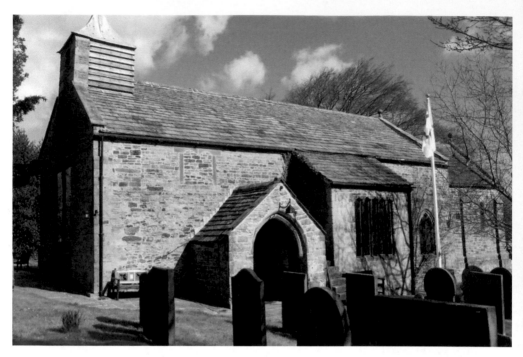

Above: Barlow Church, where Bess's first husband Robert Barlow was buried in 1544. (Author's collection)

Below Left: James V married Mary of Guise and fathered Mary Queen of Scots. From Hardy's *Arbella Stuart: A Biography* (1913; hereafter A. StBiog).

Below Right: Robert Dudley, lifelong friend of Elizabeth. (BHC)

Above Left: Thomas Seymour vowing fidelity to Edward VI in a nineteenth-century engraving. Thomas Seymour was husband of Dowager Queen Katherine Parr, and is rumoured to have seduced the young Princess Elizabeth. (Author's collection)

Above Right: Sir William Cavendish was forty years of age when he married nineteen-year-old Bess Barlow. (BHC)

Below: The execution of Lady Jane Grey, the Nine-Day Queen. Print by Paolo Mercuri based on a painting by Paul Delaroche. (Courtesy of Rijksmuseum)

Queen Mary enters London followed by her sister Princess Elizabeth. (John Byam Liston Shaw/ Getty Images)

Queen Mary was given the name Bloody Mary for the barbaric way she persecuted Protestants. (Modified sketch)

Philip of Spain, King
Consort of England.
(Modified sketch)

Princess Elizabeth,
now twenty-two,
had matured into an
attractive young woman.
(BHC)

Above: Sir William St Loe, who had served Princess Elizabeth faithfully at Hatfield House, was officially made Captain of the Queen's Guard. He then became the third husband of Bess Cavendish on 27 August 1559. Picture by Richard Keere Ltd, Derby, from the picture at Hardwick Hall. (BHC)

Below: Elizabeth was crowned queen on 5 January 1559, a date chosen as propitious by the astrologer Dr John Dee. From Odom's *Mary Queen of Scots – Her Friends & Foes* (1904; hereafter MQS F&F).

Right: Robert Dudley was made Earl of Leicester but when the body of his wife Amy Robsart was found and foul play was suspected. (Courtesy of Rijksmuseum)

Below: Katherine Grey was next in line to the throne but had married without the queen's consent and on 24 September 1561 gave birth to her son, Edward Seymour, Viscount Beauchamp, while still in custody in the Tower. Miniature by Levina Teerlinc. (Courtesy of the Rijksmuseum)

Above: Hampton Court Palace, where Queen Elizabeth was confined in October 1562 with the potentially deadly smallpox. (Author's collection)

Below Left: Henry, Lord Darnley, was in the English line of succession as a great-grandson of Henry VII, so by marrying Mary Queen of Scots they could rule together as King and Queen of England and Scotland. (Courtesy of Rijksmuseum)

Below right: Mary Queen of Scots. (MQS F&F)

Above: Bolton Castle, Wensleydale, where Mary was confined for six months but enjoyed the comfort of the first building in England to have central heating. (MQS F&F)

Below Left: Thomas Howard, 4th Duke of Norfolk. (MQS F&F)

Below Right: George Talbot, 6th Earl of Shrewsbury, was a commanding figure in his prime. After a portrait at Rufford Abbey. (BHC)

Above: Tutbury, where Mary arrived in February 1569 and which castle she always considered to be her first prison. (Author's collection)

Below: South Wingfield Manor, where Mary spent many years as a captive. (MQS F&F)

Above: The Chatsworth Estate, bought by Sir William and Dame Cavendish in 1550 for £600. (BHC)

Below: Queen Mary's Bower at Chatsworth, a belvedere where she could be confined but enjoy the open air. (Author's collection)

Sheffield Manor, 1829. (MQS F&F)

The baths at Buxton, where the Shrewsburys built a house and Mary was allowed to visit to benefit from the curative waters. From *Black's Tourist Guide to Derbyshire* by Llewellynn Jewitt (1879).

Above Left: Meg, Countess of Lennox, granddaughter of Henry VII, mother of Henry Darnley and Charles Stuart. (Author's collection)

Above Right. Arbella Stuart was in line to the English throne but lost her titles and land. Picture from Hardy's *Arbella Stuart: A Biography* (1913).

Right: William Cecil, Lord Burghley. (BHC)

The remains of Fotheringhay and its mound. (Courtesy of Andy B. under Creative Commons)

Above left: James I,
from *The Last
Elizabethan* by
Dorothea Coke
(1937).

Above right: Gilbert
Talbot, 7th Earl
of Shrewsbury,
entertained King James
I at Worksop Manor
on the king's way
south to claim the
English crown. (BHC)

Left: Mary Talbot,
wife of the seventh
earl, aunt and
supporter of Arbella.
(BHC)

Above: Hardwick Old Hall.

Below: Hardwick.

Above: Richmond
Palace today.

Left: Bess of Hardwick.
(BHC)

have promised to be mine and I yours. I believe the Queen of England and the country should like of it.'[14]

To this end, Mary agreed to be divorced from Bothwell, who had escaped to Denmark, believing that her new marital status would lead to her restoration to the Scottish throne. She was wrong. At the Perth Convention in July 1569 this idea was rejected forty votes to nine. Even worse, when news of this and Mary's plans to marry Norfolk reached Elizabeth six weeks later, she was furious. The queen and her government had been on red alert to the prospect of trouble in the north of England ever since the Scottish queen's arrival. They had heard rumours of Norfolk's involvement with the queen, although he had denied any interest in marrying her. Despite this denial, he finally admitted what he had done; Queen Elizabeth refused to permit the marriage, and charged him with disloyalty. He was arrested and sent to the Tower of London, and Mary was sent back to the hated Tutbury.

When Shrewsbury suffered a slight stroke, Henry Hastings, 3rd Earl of Huntingdon, was recruited to step into the breach. Shrewsbury and Huntingdon became joint custodians. However, finding this arrangement uncongenial, Huntingdon obtained permission to renounce the position and left Tutbury on 7 November. Unknown to people at the time, his departure coincided with a plot being hatched by Leonard Dacre with the earls of Westmorland and Northumberland to rise up in protest against Mary's enforced confinement and bring Catholicism back to England. Charles Neville, Earl of Westmorland, and Thomas Percy, Earl of Northumberland, may have been at the forefront but they were wavering and indecisive until their wives stepped in with a simple plan of their own.

Jane Neville, Countess of Westmorland, was the sister of Lady Margaret Scrope, custodian of Bolton Castle where Mary had been lodged earlier in the year, and even more significantly Jane's influential brother was the Duke of Norfolk, languishing in the Tower because he had dared to pledge his troth to the Scottish queen without permission from the English queen.

Anne Percy, Countess of Northumberland, was an equally strong-minded lady and supporter of the Scottish queen. She and her husband had hoped to be appointed Mary's custodians and had visited her soon after she'd arrived in England. Now, the two countesses devised a plan which involved the Countess of Northumberland pretending to be a midwife and attending Christine Hogg, the pregnant wife of one of Mary's French servants, Bastian Pagez, first recorded at the court of Mary Queen of Scots in 1565 as a musician. Although it has often been written that Pagez married one of the queen's ladies, Margaret Carwood, his wife's name, as recorded in the parish register of Holyroodhouse and Canongate and only a few years later in England, was Christily or Christine Hogg. The parish register entry, which is dated later in the year, records the marriage being celebrated in the Queen's House the day after Darnley's murder and Mary was present at the celebrations.[15]

Pagez had followed his mistress into exile in England where he and his family continued in her service. He and Christine Hogg were listed in Mary's household at Tutbury Castle in October 1569, which adds credibility to the plan hatched by the two countesses. Anne Percy, Countess of Northumberland, disguised as a midwife was to visit the pregnant Christine Hogg. She would then exchange clothes with Mary Queen of Scots, who would leave the castle in disguise while the countess took her place. They were both tall women, and the Countess of Northumberland was said to have been 'something like the queen in personage'.[16]

However, the simple plot seems to have miscarried, unlike Christine Hogg herself, who is recorded as having a baby born at Wingfield Manor in November 1569, by which time the northern rebellion was taking place.[17]

After their plan failed, both the countesses accompanied their husbands and some 300 armed followers to Durham Cathedral where they made their first stand. Since Henry VIII had pronounced himself head of the Church of England and banned Catholicism, in this beautiful ancient cathedral, as in other similar places throughout England, symbols of the Catholic Church had been deformed, defaced or destroyed. Here, on 14 November 1569, they decided to reverse that as they smashed the communion table and burnt the English Bible and Book of Common Prayer.

This destruction was probably impulsive, but it marked the start of the Rising of the North, followed by a Catholic High Mass said in Latin and with all the elaborate ceremony of days of old. The rebels were joined by local people who took part wholeheartedly.

Now there was no turning back, no half-measures. Their next objective was to rescue Mary the Queen of Scots.

Like Countess Anne's plan, the Northern Uprising was probably impetuous and ill organised, it's only objective being to rescue the Catholic Queen without thought for the consequences. Mary herself did not approve of this enterprise, feeling that her escape would be ruinous to any future relationship with Elizabeth and England.

Without heed, the rebel army advanced south, increasing in size as they marched. On 23 November, in view of this threatened uprising, orders were sent to Huntingdon to return to Tutbury to help Shrewsbury remove Mary from there to the walled city of Coventry. Remarkably, the original letter from Queen Elizabeth requesting the assistance of the mayor and bailiffs of Coventry in this matter survives in the city archives, stored in the Herbert Art Gallery and Museum.[18]

> Elizabeth R   By the Quene
> Trusty and welbeloved we grete you well. Forasmuche as wee have for dyvers good considerations gyven ordere to our right trusty and right welbeloved Cousyns the Earles of Shreweshury and Huntington to bring the Scottyshe Queene to that our towne of Coventrie and there to see hir safely kept and garded untyll our pleasure shall be other wyse to determine. We let your will or pleasure and commaundment is that for the better assystance of our sayd Cousyns and either of them in this charge committed unto them, you shall from tyme to tyme followe suche ordere and direction as shall for that purpose bee by them or either of them prescribed unto you in suche a wyse as they or either of them shall think fyt for the weale and furtherance of our service. Gevven under our Signet at our Castle of Wyndesor the xxvjth of November the xijth yere of our Reigne.

The government in London, as usual in ignorance of conditions in the North and Midlands, ordered that Mary would be lodged at Coventry Castle; that castle was in ruins, and all that remained was a three-storey building known as Caesar's Tower, which may have formed part of the castle's gatehouse. Although the accommodation would have been cramped, Caesar's Tower has long been regarded as the location where Mary was detained while her entourage lodged temporarily at the city's largest tavern, the Bull Inn. This did not please Elizabeth, who regarded a common inn as totally inappropriate, implying too much dangerous socialising. According to the Coventry City Annals, Mary nonetheless remained in Coventry from November 1569 until January 1570, when she returned to Tutbury.[19]

By the end of November 1569 the northern army had got as far as Bramham Moor, but, hearing of a large force being raised by the Earl of Sussex, the rebels abandoned plans to besiege York and captured Barnard Castle instead. They proceeded to Clifford Moor, but found little support. Sussex marched out from York on 13 December 1569 with 7,000 men against the rebels' 4,600. Being outnumbered and deflated, the rebels retreated northward and finally dispersed their forces. Little mercy was shown to any person implicated in the rising. Upward of 800 perished on the gallows, and fifty-seven noblemen and gentlemen were attained by Parliament and saw their estates confiscated. The Rising of the North had failed, and the Tudor revenge was strict and terrible.[20]

Norfolk couldn't be accused of being the chief architect of the Rising of the North because he was in the Tower and took no part beyond tacit encouragement. There was not enough evidence to incriminate him, and as a mark of clemency he was released from the Tower in August 1570, although he remained under surveillance.

One of the consequences of the Rising of the North was the hardening of attitudes between Catholics and Protestants. Since King Henry had broken away from the Catholic Church heresy had become a crime, and too many had died for their faith on both sides, especially in the reign of Mary I. Elizabeth had reaffirmed the Protestant faith in England, asking, 'Who am I to make windows into men's souls?' She gave her people the freedom to worship God as they believed, allowing them to follow their own faith privately without interference, provided that they conformed outwardly to the Church of England.

After eleven years on the throne of England, in light of the Rising of the North, Elizabeth was excommunicated by Pope Pius V who told her Catholic subjects that they should not support her as they no longer owed obedience to her. Large numbers of Jesuit priests were sent to England to encourage insurrection against the queen, who had no option but to strengthen religious laws. Those who refused to attend their local parish church were punished with heavy fines, imprisonment and sometimes death. In 1581 Elizabeth passed the Act of Persuasions, making it high treason to reconcile or be reconciled to the Catholic faith, and by 1585 it also became high treason for a Jesuit to set foot in England. Anyone found harbouring a priest faced a horrible death, causing an increasing number of 'recusants', as they were known, to seek refuge in Catholic countries abroad.

As Lord Lieutenant, Shrewsbury was responsible for searching and handing over anyone breaking these laws. This was an awkward situation for him, as several of his children and stepchildren belonged to the faith. His first wife, Gertrude Talbot, had been a staunch Catholic, and her family the earls of Rutland of Haddon Hall and Beaver Castle openly embraced the faith. It was a major embarrassment for Shrewsbury when in 1584 it was discovered that while Mary Queen of Scots was staying at Worksop Manor, Shrewsbury's Nottinghamshire home, she was visited by his brother-in-law the Earl of Rutland.

11

Mary's Imprisonment during the 1570s

By January 1570 Mary was back at Tutbury Castle in the sole charge of Shrewsbury, but her guard was doubled when it was discovered that Sir Thomas Gerard of Etwell, which is only a few miles from Tutbury, intended to free her and escort her to Scotland.

Warmer weather often brought outbreaks of plague, and at Tutbury there was less risk of plague if all those who came and went were questioned carefully as to where they had been and how they felt. Huge bunches of herbs were strung across the doorways of every chamber and the brisk air from the moors blew through the gardens to expel evil humours. Despite these precautions, in May 1570 a plague broke out at Tutbury Castle, and preparations were made to move Mary back to Chatsworth House.[1]

Unlike the previous year at Chatsworth, the summer of 1570 was a much more enjoyable time for Mary, who, in better health, was able to spend more time outdoors. As William Cecil informed the queen, 'Chatsworth is a very nete hous, having no town or resort where any ambush might lye.' He wrote to Shrewsbury that 'the queen might take the ayre about your howss on horseback in your lordship's company ... and not to pass from your howss above one or two myles, except it be on ye moors'.[2]

Having permission to ride meant that she did so daily, and she often joined hawking parties that went out into the deeply wooded countryside around Chatsworth. She then asked to be provided with more horses and grooms at Elizabeth's expense as she had brought only ten with her, and this meant employing three grooms and a farrier. The cost of keeping the captive queen was rising.

Chatsworth House was and still is extremely charming, with pleasure grounds boasting lawns where Mary was able to exercise her dogs. There would have been a bowling green and tennis courts, and butts set up for her to enjoy the popular sport of archery. Chatsworth gave her more freedom than any of her other stately prisons, but still she was always under close guard. As a slight concession, a moated belvedere – now known as Queen Mary's Bower and one of the few Elizabethan structures still intact – was built in the grounds near the River Derwent. This allowed Mary to spend considerable time in the open while still enclosed behind restrictive walls, with a substantial locked door or gate over which were her initials and coat of arms. It is rather like a raised playpen where the captive queen could wander or picnic, and it also provided a grandstand for entertainment in the grounds, but its main purpose as a prison was never in doubt.

Bess and Mary would have spent many hours playing the lute, working on embroidery and dressmaking. Their companionship at this time included swapping stories and gossip. Mary's life had been full and no doubt Bess, who had never ventured outside England, showed a keen interest in French court life. The two ladies undoubtedly talked freely about their lives at the French and English courts, sharing stories of indiscretions – something that Bess would bitterly regret when years later Mary used this knowledge against her.

It was during their early years together that the joint embroideries attributed to them at Hardwick Hall, Derbyshire, Oxburgh Hall, Norfolk and elsewhere must have been completed. Embroidery was to prove the great solace of Mary's long years of captivity, filling the empty hours of boredom. Some thirty of these embroideries carry Mary's cipher. Many were sent as gifts to Elizabeth. Inside the parcels of silks and sewing materials sent to Mary there were often concealed notes from her Catholic sympathisers, who were constantly plotting on her behalf.

Mary was twenty-five years old. Her beauty and her charm, the latter largely developed in her youth at the French court, meant that she quickly became a romantic and tragic figure. She met and received many local people, and enjoyed a social life with the prominent Catholic families of Derbyshire and Staffordshire – the Vernons and Manners of Haddon Hall, the Eyres of Padley, Sacheverells of Morley, Ports of Etwell and many others. They shared their enjoyment of music and musical festivals.

In the summer of 1570 there was a suggestion that her son James, by then four years old, should be brought to England. Mary was enthusiastic, but others weren't, and the scheme came to nothing. Perhaps to compensate, Mary took a special interest in the children of the household, particularly Bess's granddaughter Elizabeth Pierrepont, who was better known as Bessie. Mary called her Mignonne and referred to her as her bedfellow. When Mary's secretary Augustine Raulett died in 1574, he was replaced by Claude Nau, and Bessie later fell in love with this man. Her association with Nau led to Bessie and her father being suspected of Catholic recusancy. Anyone who grew close to the Scottish queen and her household was automatically suspected because all the socialising provided an excellent cover for secret messages to be passed.

Many of Mary's supporters, among them Shrewsbury's former agent John Hall, Francis Rolleston of Ashbourne and his son George Rolleston of Lea, were eager to take advantage of the situation. One plan was simply to carry her off as she took the air on the moors around Chatsworth. Two of the main protagonists in this plot were Sir Thomas Stanley, son-in-law of Sir George Vernon of Haddon Hall, whose land bordered onto Chatsworth, and his brother Edward. Sir Thomas Stanley was Governor of the Isle of Man for his father, the Earl of Derby, and it can be assumed that the plot was to snatch Mary and ship her off to the Isle of Man where they could rally her supporters. It was John Hall who betrayed the plot, and when it was foiled he said, 'I feared to make any man privy thereof for danger of discovery and unless many were made privy, the thing could not be done.'[3]

It's unclear whether it was these plots or her illness that ended the freedom that Mary had enjoyed during the summer of 1570 at Chatsworth, because in the autumn she was once more moved to Sheffield. Mary wrote to her envoy John Lesley, Bishop of Ross, 'My Lord of Shrewsbury, because he and others have opinion that change of air shall make us convalesce, is deliberate to transport us tomorrow to Sheffield.' The use of the words 'making us convalesce' would indicate that Shrewsbury was also unwell. Whether it was a nervous or a physical complaint is uncertain, as earlier he had complained in a letter to Cecil that 'the queen of Scots coming to my charge will make me grey-haired'.[4]

Sheffield Manor stood in the middle of a 2,500-acre deer park on the eastern side of the city, and the Shrewsbury family also owned Sheffield Castle, situated upon a steep sandstone outcrop overlooking the confluence of the rivers Don and Sheaf. The short distance between the two meant that it was much easier to move the queen between them when cleaning was necessary.[5] The fortified castle built in 1270 formed the nucleus of the structure, which covered an area of about 4 acres, and was the earliest settlement site in Sheffield. With its enormous park, Sheffield Castle was one of the largest in medieval England but by the sixteenth century it was antiquated.

In 1516, George Talbot, 4th Earl of Shrewsbury, had built the alternative residence of Sheffield Manor a mile south-east of the castle. The manor house was subsequently extended and updated by the fifth and sixth earls, and became the family's Sheffield home of preference. With a boundary fence of about 8 miles, this was one of the largest parks in England and the rights to hunt, mine and farm this land were jealously guarded by subsequent Lords of the Manor.

During the 1570s, Shrewsbury undertook a major programme of remodelling the manor house built by his father and grandfather, and a gatehouse, built in brick with two octagonal towers, was the most imposing of these developments. The turret house, built most probably around 1574, still stands on the site, with its elaborate plaster ceilings of the finest quality, and it's tempting to say that it was built as a prison for Mary Queen of Scots. At other times, it's likely to have served as a gatehouse and a hunting tower, a fashion in deer parks in the sixteenth and seventeenth centuries.

In 1570, Thomas Howard, Duke of Norfolk, was released from the Tower. This signalled the start of another conspiracy, inspired by Robert Ridolfi, an Italian banker based in London. Ridolfi's idea was to incite Philip of Spain to send an invasion force from the Netherlands. This was to be supplemented by a force of Catholics within England who would free Mary, seize

Elizabeth and place Mary on the throne of England alongside her consort, which role Norfolk was to fulfil. Norfolk was given the responsibility of sorting out the practical details alongside Mary's envoy John Lesley, Bishop of Ross. This was a rash scheme, not helped by the fact that Ridolfi was seen as a lightweight and a chatterbox, which gave people very little confidence in his plan. By March 1571, with Mary incarcerated at Sheffield Manor, news of Ridolfi's hazardous plan had trickled through to the English government. When letters in Mary's handwriting were discovered, it left no doubt that she had sanctioned the undertaking and supplied funds for carrying it out.

Bastian Pagez and Christine Hogg were listed in Mary's household at Sheffield on 3 May 1571, although once again it appears that Mary had been told to reduce the number. Mary wrote to John Lesley from Sheffield Castle in September saying she had to give up some servants, but Pagez, who designed Mary's embroidery patterns, was deemed necessary.[6] Mary informed Lesley that Pagez's inventions for her needlework were her first solace after her books. He and his wife served her well and faithfully, but had children and no support. She hoped the bishop could get him some French appointment to give him the financial security to stay with her.[7]

On 18 September Mary wrote to the French ambassador:

> By the carriers I find it is not wise safe to write unless all other means fail, in which event the best and most secret writing is with alum dissolved in a clear water 24 hours before you wish to write. To read it, it is necessary only to dip the paper in a basin of clear water. The secret writing appears white, very easily read until the paper dries again.

It was perhaps not the brightest idea to write this in a letter that she knew might be intercepted, but was Mary in fact just playing games?

Ridolfi was probably tipped off that his plot had been uncovered, because just before the government swooped he escaped abroad. Norfolk and Lesley were not so fortunate. Charles Bailly, Lesley's secretary, was arrested while carrying letters from Ridolfi and Pope

Pius V to the bishop. He admitted that Ridolfi had left England with a message from Mary Queen of Scots to the Pope and the Duke of Alva, the King of Spain's governor of the Netherlands, urging them to invade England to overthrow Elizabeth and substitute Mary on the English throne with Norfolk as her consort. On 7 September Norfolk was arrested again, and admitted sending gold from the French ambassador in London to Mary's northern supporters. He also confessed that money from the Pope would be used for the invasion too.

In November 1571, the Earl of Shrewsbury discovered that Bastian Pagez was doing more than helping Mary with her needlework project – he was sending letters in cipher from Mary to the French ambassador. Pagez had been picking up the ambassador's letters from Nicolas, an Englishman employed as an interpreter, in St Paul's Church, Sheffield. The historian Michael Bath notes one of Mary's needlework emblems on a pillow designed by Pagez was cited in the trial of the Duke of Norfolk because the emblem held a coded message.[8]

As Lord Chief Steward, Queen Elizabeth appointed the Earl of Shrewsbury to preside at Norfolk's trial, which began on 16 January 1572 while Sadler covered for him in Sheffield as Mary's jailer. Shrewsbury sat on a raised chair with a cloth of estate, set on a high scaffold 6 feet wide. On either side sat twenty-six peers and below him sat the judges. The only witness present was Richard Cavendish, who repeated on oath treasonable words that Norfolk had said to him.

Norfolk was found guilty of high treason, and Shrewsbury pronounced sentence: 'Thou shalt be had from hence to the Tower of London from thence thou shalt be drawn through the midst of the streets of London to Tyburn, the place of execution. There thou shalt be hanged, and being alive, thou shalt be cut down quick, thy bowls shall be taken forth of thy body and burnt before thy face, thy head shall be smitten off; thy body shall be divided into four parts or quarters, thy head and thy quarters to be set up where it shall please the Queen to appoint; and the Lord have mercy upon thee.' He then broke his white staff into two to dissolve the commission.

On 5 February, Shrewsbury returned to Sheffield with the news. Mary was devastated. She spent her time fasting and in prayer, observing abstinence on Monday, Wednesday and Friday, but to no avail. On 2 June, the 4th Duke of Norfolk was executed.[9]

Shrewsbury was again summoned to London, this time to witness Norfolk's execution. News of the duke's death triggered in Mary periods of persistent vomiting. Shrewsbury was informed in a letter that she 'gets worse every hour. Nothing remains in her stomach. She has vomited at least 10 or 12 times last night.' The doctors feared that she would die and Shrewsbury lost no time in returning to Sheffield. He could not afford for her to die while in his care in case he was accused of arranging to have her poisoned.[10]

Mary recovered, but in mid-June she was accused of the heinous crime of taking up arms against England. She freely admitted that she had written to the King of Spain and the King of France, the Pope and others asking for help in order to be set at liberty and restored to her own country. She insisted that her imprisonment was illegal and she was therefore justified in taking advantage of any means to secure her liberty. She also maintained that as a sovereign princess she came outside the jurisdiction of England, and although the people called for justice, Elizabeth's personal intervention prevented this.

Mary wrote, 'My head is so full of rheum and my eyes so swelled with such continuous sickness and fever that I am compelled to keep entirely to my bed where I have but little rest and am in a bad condition so that I can't now write with my hand.' Indeed, there are few of Mary's many letters written over the next fifteen years in which she doesn't refer to the constant pain she had to suffer. Her digestive upsets, stiffness, aching limbs and the pain in her side which plagued her all her life were interspersed with bouts of severe illness which on several occasions became critical and almost proved fatal. Acute pains in her arms prevented her from writing, and attacks of fever and the gradual onset of rheumatism aggravated by the dampness of some of her prisons took their toll.

Bess, who had always enjoyed robust health, probably lost all patience, particularly when Shrewsbury, who suffered occasionally from bouts of painful ill health due to his gout, came down with 'the hot ague'. His physician Dr Francis was deeply concerned due to 'the many hot choleric vapours which had found their way up to the patient's head from his stomach, when he took a fever after drinking too much cold water'. Shrewsbury may have had a stroke, and as his recovery was slow Bess wrote to Elizabeth asking for permission to accompany him to Buxton to take the curative waters. When she received no reply they went ahead with the journey, leaving Mary at South Wingfield Manor.[11]

The therapeutic quality of the water in Buxton has long been regarded as special. The Romans named it Aquae Arnemetiae after the Celtic water goddess and established it as a Roman spa. In the Middle Ages, the goddess Arnemetiae was replaced by St Anne and Buxton became famous as a place of pilgrimage attributed with many miraculous cures. With a chapel served by priests built close to the well, it would have resembled a Peakland Lourdes with the sick and lame bathing in the waters. Those who were cured left votive offerings of crutches and miniature arms and legs in gold that were hung from the walls. Then came the Dissolution of the Monasteries, and Thomas Cromwell viewed this as idolatrous superstition. He sent Sir William Bassett and his men to make a bonfire of the crutches and other offerings, melt down the gold and raze the chapel to the ground. This didn't stop the people making pilgrimages to Buxton, but among them were many poor and destitute who had previously relied upon the monasteries to give them food and shelter. Their arrival in ever-increasing numbers put an intolerable burden on the town, and the people sent a petition to Queen Elizabeth declaring that the cost of maintaining these poor wayfarers was so great that they had no money to repair their church. A year later an Act of Parliament was passed forbidding people to visit the well without a magistrates' licence or proof that they could pay for themselves during their visit to Buxton. The charges varied from £3 10s for a duke to 1s for a yeoman.

In 1572, the entrepreneurial Shrewsbury saw an opportunity to build an impressive new bathhouse in the centre of Buxton on the foundations of an earlier inn or hostelry where the warm springs surfaced. He called it Buxton New Hall.[12] He installed a fashionable doctor named John Jones, who that same year wrote the first medical book on Buxton waters, entitled *The Benefit of the Ancient Bathes of Buckstones*. Dr Jones described Shrewsbury's bathhouse as 'a very goodly house, four square, four storeys high, so well compact with houses and offices underneath and above and round about, with a great chamber and other goodly lodgings to the number of thirty. The baths also are bravely beautiful with seats round and are defended from the ambient air.'[13]

The eminent physician declared that the thermal waters were efficacious for almost every ill of the human body, and understandably this attracted great fame, and a wealthy, aristocratic clientele who flocked to take advantage of the curative properties of the healing water. Buxton became a fashionable place to spend time, but when Queen Elizabeth learnt that the Shrewsburys had left Mary alone at South Wingfield while they were at Buxton she was furious. She ordered them to return immediately, and temporary guardianship of Mary was given to the Henry Hastings, Earl of Huntingdon, Sir Ralph Sadler and Sir John Zouche.

Bess must have been angry. Their carefree lifestyle was over. Keeping their expensive royal prisoner and her entourage was a full-time chore and an unwanted, burdensome strain for the couple. They could no longer enjoy their untroubled former way of life. They were committed to Mary twenty-four hours a day, every day. They could never relax. Their lives were constantly disturbed by the intrigues of the captive queen and the suspicions of the reigning one. Having a captive queen as a permanent house guest meant that they could no longer entertain, so they were cut off from their friends and family, and now they were being told to curtail all their outside activities too. No wonder the good relationship between Bess and Mary was wearing very thin.

At the end of July the queen once again ordered Mary to be taken back to Tutbury. This was not only because the 'manor waxed unsavoury'; it was to give superior protection. Bess and her husband had to arrange and undertake the upheavals of another journey as the queen and her retinue were moved the 28 miles from South Wingfield back to the hated Tutbury.

Mary's health continued to cause concern, and on 10 August 1573 the queen eventually gave consent for Mary to visit Buxton to take the waters to seek relief from her chronic arthritis. Buxton had become the fashionable place to be, with local dignitaries and gentry mingling with many of the preeminent nobles of Elizabeth's court. Although rumours were always rife that Elizabeth herself would make an unannounced visit, the furthest north she ever got was in August 1575 when on a royal progress she stayed at Chartley, the home of the Essex family in Staffordshire.

It was the first of six visits Mary was to make to the Derbyshire spa town between 1573 and 1583, and Mary wrote to Elizabeth, 'I have not been at all disappointed thank God, having found some relief.' However, Elizabeth put tight restrictions upon Mary's liberty, and sent strict instructions that she must give an hour's notice if she wanted to leave her rooms and that no one was allowed to visit her after 9 p.m. Nevertheless, there were reports that Mary explored the town and went as far as Poole's cavern, a natural cavern formed by the action of rainwater percolating through cracks and joints in the limestone rocks over many thousands of years. According to legend, Mary ventured deep into the cave to a point now known as Mary Queen of Scots Pillar.

The other drawback would appear to be the lack of servants: 'I have few servants,' wrote Mary, 'and it is not possible that they will be able to hold out much longer. I have only one gentleman in waiting, and if he is ill, I am obliged to wait upon myself.'[14]

It's not obvious what she meant by this, as it's hardly likely she was without her usual cavalcade of female attendants, but perhaps she was hinting at some new intrigue. If this was so, she was not alone. Bess had a few secrets of her own, and during the summer of 1574 she was busy with them.

12

The Unsanctioned Marriage

Bess had one unmarried daughter, the nineteen-year-old Elizabeth Cavendish, and it was time to find her a husband. Bess had arranged advantageous marriages for her other children, but now she was aiming even higher. Her plan was to marry her daughter to a man of royal blood and her choice was Lord Charles Stuart, son of the Earl and Countess of Lennox, and great-grandson of Henry VII. The silver spoon could now be bought.

Charles Stuart's mother, Meg, Countess of Lennox, granddaughter of Henry VII, had been barred from taking the throne because of her alleged illegitimacy, but she had successfully arranged the marriage of her son Henry Darnley to Mary Queen of Scots. Henry Darnley had for a very short time been the King of Scotland. Meg's one remaining son, Lord Charles Stuart, had a definite – though remote – claim to both the Scottish and English thrones. The Lennox family had prospered during the reigns of Henry VIII, Edward and Mary, then cousin Elizabeth took the throne and things changed. There was no love lost between Queen Elizabeth and her aunt Meg.

Not only was the Lennox family heavily fined for refusing to denounce their Catholic faith, the furious Queen Elizabeth confiscated their English properties and imprisoned Meg and her husband for arranging an unsanctioned marriage between their son Henry Darnley and Mary Queen of Scots. But Meg was ambitious. Her eldest son had fathered James, the Scottish king; why shouldn't her younger son Charles Stuart, Earl of Lennox, father a future English king? There was every opportunity for the family to reverse their fortunes if Charles married into a wealthy merchant family in favour with the English queen, and the Cavendish/Shrewsburys were such a family. Their friendship and loyalty to Elizabeth was never in doubt, which made them an obvious choice.[1]

It's not clear who made the first move, but during the summer of 1574 the two countesses formulated their secret plans and in the autumn they put them into action. At Rufford Abbey, on the Derbyshire–Nottinghamshire border, Elizabeth Cavendish and Charles Stuart, Earl of Lennox, met and married. Given that royal blood was involved, the queen's permission should have been sought; it wasn't, and the parties involved had to face the royal rage. The furious queen ordered them to return to London. Meg Lennox was put on trial immediately, but it soon became apparent that the council were more interested in uncovering a plot to rescue Mary Queen of Scots than the unsanctioned wedding of Elizabeth Cavendish and Charles Stuart, Earl of Lennox.

Finding no evidence of a plot, Meg was sent to the Tower of London and the newlyweds were placed under house arrest at King's Place, Hackney. It was there that Elizabeth gave birth to their daughter – no doubt a great disappointment when all their hopes were centred on a son who could inherit the English throne. They called the baby Anabella after her fourteenth-century ancestor Anabella Drummond, Queen Consort of Scotland and mother of James I of Scotland. It's believed that a scribe's mistake changed the spelling of Anabella to Arabella which later became Arbella.

Elizabeth and Charles Stuart had been married eighteen months when in April 1576 Charles Stuart, Earl of Lennox, died of consumption. Arbella was only a few months old, and the Scottish Crown seized the Lennox estates in Scotland, the loss of which meant that Meg, already paying interest on debts outstanding to the English Crown, was now in dire financial difficulty. The Scottish Crown then decided to claim the Lennox title that should rightfully have gone to Arbella, but as the fifth earl's widow Meg refused to denounce her title. She worked unceasingly to regain Arbella's birthright, badgering, pleading and pestering anyone who might help her cause.

Meg Lennox had expected to acquire a hefty dowry from the Cavendish/Shrewsburys, which would have helped to solve her financial difficulties, but the money was not forthcoming. The Earl of Shrewsbury was pleading poverty and declaring himself in dire financial straits due to the constant demands of housing Mary Queen of Scots. In addition to being unprepared to honour the agreements drawn up by him and Bess in their 1567 marriage contract to provide a dowry for Elizabeth, he was also refusing to give £20,000 to each of Bess's sons when they reached the age of twenty-one. Shrewsbury always managed to wriggle out of parting with money where Bess was concerned, and although Bess had brought great wealth to the marriage she had no say on how her money was spent. Bess would have provided Elizabeth's dowry, but the law dictated that a married woman could have no independent finances – a situation that was bound to cause a lot of friction between Bess and Shrewsbury. To help ease the situation, and showing a business acumen that was shortly to come to the fore, Bess made Meg Lennox a loan that necessitated an annual repayment of £500 over four years.

Perhaps things were brought to a head when Bess's brother James Hardwick, who had inherited the Hardwick estate that had been Bess's childhood home, was declared bankrupt and thrown into debtors' prison. Bess asked Shrewsbury to help pay off her brother's debtors, but he refused and overreacted to Bess's imagined provocations with uncalled-for hostility.

Then, on 4 March 1578, Meg Lennox died. Although poison was suspected, it was never proved. The unsympathetic queen immediately seized all the remaining Lennox lands in England and their revenue on the pretext of the debt the countess owed the Crown. Immediately King James of Scotland tried to claim the Lennox English lands from Queen Elizabeth, but she claimed they were not available; their sale had undoubtedly paid for Meg's lavish state funeral and the magnificent monument at her burial site, which she shared with her son Charles in the south aisle of Henry VII's chapel in Westminster Abbey.

In retaliation, on 3 May 1578, just two months after Meg's death, James of Scotland officially revoked the earldom of Lennox. Queen Elizabeth wrote to him reminding him that the earldom by rights officially belonged to Arbella, but the following month, in the most callous move of all, James gave it to Robert Stuart, Bishop of Caithness.[2]

In September 1578, six months after Meg's death, Bess went to court to press for her daughter and granddaughter's claim. Queen Elizabeth promised to do what she could, but her authority did not extend into Scotland. She did, however, award Elizabeth Lennox an annual sum of £400 plus £200 for Arbella. This undoubtedly would have been a portion of the revenue from the land and property that was rightfully theirs anyway.[3]

In less exalted circumstances £600 would have been sufficient to keep a mother and child, but there was no way that Elizabeth and Arbella could continue to live at King's Place. Arbella was of royal blood, descended from Henry VII, and her mother was adamant that she had to live in a fitting style. The only solution was for them to leave London and move back to Derbyshire. The Shrewsburys were like Derbyshire royalty, but having Arbella live with them was something Queen Elizabeth had been anxious to avoid in order that Mary Queen of Scots, 'that frustrated, disappointed and neurotic captive' as she called her, could not have a detrimental influence on the four-year-old Arbella. Seeing no satisfactory alternative, the queen eventually agreed that they could move back to Derbyshire on condition that Arbella and her mother were not to share the same roof as the captive queen.

In December 1578, when they arrived in Derbyshire, Mary and the Shrewsbury family were at Sheffield Castle so Bess was forced to leave her daughter and granddaughter at Chatsworth House and continue her journey to Sheffield. She wrote to Walsingham from Sheffield Castle on 29 December 1578: 'I came hither to Sheffield of Crestoline's Eve and left my little Arbella at Chatsworth. She endured very well with travel and yet I was forced to take long journeys to be here with my lord afore ye day.'[4]

The impracticality of maintaining two households at the same time sorely tested Bess, who prevailed on Queen Elizabeth's close advisor William Cecil to allow them all to live in the same household. Finally it was agreed.

Mary Queen of Scots had been a captive in the household for ten years. She had arrived in February 1569, and for the next seven years Arbella would have had almost daily contact with the Scottish queen, who was an excellent storyteller. Arbella would have heard every aspect of Mary's colourful life and seen the subsequent consequences of her royal birth. Mary tried to use her influence in Scotland to restore the Lennox title and lands to Elizabeth and Arbella but was unsuccessful. When Elizabeth Lennox told Mary that she was suspicious that her mother-in-law's executor Thomas Fowler had absconded with the Lennox jewels, on 19 September 1579 Mary wrote to him on Arbella's behalf, issuing a warrant ordering Fowler to hand the jewels over.[5] Fowler replied from Scotland claiming that he had been waylaid and robbed on the way, but no one was surprised to hear that the priceless Lennox jewels were later found in the possession of James of Scotland. Queen Mary tried to put pressure on her son to return the jewels that rightfully belonged to Arbella, but despite all her efforts they were never returned.

While Arbella cultivated a good relationship with the imprisoned queen, Bess was finding their relationship very trying. Mary could be very kind and thoughtful, but sometimes she would be angry, hostile and tearful. Her moods changed on a regular basis. Her frequent disturbances of mind, hysteria, nervous collapse and physical prostration suggest that she may have been suffering from the hereditary disease porphyria.[6]

There was continuous friction between Bess and her husband, and by 1579 reports of their discontent had reached court. Queen Elizabeth asked them to patch up their differences, and although Bess tried, Shrewsbury just became meaner. He would explode into criticism and abuse of his wife with little or no provocation. The idyllic early years of the Shrewsbury marriage were over. Bess became more pragmatic, and after long and heated discussions they eventually came to an agreement that Shrewsbury would be excused from paying what had been agreed in their 1567 marriage settlement if he returned to Bess all the land and property she had inherited from her third husband William St Loe. It was mainly in Somerset and Gloucester, but this at last gave Bess her financial independence. Although it was necessary for her to stay in the background, she controlled events through her protégés William and Charles Cavendish.

When James Hardwick died in debtors' prison in April 1581, Bess raised enough capital to purchase the Hardwick estate of her dead brother for £9,500. She was convinced that if the estate was managed well it could produce a good return on the minerals alone. Bess was a shrewd businesswoman and superbly competent. She acquired interests in land and mineral rights, and provided a popular moneylending service to members of the nobility, dipping into the coffers stacked under her bed for loans at competitive rates.

But Shrewsbury was not a man of intellect, and argued that Bess had siphoned away his fortune into her own coffers. He started a vendetta against her, and although he'd agreed to return her property he seized rents from the estates which he had returned to her and harried her tenants. Shrewsbury's gout and finances were troubling him, making him short-tempered, and as his nervous disposition became more pronounced he reacted to his wife's imagined provocations with renewed hostility. Throughout all their quarrels, though, Bess never wronged him nor wished to be parted from him. Shrewsbury, on the other hand, was guilty of both. The marital situation was so fractious that one of Bess's gentlemen servants wrote seeking employment at Woollerton Hall in Nottingham, stating that 'this house is a hell'.[7]

On 21 January 1582, twenty-six-year-old Elizabeth Lennox died at Sheffield Manor, leaving her daughter Arbella in the care of her grandmother Bess. That same year Shrewsbury's son and heir Francis Talbot also died, and his younger son Gilbert, married to Bess's daughter Mary, became Shrewsbury's heir. The extended family with Arbella and their royal captive moved between Sheffield Castle and the other Shrewsbury homes, but being so often alone Arbella frequently found herself seeking out the company of the Scottish queen. Perhaps Mary could trust a child; she certainly couldn't trust many adults. She was a captive, a lonely, confused woman aware that even her own people were capable of plotting both for and against her. Maitland, who had been her secretary for years, could forge her handwriting and had been known to do so.

During all the years of her captivity, there were many who had been plotting the Scottish queen's escape and the overthrow of Queen Elizabeth. Mary was involved in many of these attempts to gain her freedom but all to no avail because Sir Frances

Walsingham, master of espionage, had spies watching constantly for the Scottish queen's complicity. The next major plot was the Throckmorton Plot. Sir Francis Throckmorton acted as Spanish agent between Mary and Bernardino de Mendoza, the ambassador of King Philip II of Spain, but a double agent named Charles Paget, who had entered Walsingham's services secretly in 1581, was aware of this and gave Walsingham the incriminating information he needed. Sir Francis was found carrying letters from Mary agreeing to an invasion on her behalf by Spain, and he was arrested in November 1583. Before his execution Throckmorton made a full confession implicating Mary, who knew every detail of the plan. Another plot had been unsuccessful, but Elizabeth's response was just to guard Mary more carefully. By November, according to a state paper, there were 210 gentlemen, yeomen, officers and soldiers at South Wingfield to watch the captive queen.

Walsingham had other matters to attend to; he had heard Arbella's name linked with James of Scotland. Both were of royal blood, descended from Henry VII, and both were in line for succession to the English throne. Because it could be a plot to dethrone Elizabeth, Walsingham had to investigate, particularly as it was rumoured that the suggestion had been made by Mary herself. She had written to Queen Elizabeth inferring that it was Bess's intention for her granddaughter to marry James.[8]

In the spring of 1585 Walsingham sent his cousin Sir Edward Wootton on a special mission to Scotland with instructions to speak to nineteen-year-old James on the subject of marriage. Wootton was to suggest that James took Arbella as a bride, but James had already been approached by a Danish contingent; he had the choice of Arbella or a Danish princess.[9] Wootton reported back that James had so little interest in marriage that he willingly gave a promise that he would take the advice of Walsingham and Leicester when he came to make a choice.[10] The problem was that neither Walsingham nor Wootton had any real interest in pushing Arbella's claim, whereas the Danish ambassadors were a lot more competent and did a much more thorough job. They pressed harder and were more persuasive, leaving James contemplating with reluctance the notion of his marriage to Anne of Denmark.

Meanwhile, Mary was being diverted quite pleasurably by having her portrait painted. When she injured her back getting onto a horse to go to Buxton she was allowed a coach and six horses, which from then on she used to ride through Sheffield Park. It was easy for Shrewsbury to complain of the strain of keeping Mary Queen of Scots, but everyone knew that he only pretended to despise his position as her jailor. He was besotted by the woman. Even the queen was suspicious that the earl was overly friendly with Mary. Lord Burghley had confirmed this on his visit to Buxton when they were taking the curative waters.

Rumours began to circulate that Mary had been having a long-running affair with Shrewsbury and there had been at least one child. Shrewsbury accused Bess of inventing the story; it may have been Mary herself, but she was adamant that the rumours had been started by Bess. No one seemed to know whether the stories were fact or fiction, but because no one was above suspicion, in December 1584 Bess, William and Charles were called to court to publicly deny that they had initiated the rumours of the affair between Shrewsbury and Mary.[11]

The year 1584 was to see Mary's last summer at Buxton, where in melancholy premonition she used a diamond ring to scratch a few lines in Latin on the window of her room in the New Hall – '*Buxtona, Quau calidae celebrabere nomine lymphae, Forte milhi postae non aduenda, vale*'. Translated it reads, 'Buxton, whose fame thy milk-warm waters tell, whom I, perchance, no more shall see, farewell.' She signed it Marie R.'[12] (The expression *calidae lymphae* means milk-warm, or the temperature of fresh milk.)

While the queen's favourite Robert Dudley, Earl of Leicester, had been in Buxton he had called on the beleaguered Bess at Chatsworth. They were planning a betrothal between Arbella and Robert Dudley Jnr. Neither Bess nor Leicester saw any reason why Queen Elizabeth would not approve of the union, but before they requested royal approval the secret was leaked. In a letter from the double agent Charles Paget to the Earl of Northumberland on 4 March 1584 he states, 'The queen should be informed of the practices between Leicester and the Countess for Arbella, for it comes on very lustily, in so much as the said earl hath sent down a picture of his baby son.'[13]

When Mary Queen of Scots heard of the proposed betrothal between Arbella and the young Robert Dudley, she was extremely angry. She had tried to instigate a betrothal between Arbella and her own son James, but she claimed that Bess had dashed all their hopes because of the plans she was making to marry Arbella to the young Robert Dudley. Mary wrote to the French ambassador Mauvissiere that 'nothing has alienated the Countess of Shrewsbury from me more but the vain hope which she has conceived of setting the crown on the head of her little girl Arbella and this by means of marrying her to a son of the Earl of Leicester'.[14]

Bess was doing her best to cope with the strained circumstances. She resented the demands that Mary made on their lives, feeling as much a prisoner as Mary. She was tired of being the Scottish queen's jailer. She had no freedom. She could not entertain or attend court as she had once done. Not only did they live in constant fear that Mary would escape or be assassinated, but the situation was made worse because Mary was poisoning Shrewsbury against Bess. Francis Battell, one of Bess's gentlewomen, wrote to Lady Paulet in March 1584: 'Shrewsbury gives out hard speeches of her to her great discredit if it should be believed of her friends. The cause of her Lord's hard dealing with her is that the Scottish queen cannot abide her, for how can she abide her when she is with all hatred bent against her.'

With Shrewsbury's mind growing more disturbed, his relationship with Bess cooled to frostiness. In order to retain her own sanity, Bess left him in Sheffield with Mary and returned to Chatsworth. At least there she had the freedom she lacked as the Scottish queen's jailor.

While his marriage was deteriorating or possibly because of it, Shrewsbury discussed his problems with Mary, who now used him utterly to her own ends. Bess sent many appeals to end the discourse between them, but Shrewsbury refused. His heart was full of deadly malice and hatred, no doubt inflamed by the spiteful tongue of the Scots queen. He referred to Bess as his 'wicked and malicious wife, who was a woman of base parentage', and said he was ashamed of his choice of such a creature. Such harsh words cut Bess deeply, but historians believe the words actually came from the venomous tongue of the Scots queen, who had become Bess's sworn enemy.

Mary's letters to Mauvissiere and her friends display a rising tide of hatred and fury towards Bess. She claimed betrayal by one she had been foolish enough to trust. She thought Bess 'bound to me and regardless of any other duty or respect, so affectionate towards me that, had I been her own queen, she could not have done more for me. I had the sure promise of the said countess that at any time if my life was in danger, or if I were to be removed from here, she would give me the means of escape and that she herself would easily elude danger and punishment in respect of this'. Mary assured Mauvissiere that at the time she had accepted these assurances without question.

All Bess's supporters became targets for Mary's slander, but her main aim was to display Bess as disloyal to Queen Elizabeth. She said that Bess had commissioned an astrologer who foretold that she, Mary, would replace Elizabeth on the English throne, and would be followed by her son James and his wife Arbella. If this was true it would be treachery, but when no action was taken Mary announced that she was prepared to unleash such revelations that rumours of her intimacy with Shrewsbury would be left in the shade. Her most venomous plan was to reveal facts allegedly told to her by Bess in those early companionable days when they sat sewing together. Bess had no doubt passed on court gossip, exchanging like for like with the Scottish queen, who was aware of all the gossip of the French court. Now Mary, 'without passion and with true sincerity', was preparing to reveal facts of the most indelicate nature and divulge lurid details of alleged episodes at court that she had heard from Bess's own lips.

She wrote a letter quoting Bess as telling her that 'Elizabeth had made the Earl of Leicester a promise of marriage, and she had slept with him an infinite number of times with all the familiarity and licence as between man and wife'. Mary wrote how Bess had portrayed Elizabeth as a raging nymphomaniac, taking new lovers as she pleased, and laughing loudly at her own suggestion that it would be to her advantage if Mary allowed her son James to become Elizabeth's lover. Mary describing how Bess and the other attendants had made jokes behind Elizabeth's back, mocking her vanity and immorality.

Mary raged on and on, shooting poison arrows with each sentence, but it is unlikely that this letter – named 'the scandal letter' – ever reached Elizabeth. Someone kept it concealed until after Mary's death, but the fact that she wrote it in the first place shows her venomous character, attacking someone who had been her friend and companion, not a detached and dispassionate jailer, for sixteen years.

It was inevitable that the rest of the family were drawn into the incessant quarrels and disputes. Shrewsbury's son Gilbert Talbot, now heir to the earldom, tried to act as mediator between the battling elders without success, and as the persecution continued the careworn Bess was no longer able to live with Shrewsbury at Sheffield Castle. With Mary still dropping hints of the catastrophic revelations she could make if she so wished, Bess moved to Chatsworth, which was a Cavendish property willed by Bess's second husband to her throughout her lifetime, then to their eldest son and heir Henry Cavendish.

But no sooner had Bess moved in than Henry decided that he was going to evict her and take early possession of Chatsworth. When Bess heard this, she promptly transported all the best furniture and furnishings to Hardwick. Henry Cavendish was so angry that he changed his allegiance and sided with his stepfather (and father-in-law) against his mother in the family dispute. With Henry Cavendish as his ally, Shrewsbury's harassment of Bess became extreme, and things came to a head in July 1584 when Shrewsbury's men mounted an armed attack to forcibly take possession of Chatsworth. Feelings must have been running high when William Cavendish, trying to ward off the confrontation, took to the battlements with halberd in hand and a pistol under his girdle. He managed to hold off the attackers while Bess fled to Hardwick, where she took refuge in fear of her life. Henry Cavendish complained to the authorities, claiming that he was the rightful owner and was only trying to take what was rightfully his. The law sided with Henry Cavendish; his brother William was subsequently thrown into the Fleet Prison, and Henry took possession of Chatsworth.

Bess must have been devastated. For thirty years she had devoted all her money, time and energy into building Chatsworth House. She had overseen every stage of the building and the decoration, and now she was being forced to leave her beloved home. It was under this immense pressure that Bess surveyed the farmhouse and buildings at Hardwick that had grown piecemeal since she had lived there as a girl, with additions and repairs undertaken when money was available. It was damp and unwelcoming and not in a fit state to accommodate Bess and her household, having stood empty since her brother's death. She must have been at her lowest ebb when in April 1584 she wrote to Walsingham: 'For myself I hope to find some friend for meat and drink and so to end my life.'

But Bess was a survivor, and with her independent income she rebuilt the old house in a modest style to provide her with a roof over her head. Later she would start making plans and eventually embark upon a large remodelling scheme that would reflect her lifestyle.

13

Mary's Final Years of Captivity

At last someone in authority realised that Shrewsbury could not continue to guard the Scottish queen effectively on his own without Bess, and that autumn he received the news that Mary Queen of Scots was being moved away from the Shrewsbury household. He wrote to the queen to thank her for setting him free of two devils: his wife and Mary.

The reluctantly appointed new gaoler was the gaunt, elderly Sir Ralph Sadler, who had served four Tudor monarchs. In November 1584, Sadler officially took over from Shrewsbury as Mary's new guardian. Mary was once more back at South Wingfield Manor, but her stay there was brief as Sadler received instructions to move her to Tutbury. For the sickly Mary the prospect of once again having to inhabit that hated castle did not appeal, but she had no say in the matter. Sadler was instructed to make the journey in one day but the weather was poor and he replied that, 'the ways being so foul and depe', it would be necessary for them to break their journey at Derby, which was 17 miles from South Wingfield, and 10 miles from Tutbury.

But there was an added complication. The Quarter Sessions were being held at Derby, making the town particularly busy. With so many strangers in town this would have created a perfect opportunity for Mary's supporters to plan her escape, an opportunity that was obviously not seen or taken but which was not overlooked by Sadler. On 13 January 1585 the party set off, but not before secret orders had been given to two bailiffs, Thomas Ward and Robert Wood, to keep the proposed route through the town clear in the latter half of the day.

Towards evening the carriage drove slowly over St Mary's Bridge, which still spans the River Derwent at Derby, and rattled into town towards St Peter's Church. It pulled up outside Babington Hall and Mary alighted. Limping from her rheumatism, she was introduced to her hostess, Mrs Beaumont, ironically to spend her last night in Derbyshire at Babington Hall, the family seat of Anthony Babington, the ardent Catholic who was at the forefront of a new plot to free her from captivity.

The Shrewsburys had been given custody of Mary in 1569, two years before the ten-year-old Anthony Babington joined their Sheffield household to become a page to the twenty-six-year-old Mary. At the age of twenty he went to London to study law, then to France where he met Thomas Morgan, who was living in Paris. Morgan had been Shrewsbury's secretary and had become a fanatic, believing it was his destiny to kill Queen Elizabeth.

Anthony Babington would have been aware of the attempts to free Mary. He may have been involved in the plots, and would have been hugely disappointed when they failed. Over the years he grew infatuated by Mary, and must have seen himself as her champion, destined to liberate her from her life of imprisonment. The Babington family owned several Derbyshire properties, including a relatively modest country house at Dethick, where Anthony was born in 1561, and Babington Hall in the centre of Derby, where Mary stayed that night in 1585.[1]

Anthony Babington's first ill-conceived plan to put Mary on the throne of England was formulated while she was imprisoned at South Wingfield Manor. With the manor impregnable on all sides, the escape plan allegedly involved taking Mary through a series of tunnels over the 2.5-mile distance from South Wingfield Manor to Babington's country house at Dethick. This may be a local legend, but what gives it credence is the fact that part of the neighbouring Peacock Inn at Oakerthorpe, which sits on an old Roman road, dates back to the eleventh century and was an early monastic establishment with tunnelling dug by the White Monks in the 1400s to extract coal or lead; this digging had continued after the Dissolution of the Monasteries when many monks were forced to survive by whatever means they could. It is possible that these monks gave spiritual guidance to the Catholic queen during her enforced confinement at South Wingfield Manor, and with their allegiance to the Catholic queen the monks could have extended these tunnels all the way to Wingfield Manor. This could have been her means of escape, but as the tunnels are now impassable we can only speculate. Nevertheless, Mary's escape through the tunnels never happened because she was moved from South Wingfield to Tutbury.

The Shrewsburys had managed sixteen years with very little thanks or help, but the responsibility of guarding the Scottish queen proved to be too much for Sadler after just a year. Although Mary was to remain at Tutbury Castle, there was going to be another gaoler, Sir Amias Paulet, an odious, extremely severe man in his early fifties. He was well known for his strong anti-Catholic feelings, and it was obvious that he intended to treat Mary more like a common criminal than a crowned queen. Paulet was intent upon reducing the number of servants that surrounded the captive queen, and wrote, 'If Bastian's wyfe be discharged yt is like that Bastian will desire to go with his wyfe, wherein there were no greate losse because he is cunning in hys kynde, and full of sleightes to corrupt yonge men.'[2]

Paulet gave orders that all private letters and messages would be stopped, the Scottish queen would not be allowed to leave her room without an escort and under no circumstances was she to be allowed outside. Security was tightened, visitors were searched and questioned, and family members only allowed to visit her individually and for ten minutes a day.[3]

Amias Paulet was theoretically in charge, but he found the accommodation utterly unacceptable and so planned to stay at the nearby Tutbury Priory. This was another Cavendish property that had passed to Bess's son and heir Henry Cavendish – the one who had forced Bess from Chatsworth House claiming it was his birthright. He in fact hadn't moved into Chatsworth, because he had no money to replace the furniture and fittings that Bess had transported to Hardwick Hall. As a result, Chatsworth lay empty and Henry Cavendish lived at Tutbury Priory. He now informed

Paulet that in exchange for £100 a year he would be willing to allow him to move in. When this was considered unacceptable he asked that the queen lend him £2,000 towards the payment of his debts, but the queen was not prepared to deal.

Despite being in charge, Paulet seems to have been a remote authority figure because the Shrewsbury family were still living at Tutbury Castle. Tired of being asked to give reasons every time she passed through the gates, Mary Talbot, as lady of the house and female authority figure, wrote to Queen Elizabeth objecting in the strongest possible terms. Famous for her grim defiance of authority, Mary Talbot resembled her mother Bess in temperament. She was also an obstinate recusant Catholic and non-attender of Anglican services, so her sympathies were with Mary.

Since arriving in Derbyshire and being placed in the care of the Earl and Countess of Shrewsbury sixteen years earlier, Mary had been moved forty-six times. Now Queen Elizabeth decided it was time for a new jailor and a new jail, and moved the captive queen 12 miles from Tutbury Castle to Chartley Castle in Staffordshire.

Walter, Lord Ferrers, 1st Earl of Essex, had built a beautiful hall on the site of an earlier one. He had married the queen's cousin, Mary Boleyn's granddaughter Lettice Knollys, and when he died suddenly their eighteen-year-old son Lord Robert Devereux became 2nd Earl of Essex and inherited Chartley. Lettice Knollys, the widowed Countess of Essex, married the queen's favourite Robert Dudley on 23 September 1578, and when Elizabeth heard the news she was deeply saddened. Dudley was out of favour for months, and Elizabeth never forgave Lettice. Dudley's place as the queen's favourite was taken by his stepson Essex, but he was a flirt and had rather too many dalliances with the court ladies. The jealous queen took this personally and decided to settle this score with Essex for his blatant indiscretions by insisting that he became the guardian host of Mary Queen of Scots. Essex was appalled at the prospect of having Mary at Chartley, and ordered that all bedding and furnishings should be removed immediately so that he could plead poverty. Elizabeth was not amused, and despite everything Mary was moved there on Christmas Eve 1585. There this unwanted guest remained for nine months.

Through his many agents, Walsingham mounted a new stage in his campaign to incriminate the Scottish queen. On 4 January 1586 the double agent Charles Paget wrote to Mary that he would try to introduce a Catholic priest into the house under the name of Master Alisson. His innocent letter of introduction would be brought to her embroiderer Bastian Pagez, because if there was a problem the secretaries would not be compromised. Paget's letter was intercepted, deciphered, copied and signed on the back by Burghley, Hundsdon, Cobham, Shrewsbury and Walsingham.[4]

Walsingham was looking for verification that it was too dangerous to keep Mary alive, and set about enmeshing her in two separate conspiracies that formed the bogus machinations of a dubious assassination plot known as the Babington Plot. Despite the failure of his earlier attempts, Anthony Babington was formulating a much more ambitious and lethal plot.

On 16 January 1586 Mary received the first secret message in this plot via the local brewer, who concealed the letters in a cavity in casks of ale. Mary was told to use the same method to smuggle out her own notes, but she little realised that treachery was afoot. All her mail, her most private thoughts and schemes, were going directly to her jailor Paulet and her enemy Walsingham in London. Mary had fallen into the trap that had been laid for her and those trying to free her. Babington wrote to Mary telling her of his plans, and these plans carried the inevitable goal that Elizabeth should be deposed and Mary seated on the English throne. Philip of Spain was poised to devote his resources to restoring England to the Catholic fold, and the English conspirators were led to believe that a Spanish invasion was certain. But among the conspirators were renegades and double agents secretly in the pay of the English government. So long as she lived, the 'bosom serpent', as Walsingham called her, would continue to be the hope of all Catholics. Paulet and Walsingham waited, patient as sparrowhawks, for Mary to encourage Anthony Babington in his plans. Mary's consent would make her an accessory to treason.[5]

In June 1586, Mary wrote to Babington approving the plan. By August Mary's hopes of release began to rise, but she had no idea that her conspirators were systematically being arrested. On 11 August, when the English authorities decided to act on the plot, Mary was out riding with a group that included Pagez and her doctor Dominique Bourgoing. Seeing a group of armed soldiers heading towards them, they thought initially that it was the rescue attempt. It wasn't. Mary was taken to Tixall Hall, where she was held for two weeks while her apartments were searched and her servants were interrogated and arrested.[6]

When Mary was returned to Chartley two weeks later Pagez was offered the keys to Mary's room, but the queen told him not to accept and had an English officer open her things. She found her papers had been taken away, at which point she said two things could not be taken from her: her English blood and her Catholic religion.[7]

On 18 August, Anthony Babington made the first of his forced confessions. Mary was incriminated, and on 20 September, Babington, with thirteen fellow conspirators, was brutally hanged. The following day Mary left Chartley on a journey that would last five days until the party arrived at the grim castle at Fotheringhay in Northampton.[8].

Her French doctor Bourgoing left an eyewitness account of Mary's last journey in his journal, and according to this she rode in a coach because she was too infirm from rheumatism to ride a horse. The first night after a gruelling 7-mile journey they arrived at Hall Hill near Abbots Bromley, an ancient parish 6 miles south of Uttoxeter. It originally belonged to Burton Abbey, but after the Dissolution of the Monasteries it was granted to Sir William Paget. It is here that one of Mary's supporters is accredited with writing a Latin verse on a pane of glass which is now in the William Salt Museum in Stafford. The inscription, '*Maria Regina Scotiae quondam transibat istam villam 21 Septembris 1585 [sic] usque Burton*', roughly translates as 'Mary Queen of Scots once stayed at this house 21 September 1586 on the way to Burton' (date corrected).[9]

The following day she was moved 11 miles to Burton on Trent where two inns both claim to have played host to the royal guest, the Three Queen's Hotel and a former hostelry called the Crown Inn. On Thursday 22 September, they travelled a further 7 miles to the castle at Ashby-de-la-Zouch and from there to Leicester, where they entered the town through the medieval North Gate. It has previously been claimed that Mary Queen of Scots lodged at

Huntingdon Tower on the High Street (the tower was demolished in 1900). However, a note in Dominique Bourgoing's account of the journey contradicts this. He wrote that Mary stayed at a hostelry called the Angel Inn, situated just inside the town wall, close to the East Gate. The town records state that three men were paid 2s for watching 'Sir Amias Pollett's' carriages for two nights. This would indicate that Mary stayed in Leicester for two nights before setting off again on 25 September for Fotheringhay.

Leaving the city of Leicester, they travelled along the rather lugubriously named Gallowtree Gate, now a major shopping street. Crossing the county border of Leicestershire and into Rutland, they soon encountered Withcote Hall near Oakham. Next was Collyweston, a royal palace owned by Elizabeth and once the home of Mary's grandmother Margaret Tudor, sister of Henry VIII, prior to her marriage to King James IV of Scotland. Ironically, their marriage was intended to unite England and Scotland. Another 7 miles south beyond Collyweston Palace lay their final destination, Fotheringhay Castle. As they approached Fotheringhay, the name of the road was Perio Lane. On hearing this, Mary is said to have expressed deep anguish. In Latin, *pereo* means 'perish'.[10]

The royal procession would have seen Fotheringhay Castle from some distance across the flatlands of Rutland and Northamptonshire. A typical Norman motte-and-bailey castle, it was probably built around AD 1100 by Simon de Senlis, Norman Earl of Northampton and Huntingdon. On his death, his widow Maud married David, King of Scotland, and the castle became a Scottish possession. It returned to English hands in the reign of King John, eventually falling to Edmund Langley, 1st Duke of York, after which it remained in the hands of the Yorks. Richard III was born at Fotheringhay Castle in 1452, but when he lost his head and his crown in 1485 at the Battle of Bosworth, Fotheringhay went into decline.

Henry VIII gave Fotheringhay Castle to his first queen, Katherine of Aragon, who spent large sums of money on it. After their divorce, Katherine moved a few miles away to Buckden Towers before being sent to Kimbolton Castle to live out her days, and Fotheringhay Castle then passed to each of Henry's wives in succession.

Mary Queen of Scots arrived at Fotheringhay Castle on 25 September 1586, and on 1 October she had a visit from

Amias Paulet, who informed her that she would be interrogated by certain lords and suggested she should confess her guilt. She replied that she was unaware of any fault for which she should give account to anyone but her maker.

On 8 October commissioners were appointed in London to sit in judgement of Mary, who was brought to trial under the Act of Association, which had been passed by Parliament the year before, undoubtedly hurried through with the fate of Mary Queen of Scots in mind. It stated that twenty-four peers or Privy Councillors should try any plot or attempt on the life of Elizabeth by any person who purported to claim her crown for their own person.[11]

The trial began on 14 October 1586 in a room above the Great Chamber at Fotheringhay Castle. It lasted two days, presided over by the Lord Chancellor, Lord Burghley. As Earl Marshal, Shrewsbury, who had been Mary's jailor for almost eighteen years, had to be in attendance. Mary Stuart was found guilty of treason on 25 October 1586, but Queen Elizabeth was reluctant to sign her death warrant.

When James heard about his mother's arrest at Chartley and her move to Fotheringhay, he made the heartless comment that she should have contented herself with drinking ale and meddled in nothing but prayer. He showed no concern that she was on trial for her life. A trial for high treason was a foregone conclusion as far as the result was concerned, but her plight did not stir any filial sympathy in him.

Around this time, Mary disowned James and willed her English succession to Philip of Spain. In a fit of pique, James threatened that if he was excluded from the succession he would make war on England. It was probably an empty threat, but Cecil considered it too risky to leave the matter open. Good relations could be maintained between the two kingdoms so long as James thought he would succeed Elizabeth on the English throne.

James was always short of money to spend on personal projects or to grant gifts to friends and favourites, and records show that although payments were irregular and unpredictable, he was being paid quite considerable sums by the English government. The English called the payments a gratuity or pension, and the Scots called them an annuity, claiming that James VI was entitled to an income from his grandmother's Lennox estates in England. This seems grossly unfair when that income should rightfully have been given to Arbella.

In 1586, when a secret treaty was signed between Scotland and England, James received £4,000 as his first subsidy. However, the money always came with the expectation that James would act in a way beneficial to Cecil and the English throne. For instance, James was assured of a substantial sum of money when he married and when he had a son. His sexual preference was for men, but the general populace would not be aware of his sexual orientation if he was married with sons, and if he married and sired sons this would theoretically ensure a male succession and long-term dynastic stability. James was a puppet dancing to Cecil's tune; the Privy Council wanted a king. They blamed all the political and social ills of the decade on the fact that England was ruled by a woman with the weakness of character this supposedly entailed. A male monarch offered a welcome return to what they considered to be normality.

Between midnight and one o'clock on the night of Sunday 29 January 1587, Mary's rooms at Fotheringhay Castle were illuminated three times by a great flame of fiery light, bright enough to read by. It was probably a comet, but the superstitious public considered this phenomenon to be some sort of evil omen that, according to reports, was seen nowhere else in the castle.[12]

If it was a bad omen then it was certainly borne out by events, as two days later, on 1 February 1587, at her court at Greenwich, Queen Elizabeth eventually signed the warrant for Mary's execution. She gave instructions that it was to be held in private in the great hall of Fotheringhay Castle, then dismissed the subject, stating that she wished to hear no more until the execution was successfully completed.[13]

Shrewsbury's connection with Mary was not yet over. He was reluctant to take part in the trial, but it was made clear that his absence would not be tolerated. He was also given the responsibility of taking Mary's death warrant to Fotheringhay, and on the evening of 7 February 1587 he told her that she had been found guilty and condemned to death. Mary was told that her execution would take place the following morning at eight o'clock, and she replied, 'I thank you for such welcome news. You will do me a great good in withdrawing me from this world out of which I am very glad to go.'[14]

She was refused the services of her chaplain but offered those of the Protestant Dean of Peterborough. She refused, then drafted a will and a letter to her chaplain in lieu of a confession. Mary's last letter was to her brother-in-law King Henri of France, relating how abruptly her sentence had been broken to her. She went through all her possessions, dividing them up between her servants, friends and foreign relatives, and then lay down on her bed fully clothed. It was two in the morning. She rose four hours later and prayed. She was then dressed in a black satin dress embroidered with black velvet and set with black acorn buttons of jet trimmed with pearl. On her head she wore a lace-edged white veil that flowed down her back to the ground. Her stockings were edged with silver and she wore black Spanish leather shoes.

A stage had been erected with the block and the axe in the centre of the great hall at Fotheringhay, and there waited the lords, the ranks of soldiers and about 300 spectators. As Mary was escorted into the hall she was perfectly calm; her bearing was regal and she showed no sign of fear or distress. A contemporary observer even described her as cheerful and smiling.[15]

Assisted by her ladies Jane Kennedy and Elizabeth Curle, Mary undressed. Stripped of her black, she stood in her red petticoat above which was a red satin bodice trimmed with lace. One of her women passed her a pair of red sleeves, so the Scottish queen went to her death dressed all in red, the liturgical colour of martyrdom. Mary retained her composure and dignity throughout, even when the executioners requested the queen's belongings, which custom allowed them to take. She refused to hand over her gold rosary and offered money in its place.

It was exactly eighteen years previously that Mary had arrived in Derbyshire in February 1569 to be placed in the care of the Earl and Countess of Shrewsbury. In the final act of this macabre drama, the earl sat on a stool upon the scaffold with his son and heir Gilbert Talbot. It was Shrewsbury's unpleasant duty to signal Mary's end to the executioner, who stood ready with the axe. As he raised his white baton of office, Shrewsbury turned his head away, too upset to speak to the crowd, his face wet with tears.

The first blow missed Mary's neck and cut into the back of the head, necessitating a second blow to sever the neck. The executioner then took hold of Mary's hair to hold her head aloft, but as he held the auburn tresses they came apart from the skull and the head dropped to the floor. Mary had been wearing a wig.

One of the spectators, Robert Wynckfield, wrote a report endorsed in the handwriting of Cecil: 'Then her head appeared as grey as one of three score and ten years old polled very short, her face in a moment being so much altered from the forme she had when was alive, as few could remember her by her dead face. Her lippes stirred up and down a quarter of an hour after her head was cut off.'[16]

It was then that Mary's little Skye terrier, who had managed to accompany her into the hall, crept out from under her skirts and would not be coaxed away from his decapitated mistress. The weeping women were pushed aside and locked in their rooms and the castle gates were shut so that no one could break the news to the outside world. Severe restrictions were put in place to prevent even a drop of Mary's blood being taken as a martyr's relic. To prevent anything of hers being venerated, the crucifix and book she had carried, her bloodstained clothes and even the block on which she laid her head were burnt in Fotheringhay Castle's courtyard.

Mary's body was embalmed, wrapped in a wax winding sheet and placed in a heavy lead coffin. Her request to be buried in France was ignored.[17] Walsingham specified that the coffin should be 'bestowed by night on an upper shelf of the local Fotheringhay church'; it wasn't. Her body was kept at Fotheringhay Castle until it had decomposed enough to make it unfeasible for her supporters to remove it. At midnight on Sunday 30 July 1587, Mary's body finally left the castle by torchlight. It was carried in silent procession to Peterborough Cathedral, where she was buried. The simple service was short, and no Scots attended.

It was predicted that the execution of Mary would have far-reaching repercussions, that Scots would take up arms or seek some form of reprisal. However, James of Scotland made no move to avenge his mother's death. He was prepared to swallow the insult to his family and his nation as long as the English crown dangled within his reach – that is all he was interested in. He was being paid to prevent any form of retaliation, so he did nothing.

He didn't even mention her wish to be buried in Rheims with her mother. However, in 1612 he would order her body to be exhumed and reinterred in the Henry II chapel in Westminster Abbey, only 30 feet from the grave of her cousin Queen Elizabeth. For almost twenty years, Mary, whose monument is slightly larger than Queen Elizabeth's, had longed to be this close to her cousin, and now in death it was too late. On Mary's tombstone it reads, 'Mistress of Scotland by law, of France by marriage, of England by expectation.'

While at Fotheringhay, Mary wrote a poem:

> Alas what am I? What use has my life?
> I am but a body whose heart's torn away
> A vain shadow, an object of misery
> Who has nothing left but death-in-life
> O my enemies, set your envy all aside
> I've no more eagerness for high domain
> I've borne too long the burden of my pain
> To see your anger swiftly satisfied
> And you my friends who have loved me so true
> Remember lacking health and heart and peace
> There is nothing worthwhile that I can do
> Ask only that my misery cease
> And that being punished in a world like this
> I have my portion of eternal bliss

14

Suitors and Building Sites

Queen Elizabeth I, unmarried and without a direct heir, had removed her legal successor to the throne; however, still she refused to name another. Elizabeth feared all potential candidates. She viewed them as rivals, and that made her feel insecure. The Scottish queen had been the foremost Catholic claimant, but had disowned her son and heir presumptive and willed her English succession to Philip of Spain, the husband of her late aunt Queen Mary I. In the years following his wife's death Philip of Spain had proposed marriage to his sister-in-law Elizabeth, but the old friendship with Spain had soured over religious differences and the work of English privateers, seizing Spanish gold brought back from their colonies in the New World.[1]

Suitors for Elizabeth had come and gone for three decades. In her mid-forties, Elizabeth's name had been linked with the twenty-four-year-old Duke of Anjou, younger son of Catherine de Medici and Henri II of France. If Elizabeth had taken Anjou as her husband then France might have ceased to press for Mary Queen of Scots' claim, and Philip of Spain might think twice before moving against an Anglo-French alliance. However, the Anjou match came to nothing like the others before it. The possibility that a foreigner could step in and claim the throne of England must have really alarmed Elizabeth.

Elizabeth was approaching sixty, no longer the youthful virgin queen in looks or vigour. The pretence that she would ever marry was at an end. But Elizabeth had a plan. James's ambassador was insisting upon a formal written document proclaiming him to be the rightful heir to her throne, but in response Elizabeth promptly and openly acknowledged that there was another in the running. She then invited Arbella Stuart down to the royal court at London. Elizabeth intended to offer Bess's granddaughter in marriage, in the same way that she had once offered herself.

Arbella was now in her twelfth year, and was about to face the most daunting and exciting challenge of her young life. Every suitor was anxious to see her, the only princess of royal blood, who had been hidden away in remote Derbyshire for years. Queen Elizabeth had spent almost thirty years as queen, and at their first meeting everyone was aware that this unsophisticated and unknown child could be their next sovereign. For Elizabeth it was a stark reminder of her own mortality.

The English court was like nothing Arbella would have ever encountered. It was a brilliant, noisy extravaganza, a spectacle of music, pageantry, dancing and feasting. It wasn't long before court life whirled around her young head, intoxicating her with its life. There were vast numbers of servants, courtiers and ladies-in-waiting, but as the only princess of the blood in England she took precedence over all the other ladies and was treated with all the deference due to her rank. She may have gotten a bit above herself, but that was to be expected. She enjoyed speaking to foreign dignitaries in their own tongues and pitting her wits against learned scholars. She was keen to put her knowledge to good use, and the fact that she made such an impact at court with her lively mind and eloquence was thanks to the education her grandmother Bess had insisted upon.

One of the main topics on everyone's lips was the offensive against England being planned by Philip of Spain as a direct result of the execution of Mary Queen of Scots, but Queen Elizabeth was not anxious to subject her people to the financial and human suffering a war would entail. She considered war to be a wasteful extravagance to be avoided if at all possible, so she was looking for a way out of a costly war – and that's where Arbella came into the scheme. The queen suggested a betrothal between Arbella and Ranuccio Farnese, eldest son of Alexander Farnese, Duke of Parma, and Maria of Portugal. The Duke of Parma was the

Spanish Governor General of the Netherlands and general of the Spanish army, which was at the time fighting against England and its allies. The proposed marriage was a cunningly devious plot to avoid a threatened military offensive, and Arbella's visit to court was to let Spain know that the queen was serious. Knowing that it would get back to Philip, she said to de Chateauneuf, the French ambassador, 'Look at her well. She will one day be even as I am.'² Queen Elizabeth was offering Arbella and the throne of England in exchange for peace with Spain.

For Arbella, 1587 must have seemed a time of absolute personal triumph. She was young and naïve, and didn't perceive the falsity that existed in the court and its social intrigues. As winter approached and no decision on Arbella's proposed marriage had been reached, things were looking rather uncertain. Spain's mighty armada of 130 ships was already on the seas, and England moved onto a war footing, building ships, requisitioning stores and erecting warning beacons on hilltops across the land.

By the early summer of 1588, with her head filled with stymied dynastic ambitions, Arbella fell for the charms of Lord Robert Devereux, 2nd Earl of Essex. He was twenty-two, tall, attractive and exciting. His skills as a showman and flatterer no doubt made her laugh and blush, and she was smitten. Born into an ancient but impoverished family, Essex set much store by his noble birth. It was widely accepted that he was the great-grandson of not one but two of Henry VIII's mistresses: Anne Stafford, Countess of Huntingdon, and Mary Boleyn, sister of Queen Anne Boleyn, the mother of Queen Elizabeth I.

The son of Walter Devereux, 1st Earl of Essex, and Lettice Knollys, Robert was brought up on his father's estate at Chartley Castle, Staffordshire, where Mary Queen of Scots was imprisoned after leaving Tutbury. He was nine years old when his father died and he inherited the earldom of Essex. He became a ward of William Cecil, and moved into his household to be brought up alongside his son Robert, but the two boys were never friends. In 1578 his mother married Robert Dudley, Earl of Leicester, Elizabeth's long-standing favourite, and when Essex joined Elizabeth's Privy Council, one of his fellow councillors was his childhood acquaintance Robert Cecil. The two boys had turned into men vying for the queen's favour, and before long Essex had replaced his stepfather in the affections of the ageing queen.

By the end of June it was clear that the offer of Arbella's marriage to Ranuccio Farnese was of no consequence and would not stop the Spanish fleet that was preparing to attack Britain. Elizabeth was frantically trying to conduct peace negotiations as late as two days before the armada's first sighting off the Lizard peninsula in Cornwall. Arbella's presence in court no longer had any significance, and on 13 July she left London to return to Derbyshire and her former quiet, uneventful lifestyle. Some said it was because her value was gone, while others said it was down to the fact that she could be taken hostage. Still others said it was because of her childishly assumed airs or because she was mooning over Essex. Realistically, it was most likely because she had served her purpose and the queen and council simply had no further use for her as negotiations had failed. Arbella had been at the heart of the court, surrounded by activity and intrigue, but back in Derbyshire she felt abandoned, alone and ill-informed.[3]

By 1587, Elizabeth's former lover Leicester had grown old. He was florid and sickly, and just a few weeks after the defeat of the armada he wrote to Elizabeth from his home at Kenilworth in Warwickshire. Six days later he was dead. Elizabeth sorrowfully wrote 'His last letter' on it, and put it in a cabinet by her bed where she kept her most precious and personal possessions.[4]

The death of Leicester signalled the passing of the old order. The court was in flux. The old guard – men like Leicester, Walsingham and Cecil – were either dying or retiring, and a new generation of men at court were making the decisions. Cecil was increasingly handing over power to his son Robert, and Leicester's replacement was his stepson, the tall, handsome Robert Devereux, 2nd Earl of Essex.

There was still a lot of interest in Arbella and the question of who would succeed the ageing Elizabeth, but she remained obdurately silent on the topic of her succession. On 23 November 1589, James of Scotland married Anne of Denmark and started a family. Marriage and children meant that James was fulfilling the necessary requirements secretly imposed upon him by the English court, and not only did he receive a substantial sum of money but he felt assured of the English throne.

The Shrewsbury quarrels were still causing a public scandal. Queen Elizabeth ordered them both down to London in March 1587 to try to sort out their marital discontent. Powerful means of persuasion by the queen were used to force Shrewsbury to take Bess from London to South Wingfield Manor, where they were ordered to 'keep house together'. The queen considered South Wingfield to be neutral ground; it belonged to Shrewsbury, but a clause in their marriage contract gave Bess a life interest. He was ordered to pay Bess the £2,000 in rents he had collected on her properties that year and drop all legal suits for the return of plate and furnishing. She was to be allowed to occupy and enjoy all her properties, and in return she was to pay him £500 per annum for their use. Bewildered, hurt and angry, Shrewsbury wrote to the queen protesting and begged her to 'give some remembrance of your good liking for my long service'.[5]

Leicester had replied on behalf of the queen:

My Lord, you must not think that Her Majesty doth this for special favour more to my Lady than to you, but she doth think my Lady hath received some hard dealing and doth not find sufficient material to charge her ... the deeds and grants as your Lordship has conveyed to my Lady ... [were intended] that my Lady should enjoy all these gifts.[6]

Shrewsbury was not pleased. He protested that he had become his wife's pensioner and due to the queen's ruling would be £2,000 per year worse off.

Under the agreement, at the end of April 1587 the couple returned to Derbyshire. Bess went to South Wingfield Manor but Shrewsbury went to Handsworth Manor, Sheffield, where he consoled himself with his mistress Eleanor Britton. The queen no doubt understood the situation better than she admitted, and as a sweetener she awarded Bess some Crown lands in the Peak Forest near Buxton as a reward for her travails. On the subject the Bishop of Coventry cited the teachings of St Paul, stating, 'If shrewdness and sharpness be a just cause of separation between husband and wife, I think few men in England would keep their wives long ... it is common jest that there is but one shrew in all the world, and every man hath her.'' Bess spent a considerable amount of time at court, serving in the Privy Chamber and the Bedchamber, which gave her intimate access to the queen. Because Shrewsbury was denied this he sent vindictive letters to her, yet she always replied politely and patiently.

Bess and the Earl were permanently estranged by 1589. Bess was busy with her business interests, and as money became available she was enlarging the old Hardwick Manor house. Then, in November 1590, George Talbot, 6th Earl of Shrewsbury, died. His son and heir Gilbert became the 7th Earl of Shrewsbury, bringing new and different conflicts within the family.

Bess still enjoyed the queen's confidence and friendship, and there is no evidence that she ever tried to exploit this situation. Because they were both very strong women, even if they disagreed Bess had the sense to keep her own council and her bearing. She gave the queen costly and sumptuous gifts, but she could afford to – she was now the richest woman in England beside the queen. Shrewsbury's death meant that once again she was mistress of all her old lands and incomes from the Barlow, Cavendish and St Loe estates, and could claim one-third of the income from the Shrewsbury estates, said to be £3,000 per annum in the 1590s.[8] She was also entitled under her prenuptial agreement to a life interest in many of the Shrewsbury properties. Included in this list were Shrewsbury House in Chelsea and several properties in Derbyshire and Yorkshire, including Bolsover Castle and its surrounding coal mines, and Wingfield Manor and its lead mines.[9]

With all the necessary raw materials on land she owned, Bess was provided with everything she needed to build a magnificent new hall within a few hundred yards of the old Hardwick Manor house. Materials were gathered: sandstone from the quarry at the base of the hill on which Hardwick Hall stands, alabaster from Tutbury, limestone from Skegby and Crich, timber from woods at Teversal, Pentrich and Heath, and black marble for fire surrounds and the chapel columns from Ashford-in-the-Water. Although everything came from within 20 miles of Hardwick, it had to be hauled in carts pulled by oxen or carried on packhorses, which was a major project. Skilled and sought-after craftsmen were hired and an overseer of the building appointed.[10]

The date on which building commenced can be pinpointed almost exactly. The fortnight's accounts, beginning on 26 October, show ten labourers for the first week, increasing to twenty-three by 21 November. This sudden increase in labour was required for digging through to the bedrock of a bleak and windswept Derbyshire hilltop and laying the foundations. The new Hardwick Hall was a house of substance, with a simple but ingenious plan based on a Greek cross, a rectangle surrounded by six turrets. To give shape to her vision Bess employed the services of Robert Smythson, who had worked on some of the most exuberant, inventive and romantic houses of sixteenth-century England. She employed two competent overseers, as well as stone getters and stone breakers, masons, builders, carpenters and joiners, and by the end of December the fleaks, or hurdles, which formed rudimentary scaffolding for the ground floor were in place. The names of 375 workmen appear in the building accounts book. Bess was in her element, and took a lively interest in every aspect of the construction. It was smaller than her previous projects at forty-six rooms excluding service rooms compared to ninety-seven rooms at Chatsworth and fifty-five in the Old Hall.[11]

Two features of Smythson's plan, unusual for its time, are the use of symmetry and glass. Both are displayed to maximum effect at Hardwick, which glories in great expanses of status-enhancing glass. The state rooms on the second floor are large and light due to the sheer amount. As Francis Bacon wrote, 'You shall sometimes have faire houses so full of glasse, that one cannot tell where to become to be out of the sunne or cold.' When Cecil was asked about Hardwick, he is reported as saying, 'Hardwick Hall? More glass than wall.'

Bess's business interests continued to occupy most of her time. She hardly ever sold land, but if it could not be used profitably she wouldn't hesitate to lease it out, take the rent and let someone else worry about it. Likewise, she would lease out unproductive mines. This was a time when the very rich were beginning to build great country houses in the English Renaissance style, and Bess didn't underestimate the value of the building materials found on her estates – stone, slate, clay, iron and lead. With foundries to extract these raw materials and kilns to bake the bricks, Bess used the skills of French glassmakers brought to Sussex in the 1560s to set up her own small-scale glasshouse at South Wingfield where Sylvester Smith had the responsibility of turning wood ash and sand into vastly improved, clearer window glass. Medieval glass had previously been limited to the small-scale production of forest glass with its characteristic variety of greenish-yellow colours.

With her eye for business, Bess set up better sales outlets and transport systems to London. She was a woman ahead of her time, an entrepreneur revelling in the challenge and rewards of her enterprise. Not just content to oversee the building of Hardwick, she also built a house at Owlcotes (often referred to as Oldcotes) barely 3 miles away from Hardwick for the use of her son William and his family. Work began on Owlcotes on March 1593.[12]

In the late summer of 1591 Arbella was again called down to London in another visit dictated by politics. War in the Netherlands continued to sap England's resources, and because Elizabeth was reluctant to send more money and troops to the French king it was decided to use Arbella again as a means to secure peace. Despite Elizabeth's best efforts nothing came of these plans either, and Arbella was sent back to Derbyshire. Others were interested in Arbella, however, and a plot to kidnap her was uncovered. When Bess heard of this, she wrote to Cecil:

> My good lord ... I was at first much troubled to think that so wicked and mischievous practises should be devised to entrap my poor Arbella ... but will use such diligent care to prevent whatever shall be attempted by any wicked persons against the child. I will not have any unknown or suspected person come to my house. Arbella walks not late; at such time as she takes the air it shall be near the house and well attended on. She goeth not to anybody's house at all. I see her almost every hour in the day... and she lieth in my bedchamber.[13]

Arbella wasn't just being kept in a protected environment, she seemed to be positively stifled by her overprotective grandmother. News was received that the Duke of Parma had died, which meant that his son was no longer considered of any political worth, so the Farnese marriage negotiations were definitively terminated. How Arbella reacted to this news is unrecorded, but she must have been ecstatic when on 10 November 1595 the Earl of Essex and his men spent two nights at Hardwick. The visit coincided with Arbella's twentieth birthday celebrations, and although she had been away from court for three years she was still smitten with the queen's favourite. Inviting Essex to Hardwick may have been Bess's idea to remind the queen that Arbella was now available and ripe for marriage. If that was so, the plan worked and Arbella was summoned to court.[14]

Henri VI of France was actively seeking an annulment of his marriage to his barren wife Marguerite de Valois and discussing the possibility of marriage to Arbella. Rumours of the match circulated around Europe as Elizabeth and her ministers tried to promote a new treaty with France against Spain. In Vatican correspondence it was written that 'Queen Elizabeth has promised him a near cousin of her own, whom she loves much and intends to make her heir and successor'.[15] But Henri was wise to Elizabeth's tactics, and said he would have no objection and would not refuse Arbella if, 'since it is said the crown of England really belongs to her, she were only declared presumptive heiress of it'.

In the spring of 1596, in joint command with Sir Walter Raleigh, Essex sailed to Spain on a mission to destroy the new armada being built in Cadiz. Having succeeded, he returned a hero. The Hardwick account books show that there was a considerable amount of entertaining, but no further reference to any visit by Essex at this time. Perhaps this was because Bess had assured the queen that she would do nothing to promote her granddaughter's marriage prospects. Her allegiance to the queen was too strong to consider a marriage other than one that the queen might suggest, and Elizabeth wasn't prepared to suggest a union between her favourite and Arbella.

In 1596 Arbella came of age and her grandmother Bess presented her with land and property, which gave her the opportunity to be independent and run her own household. The fact that she was not yet betrothed was a source for constant rumours, but the responsibility for her marriage rested with the queen and her advisers. After Henri of France they seemed in no great hurry to suggest another match, and Arbella remained in Derbyshire with her grandmother, who was leading a quiet, busy life overseeing her business affairs. On 4 October 1597, Bess, her extended family and seventy-four servants moved into the new, still unfinished Hardwick Hall. It's been suggested that the date was to coincide with Bess's seventieth birthday because there was plenty of celebrating that day. Together the two halls created by Bess of Hardwick were like a small village, with a bakehouse, brewhouse, dairy, chandlery, smithy and stillhouse.[16]

Life at Hardwick settled into routine, and year after year Arbella continued to live the lonely life the queen and Bess had assigned to her. Years later she was to refer to this time as 'that unpleasant life in the home of her grandmother with whose severity and age she, being a young lady, could hardly agree'.[17]

As she aged, Arbella's chances of attracting a suitable husband – and thus her use to the queen – diminished. Left to her own devices, it's very probable that Arbella would have married Essex (who subsequently married), but he had fallen out of royal favour. He had been given command of an Irish expedition force of 15,000 men but everything went wrong. Hundreds of his men died in battle or of disease until he had less than 400. Faced with deserters and disaster, he took it upon himself to negotiate a peace treaty which was disadvantageous to England and he was ordered back to explain himself. Elizabeth had forgiven him on many previous occasions and he expected her to forgive him again, but she didn't. He was found guilty of disobedience and dereliction of duty, stripped of all his titles and placed under house arrest. When he attempted to stage a coup, he was arrested, found guilty of treason and, on 25 February 1601, executed. Arbella was heartbroken and inconsolable. It's now hard to judge just how deep their relationship was because no correspondence between them survives, but it may not be an exaggeration to say Essex was the love of Arbella's life.

That year Bess wrote a full inventory of her properties, wrote her will and built almshouses in Derby for the perpetual relief of eight poor men and four poor women who were 'to be of good and honest conversation and not infected with any contagious disease'. The inmates of the workhouse were to parade in the Church of All Hallows (now Derby Cathedral) twice a day, and when the time came for Bess to be buried there, they were to pray before the tomb of their foundress. She installed a warder named Richard Hayward and his wife Dorothy, and among other duties, when the time came they were to sweep and clean Bess's monument. It is perhaps unsurprising that, having decided this, she also organised her final resting place at this time.[18] She had an elaborate tomb built to a design by Robert Smythson and on 27 April it was finished, requiring nothing more but to be set up at All Hallows. Her accounts show the costs, including the payment to the vicar, labourers to prepare the site, the chief stone getter and his men, and for teams of horses to drag forty loads of stone from the quarries to Derby. She was still in good health and sound mind, but she was preparing for the inevitable.

She no longer travelled to London, and had not seen the queen for eight years, but sent her frequent letters and extravagant gifts. Bess realised that the queen gave little thought to Arbella, so she made a point of mentioning her in most of her letters. Arbella had become a big worry for Bess. She spent her days moping around Hardwick, and her restless mood irritated her grandmother. Bess was still very active, and thoroughly involved with her business empire, so she couldn't understand why her granddaughter couldn't find something equally satisfying to occupy her time. She regularly berated Arbella and their affectionate relationship deteriorated to the extent that Bess was apt to admonish her with a sharp slap and angry words. Arbella wanted a life, a husband and family, and despite being in a position to secure a brilliant match for her granddaughter Bess's hands were tied. The queen had made it crystal clear that Arbella's marriage was state business. Arbella was in the depths of depression, and family chaplain Starkey wrote that 'her distress seemed no feigned, for oftentimes, being at her books she would break forth into tears'.[19]

As Arbella reached the age of twenty-seven, she had been cooped up at Hardwick for more than thirteen years. She had no reason to be grateful to the queen for her solitary and introspected life, but now she felt betrayed by those she thought she could trust. She had become a prisoner, and life was passing her by. As neither the queen nor her grandmother would find her a husband she decided to find her own, and soon she had begun negotiations for her marriage to Edward Seymour, grandson of the Earl of Hertford. They were both claimants to the throne, and a marriage between them would unite the two lines of descendants of Henry VIII's sisters Mary and Margaret and create a joint candidacy capable of attracting widespread support. They would produce heirs with a very strong claim to Elizabeth's throne, but because it was a proposal that was not likely to have the agreement of the queen, the matter had to be conducted in total secrecy.

But secrets have a way of leaking out. Robert Cecil (who had replaced his father William by his death in 1598) was alerted, and on 3 January 1603 Sir Henry Bronker (sometimes written Brounker), the queen's commissioner, was sent to Hardwick to learn the facts. Bronker's arrival was met with a mixture of surprise and apprehension. Arbella's stammered response to Bronker's questions prompted Bronker to write that Arbella 'hath vapours on her brain', but when Bronker was satisfied that there was no grand plot, no Catholic involvement and no harm intended to the queen, he wrote his report and Arbella signed it. The reserved Arbella had asserted herself for the first time in her life. She had hoped to gain the support and sympathy of her grandmother, but when she asked for Bess's blessing she was met with a volley of bitter and injurious words.

In Bess's eyes this was a crisis; an unpermitted royal marriage could be viewed as treason. Bess wrote to the queen, exonerating herself from all knowledge of Arbella's folly. She claimed Arbella was deceitful and asked the queen to take the duplicitous Arbella off her hands: 'I am desirous and most humbly beseech your majesty that she may be placed elsewhere, to learn to be more considerate, and that after it may please your majesty either to accept of her service about your royal person, or to bestow her in marriage, which in all humility and duty, I do crave your majesty, for I can't now assure myself of her, as I have done.'[20] Bess was not to know when she wrote this letter that she would never again hear from the queen. In March 1603 Elizabeth had retired to Richmond Palace. She was old and tired; she was dying.

Arbella wrote countless letters appealing to Bronker, Cecil and Stanhope for her freedom, but her pleas fell on deaf ears. Bess was also keeping Bronker informed of everything that was happening at Hardwick, and he was passing the information to Cecil, but the timing was wrong. Elizabeth's end was fast approaching, and it's doubtful that they bothered to inform the dying queen of events. She had shown no concern for Arbella Stuart and her problems in the past, and was hardly likely to care when she was dying.

15

The End of the Tudor Era

Elizabeth had become queen in 1558. Now, at almost seventy years of age, there were finally reports of her human frailty. She had to have a stick to walk up the stairs, and during the opening of Parliament she almost fell under the weight of her heavy robes. She had continued her annual routine of a short summer progress and Christmas revels, but by the late winter of 1602/3 Elizabeth was feeling unwell. In early February she had caught a chill, complaining of a sore throat as well as aches and pains, and by the end of the month she had developed pneumonia.

It was generally believed that the dying queen had been asked if she wanted the King of France to succeed her, to which she gave no answer. She was asked if she wanted the King of Scotland to succeed her; again, she gave no answer. She was asked if she wanted Lord Beauchamp, the son of the Earl of Hertford, to succeed her, and she replied, 'I will have no rascal's son in my seat.' Arbella was not mentioned.

Cecil, as head of the Privy Council, had already prepared the proclamation announcing the transfer of the crown to James of Scotland, and had sent it north for his approval.

On 20 March 1603, Bess added a codicil to her will, drawn up in April 1601:

Forasmuch as I have changed my mind touching my bequest and legacies to my grand-daughter Arbella Stuart, and my son Henry Cavendish; I have fulled determined and resolved that neither my said grand-daughter nor the said Henry Cavendish, or either of them, shall have any benefit by any such gift or legacy. I therefore declare by this codicil, that every gift or legacy by me appointed to them, be utterly frustrated, void and of non effect.

Two days later Arbella was removed from Hardwick, never to live there again. She was sent to Wrest Park in Bedfordshire.[1]

The dying Queen Elizabeth would stand for hours on end before resting in a low chair by a fire, refusing to let doctors examine her. As the days passed, her condition slowly worsened until finally she was persuaded to lie on cushions on the floor in her private apartments. She rested there for two days, not speaking. A doctor ventured to ask how she could bear the endless silence, to which she replied simply, 'I meditate.' For the third and fourth days, she continued to rest in silence, with a finger often in her mouth. She could not be persuaded to leave the cushions for the comfort of her bed.

Cecil visited and beseeched her, 'Your Majesty, to content the people, you must go to bed.' Elizabeth replied, with some of her old spirit, 'Little man, little man, the word "must" is not used to a queen.' Although nothing was said, she knew that those around her were preparing for the time when her reign would be over. Being a monarch had been a difficult, demanding and often very lonely task, and Elizabeth was tired both physically and emotionally. She herself had said, 'To be a king and wear a crown is a thing more glorious to them that see it than it is pleasant to them that bear it.'

Finally, Elizabeth grew so weak that they could carry her to bed. She asked for music, and for a time it brought some comfort. As her condition deteriorated, Archbishop Whitgift, her favourite of all her Archbishops of Canterbury, whom she once called her 'little black husband', arrived to pray at her side. He was old and his knees ached terribly, but he knelt at the royal bedside until she finally slept. Those in vigilance around the queen's bed left her to the care of her ladies, and, at last, as the courtiers watched and waited, her steady breathing stopped.

Queen Elizabeth died in the early hours of Thursday 24 March 1603. She had reigned over England for forty-four years, four months and seven days, and must have seemed immortal to many. It was the eve of the Annunciation of the Virgin Mary, perhaps an apt day for the 'Virgin Queen' to die. The Elizabethan calendar was different to ours as they still used the Julian calendar, with the New Year beginning on 25 March.[2] Thus it was that the last day of 1602 also saw the final hours of the last Tudor monarch. The New Year would bring a new reign, and there was going to be a new ruling dynasty, the Stuarts, and consequently a new era in British history. With Elizabeth's death, the world as they knew it was about to change – and who knew what the future held?

At dawn, the chief councillors left Richmond and rode to Whitehall where Cecil drafted the announcement of the queen's death and the proclamation announcing the transfer of the crown to James VI of Scotland, who was proclaimed King James I of England. The grandees of the land, heralds, Privy Councillors, lords and courtiers spread the news throughout the country. At ten o'clock, on the green opposite the tiltyard at Whitehall, Cecil read the proclamation aloud, proclaiming King James VI of Scotland to be the new King James I of England. The proclamation was read again at St Paul's and Cheapside Cross, and then the councillors formally demanded entrance to the Tower of London in the name of King James I of England.

The new king received the news of his accession three days later on 27 March, for the ambitious Robert Carey had ridden at top speed to Edinburgh; his journey was so quick that its speed would not be matched until 1832. That same day, James wrote to Cecil praising him and his fellow councillors for their care in overseeing what he described as an unprecedented event: 'the translation of a monarchy'. The supporters of the unmarried Arbella did nothing. Bess would never see her granddaughter proclaimed queen. Her dream of nearly thirty years had vanished.

As the queen had wished, there was no post-mortem. Her body was embalmed and placed in a lead coffin. A few days later she began her last journey, by water to Whitehall, and was laid in state before being taken to Westminster Hall. There her body was to remain until the new king gave orders for her funeral. He left Scotland on 5 April but had not reached London by 28 April, the day arranged for the funeral of Queen Elizabeth.

Arbella, being the only royal princess, was ordered to attend the funeral but refused. Elizabeth had never shown her any love, support or concern. She had not been allowed into the royal presence for many years, so she 'refused to be brought upon the stage now as a public spectacle'.[3]

The queen was given a magnificent funeral. The procession to Westminster Abbey was composed of more than 1,000 mourners. Her coffin, covered in purple velvet, was drawn by four horses draped in black. Behind the queen came her palfrey, led by her Master of Horse. The chief mourner was Elizabeth's step-aunt by marriage, the Marchioness of Northampton. She led the peeresses of the realm, all dressed in black, and behind them came all the important men of the realm, as well as over 200 poor people. The streets were crowded with those who had come to pay their last respects to the queen who had ruled them so wisely as she made her way to her final resting place at Westminster Abbey. An effigy of the great queen, dressed in the robes of state with a crown on her head and a sceptre in her hands, lay on the coffin beneath a mighty canopy held by six knights. Many wept when they saw the lifelike effigy of the queen. John Stow, who attended the funeral, wrote:

> Westminster was surcharged with multitudes of all sorts of people in their streets, houses, windows, leads and gutters, that came to see the obsequy, and when they beheld her statue lying upon the coffin, there was such a general sighing, groaning and weeping as the like hath not been seen or known in the memory of man, neither doth any history mention any people, time or state to make like lamentation for the death of their sovereign.

The grief of the nation was unprecedented, and was a tribute to the remarkable achievements of a remarkable woman. Elizabeth's tomb in Westminster Abbey, where she rests alongside her half-sister Queen Mary I, was paid for by the new king, but it is less impressive than that provided to his disgraced mother Mary Queen of Scots, and cost far less.

Gilbert Talbot, 7th Earl of Shrewsbury, was one of the earls who signed the proclamation of Elizabeth's successor on her death.

To show his allegiance, on 30 March he wrote a letter to his agent John Harper from Whitehall Palace, London:

> Mr Harper, it may be I shall be very shortly in the country and perhaps may be so happy as to entertain the King our sovereign at Worksop. I would entreat you to let all my good friends in Derbyshire and Staffordshire know so much, to the end that I may have their company against such a time as his Majesty shall come hither. I know not how soon. If it so happen as I shall know when in a few days certain; but then it will be too late for your horses or anything else to be prepared unless you prepare them presently upon the receipt hereof. All things here are well and nothing but unity and good agreement. God continue it. Amen. At my chamber in Whitehall Palace, this 30th March being Wednesday night, in very great haste. 1603. Your friend, most assured, Gilbert. Shrewsbury. I will not refuse any fat capons and hens, partridges, or the like if the King comes to me. GSh.

The king replied, accepting Gilbert's invitation to stay at Worksop.[4] Worksop Manor was the showpiece that Gilbert's father had built to entertain Queen Elizabeth. She never visited, but now James stayed there overnight on 20 April 1603. Gilbert Talbot obviously wished to show his hospitality and allegiance to the new king, particularly as his niece Arbella might be regarded as James's rival for the throne.

Bess did not leave Hardwick. She did not journey to London to attend the queen's funeral. She probably preferred to remember her as that seventeen-year-old princess who had been godmother to her first son Henry Cavendish, or the woman who had imparted her secrets to Bess in her bedchamber. As far as the queen allowed herself to have friends, Bess had been a constant, lifelong friend. And now she had no wish to meet the new king despite him staying overnight at Worksop Manor, one of the properties in which she had a lifetime interest. However, her daughter Mary Talbot, Gilbert's wife, took the opportunity to speak to James about Arbella. As the chosen one, James could afford to be magnanimous towards Arbella and free her from the previous lonely life, and she was invited to attend his court.

Although Bess now hardly left Hardwick, she was still kept informed of events. She would have heard about the king's coronation, blighted by yet another London plague. She would have heard of the plots to remove him and how Arbella, although not directly involved, was pivotal to any plot to depose him. Arbella was living at court and had formed a close relationship with James and his wife Anne. As a mark of this friendship, Arbella was given a patent for a peerage. With the name left blank, she could give it to anyone, and although he wasn't her first choice she gave it to her uncle, and Bess's son, William Cavendish. In the spring of 1605, hearing that her grandmother was unwell, she returned to Hardwick but was met with cold hostility from Bess; however, her forgiving spirit came to the fore when Arbella gave William the peerage patent. Bess knew the value of a title for her dynasty and the privilege it brought.

By the winter of 1607 Bess had reached her eighties, and in January 1608 she showed the first signs of deterioration. Her ladies-in-waiting were in constant attendance and took turns to nurse her. On 2 February, Dr Hunton, who had been Bess's physician for ten years, moved into Hardwick to nurse his patient, but Bess, like her old friend the queen, had a tough constitution and lay for a further eleven long days. She died on 13 February 1608, her precise age unknown. William wrote, 'Given to Dr Hunton at my Lady Shrewsbury's departure £13 6s 8d, exactly forty marks.'[5]

Bess's body was drained of blood, disembowelled and embalmed before being sealed in wax and laid in a lead coffin. She was to lie in state in the great chamber at Hardwick for three months with the room draped in huge amounts of black cloth. Sometime in May, the procession taking Bess on her last journey set out from Hardwick Hall. Crowds of sightseers lined the route, and when the cortege arrived in Derby, the town witnessed the most inexcusable scenes of drunkenness and brawling as people clambered for the customary funeral dole. Bess had requested that her funeral should not be overly sumptuous, yet she left £2,000 to cover expenses and a further £1,000 to be shared among her servants. In total the cost of the funeral appears in the Cavendish account books as a staggering £3,257.[6]

At the head of the funeral cortege as it entered the church was a mourning knight carrying a banner emblazoned with Bess's arms. He was followed by heralds and officials of the College of Arms, then the coffin carried by six gentlemen. A black velvet pall, the corners of which were held by four knights, covered the coffin, which was followed by two hooded gentlemen ushers carrying white rods. Mary Talbot, Countess of Shrewsbury, followed as the chief lady mourner. She was supported by two hooded barons, and her train was carried by one of her waiting women; then came Bess's family, her servants, mourning women hired for the occasion and finally the twelve poor folk from the almshouses in Derby that she had built. Each of them had been given 20s and mourning clothes. The Archbishop of York, Toby Matthew, preached a funeral sermon and Bess was laid to rest in the vault beneath the vast, sumptuous monument made by her architect Robert Smythson.

Born in 1527 in the reign of Henry VIII, Bess, Countess of Shrewsbury – better known as Bess of Hardwick – had seen a sickly youth and three queens sitting on the throne of England: Jane Grey, Mary Tudor and Elizabeth Tudor. She had known them all personally, yet Bess of Hardwick was born the fourth daughter of a Derbyshire farmer with no prospects or property. She had been in service in the Grey household and companion to the infant Jane. Mary Tudor had been godmother to Bess's fifth child, Charles Cavendish. Elizabeth Tudor had been a lifelong friend and confidant who had entrusted Bess with the responsibility of guarding her rival, Mary Queen of Scots. The Scottish queen had been Bess's friend and foe, living in her household for sixteen years. Four queens, and the countess had known them all – as friend, confidant, companion and jailer.

Notes

1 Four Wardships and a Wedding

1. Bess of Hardwick: Portrait of an Elizabethan Dynast. David Durant. pp. 2–3. Peter Owen Publishers. 1977. Revised edition 1999
2. Tudor Derbyshire. Joy Childs. The Derbyshire Heritage Series 1985. pp. 3, 36
3. National Trust Handbook; Hardwick Hall back page. The Arms hung in the Drawing Room on the first floor listed in the 1601 inventory as Lady Shrewsbury's Withdrawing Chamber, not to be confused with the one on the second floor.
4. 'Bess of Hardwick's Building and Building Accounts'. Basil Stallybrass. Journal of the Society of Antiquaries 12.6.1913. pp. 1–2
5. John Hardwick's Inquisition Post Mortem and Will. Public Record Office; E/15/743/8
6. Derbyshire Archaeological Journal vol. CVII. 1987. pp. 41–54, op. cit.
7. Birth, Marriage & Death: Ritual, Religion and the Life Cycle in Tudor and Stuart England. David Cressy. pp. 117–118
8. Public Record Office: E150/743/8
9. Notes on churches of Derbyshire. Cox. vol. 1. p. 246
10. Public Record Office: C/142/50/102. Deposition re Hardwyck taken 8 September 1530
11. Bess of Hardwick: Portrait of an Elizabethan Dynast. David Durant. p. 6 Peter Owen Publishers. 1977. Revised edition 1999
12. Plantagenet Ancestry: A Study in Colonial and Medieval Families. Douglas Richardson. Royal Ancestry Series ed. Kimball G. Everingham. 2nd edition 2011. p. 210.
13. *The Six Wives of Henry VIII*. Alison Weir. 2007. p. 324
14. Anne Boleyn. Marie Louise Bruce. Warner Paperback Library edition. 1972. pp. 40, 162.
15. A Who's Who of Tudor Women. Compiled by Kathy Lynn Emerson to update and correct Wives and Daughters: The Women of Sixteenth Century England. 1984
16. A Material Girl: Bess of Hardwick. Kate Hubbard. Short Books. 2001. p. 16
17. Public Record Office, Kew, London. STAC 2/19/310
18. Genealogy & Family History. Bosville of Warmsworth

19 Public Record Office, Kew, London; C1/1101

20 Public Record Office, Kew; C1/1101

21 Margaret, Duchess of Newcastle (1623–73), became the second wife of Bess's grandson William Cavendish in 1645. He called her Peg, but she was known as Mad Madge of Newcastle for her philosophical books and outlandish behaviour. She was a prolific poet, playwright, essayist, philosopher, writer of prose, fiction and science fiction who published under her own name at a time when most women writers published anonymously. Previously if a woman was gifted intellectually this never found an outlet, other than indirectly, through guiding sons or husbands, but things changed under the rules of Mary and Elizabeth. Margaret, Duchess of Newcastle, has been championed and criticised as a unique and groundbreaking seventeenth-century woman writer.

22 Chatsworth Archives; Rolls 691; drawer 367

2 Divorced, Beheaded, Died; Divorced, Beheaded, Survived

1 The Life and Political Significance of Henry Fitzroy, Duke of Richmond 1525–1536. Beverley Anne Murphy. PhD. Diss., University of Wales. 1997. pp. 80–81. Fitzroy was endowed with lands with revenues amounting to £4,845 in the first year. He was appointed warden-general of the marches towards Scotland, installed into the Order of the Garter, and became Lord Admiral of England.

2 Elizabeth: Apprenticeship. David Starkey. Chatto & Windus. 2000. pp. 12–13

3 Henry VIII. J. J. Scarisbrick. University of California Press. 1968. p. 349

4 Ibid. p. 154.

5 This series of letters, by some quirk of fate, is now in the Vatican Library. Elizabeth: Apprenticeship. David Starkey. Chatto & Windus. 2000. p. 13

6 Henry VIII. Michael Graves. Pearson Longman. p. 132

7 The Wives of Henry VIII. Antonia Fraser. 1992. p. 171

8 A Treasure of Royal Scandals. Michael Farquhar. Penguin Books. 2001. p. 67.

9 Six Wives: The Queens of Henry VIII. David Starkey. pp. 462–64

10 Henry VIII and His Court. Neville Williams. 1971. p. 124

11 The Wives of Henry VIII. Antonia Fraser. 1992. p. 195

12 Elizabeth: Apprenticeship. David Starkey. Chatto & Windus. 2000. pp. 2–3

13 Six Wives: The Queens of Henry VIII. David Starkey. 2003. p. 508

14 Elizabeth: Apprenticeship. David Starkey. Chatto and Windus, London. 2000. pp. 2–3

15 Henry VIII and His Court. Neville Williams. 1971. pp. 128–31

16 Letters & Papers Foreign & Domestic. Henry VIII. VI 1125; http: www. elizabethfiles.com/elizabeth-is-christening-10th-september. The gown traditionally thought to have been worn by Princess Elizabeth at her christening on 10 September 1533 is on display at Sudeley Castle, Winchcombe, Gloucestershire. In the 1880s experts authenticated the garment that could have been sewn and embroidered by her mother Anne Boleyn.

17 Elizabeth's Women: The Hidden Story of the Virgin Queen. Tracy Borman.

18 Six Wives: The Queens of Henry VIII. David Starkey. 2003. p. 512.

19 Elizabeth I. Anne Somerset. Phoenix. 1997. pp. 5-6.

20 The Life and Death of Anne Boleyn. Eric Ives. 2004. pp. 231–60

21 The Wives of Henry VIII. Antonia Fraser. Knopf. 1992.
22 Six Wives: The Queens of Henry VIII. David Starkey. 2003. pp. 552–54.
23 The Six Wives of Henry VIII. Alison Weir. 2007. p. 324
24 Tower Of London: A History of England From the Norman Conquest. Christopher Hibbert. 1971. pp. 54–55

3 Elizabeth's Formative Years

1 A manuscript in the Vatican archives reveals that in France the papal nuncio heard that they were married already. Archivum Secretum Vaticanum, Serg, St Francia, Vol 1B, f.40r
2 Elizabeth's Women: The Hidden Story of the Virgin Queen. Tracy Borman
3 Mary Queen of Scots. Antonia Fraser. p. 26
4 Time Out Guide: 1000 things to do in London for under £10. Edbury. p. 215. Greenwich Palace now lies under the Old Royal Naval College. Archaeological digs have unearthed multiple artefacts from the palace, and these are now on show in the visitor's centre.
5 The Education of a Christian Woman. Juan Luis Vives. 1524
6 Mary Queen of Scots. Antonia Fraser. p. 38
7 For a detailed discussion on this Act of Parliament see Eric Ives 'Tudor Dynastic Problems Revisited'.
8 Tudor: The Family Story. Leanda de Lisle. Chatto & Windus. 2013. p. 239
9 Ibid. p. 245
10 Edward VI: The Lost King of England. Chris Skidmore. Phoenix. 2007. pp. 71–87
11 The First Elizabeth. Carolly Erickson. Summit Books. 1983. pp. 53–54
12 Elizabeth the Great. Elizabeth Jenkins. Coward-McCann. 1959
13 The First Elizabeth. Carolly Erickson. Summit Books. 1983. pp. 65–79
14 The Six Wives of Henry VIII. Alison Weir. 1998. pp 14–15
15 The Virgin Queen: Elizabeth I, Genius of the Golden Age. Chris Hibbert. Da Capo Press. 1992. p. 29
16 Edward VI: The Lost King of England. Chris Skidmore. Phoenix. 2007. pp. 71–87
17 Ibid. p. 103
18 The First Elizabeth. Carolly Erickson. Summit Books. 1983. p. 84
19 Elizabeth: Apprenticeship. David Starkey. Chatto & Windus. 2000. p. 65
20 Edward VI: The Lost King of England. Chris Skidmore. Phoenix. 2007. pp. 102–04
21 Durham Palace, the former residence of the prince-bishops of Durham. It was acquired by. Elizabeth who did a swap with John Dudley, the Duke of Northumberland, who was intent upon acquiring landholdings in Northumberland and the prince-bishopric of Durham to give substance to the title. Built in the new Italian style with its impressive frontage to The Strand, it was the largest, newest, most magnificent private house in London occupying a prime site from The Strand to the River Thames, now the site of The Adelphi.
22 Elizabeth: Apprenticeship. David Starkey. Chatto & Windus. 2000. pp. 92–99

4 Bess and the Colourful Greys

1 *Bishop Percy's Folio Manuscript: Ballads and Romances 3. Thomas Percy, ed. J. W. Hales and F. J. Furnivall. 1868. p. 258*

2 Storia d'Italia, Lib. XII. Francesco Guicciardini. Cap. 9

3 Dictionary of National Biography Volume 36. pp. 397–400

4 Lady Jane Grey: A Tudor Mystery. Eric Ives. Wiley-Blackwell. 2009. P 52

5 History of the Court of Augmentations. p. 55; Bess of Hardwick: First Lady of Chatsworth. Mary Lovell. Abacus. 2006. p. 40

6 Bess of Hardwick: First Lady of Chatsworth. Mary Lovell. Abacus. 2006. p. 42; Bess's household account book in Folger Xd 428

7 Calendar of State Papers; L7P 1538, P. 281.

8 Public Record Office; E117/14/44

9 Public Record Office: E 101/424/10 William Cavendish's statement in the Star Chamber in October 1557.

10 Trevelyan papers. Payne Collier. Camden Society. 1857. p. 195

11 Historical collections of the noble families of Cavendish. Collins. p. 11. Anno 2 RE 6 stands for the 2nd year of the reign of Edward VI 1548.

12 Lady Jane Grey: A Tudor Mystery. Eric Ives. 2009. pp. 47–49

13 Bess of Hardwick: First Lady of Chatsworth. Mary Lovell. Abacus. 2006. P.64

14 Household book of Edward VI, in the Trevelyan papers. Payne Collier. Camden Society. 1857. pp. 195-6

15 Bess of Hardwick: First Lady of Chatsworth. Mary Lovell. Abacus. 2006. p. 67

16 Calendar of State Papers. Letters and Papers September 1536. pp. 166, 170-171 and 181

17 The term Dame, which is how Bess is described in the deed, is a courtesy title used for all upper-class women.

18 Calendar of State Papers. Letters and Papers 1538. p. 281

19 Bess of Hardwick: First Lady of Chatsworth. Mary Lovell. Abacus. 2006. p. 72

20 Ibid. p. 71

21 Public Record Office; E117/14/44

22 Bess of Hardwick: First Lady of Chatsworth. Mary Lovell. Abacus. 2006. p. 76; The Trevelyan Papers. Payne Collier. Camden Society. 1857. pp. 195-6

23 Levy of Household Stuff; the 1601 Inventories of Bess of Hardwick. pp. 33-34; Historical Collections of the Noble Families of Cavendish. Collins. p. 11. Bess of Hardwick: First Lady of Chatsworth. Mary Lovell. Abacus. 2006. p. 77

24 Bess of Hardwick: First Lady of Chatsworth. Mary Lovell. Abacus. 2006. p. 79; Household Book of Edward VI in the Trevelyan Papers. Payne Collier. Camden Society. 1857. pp. 195–6

5 A Problem of Succession

1 Bess of Hardwick: First Lady of Chatsworth. Mary Lovell. Abacus. 2006. p. 82

2 Ibid. Part of Jane's reluctance was probably because she was contracted to marry Edward Seymour, son of the executed Lord Protector, and Guildford Dudley was betrothed to Jane's cousin Margaret Clifford, daughter of her aunt Eleanor *nee* Brandon.

3 Lady Jane Grey: A Tudor Mystery. Eric Ives. 2009. p. 321. 2009; Tudor: The Family Story. Leanda de Lisle. Chatto & Windus. 2013. pp. 93, 304

4   The Tudors. Richard Rex. Amberley Publishing. 2009. p. 114
5   Public Record Office. E101/424/10; Bess of Hardwick. David Durant. p. 26
6   Bess of Hardwick: First Lady of Chatsworth. Mary Lovell. Abacus. 2006. p. 84
7   Mary Tudor: The First Queen. Linda Porter. Little Brown. 2007. p. 203; Sovereign Ladies: The Six Reigning Queens of England. Maurene Waller. St Martin's Press. 2006. p. 52
8   Mary Tudor: A Life. David Loades. Blackwell. 1989. pp. 176–181
9   Mary Tudor: The First Queen. Linda Porter. Little Brown. 2007. p. 210
10 Sovereign Ladies: The Six Reigning Queens of England. Maurene Waller. St Martin's Press. 2006. pp. 57–59
11 Mary Tudor: A Life. David Loades. Blackwell. 1989. p. 191
12 The Tudors. Richard Rex. Amberley Publishing. 2009. p. 122
13 Mary Tudor: A Life. David Loades. Blackwell. 1989. pp. 199–201. Mary Tudor: The First Queen. Linda Porter. Little Brown. 2007. pp. 265–67
14 Mary Tudor: The First Queen. Linda Porter. Little Brown. 2007. p. 310
15 A fuller description of Mary I's coronation ceremony can be read in Mary Tudor: Princess, Bastard, Queen. Anna Whitelock. Chapter God Save Queen Mary.
16 Lady Jane Grey: A Tudor Mystery. Eric Ives. pp. 262–67
17 Bess of Hardwick: Portrait of an Elizabethan Dynast. David Durant. Peter Owen. 1977. Revised edition 1999. p. 27
18 Longleat; Thynne Papers, vol. 11, f.227, Sir William Cavendish to Sir John Thynne. 3 March 1555 and vol. 11, f.250, ditto, 24 June 1556
19 Bess of Hardwick: First Lady of Chatsworth. Mary Lovell. Abacus. 2005. p. 87; also History of the Annals of England, Camden
20 The Sisters Who Would Be Queen. Leanda de Lisle. p. 131
21 Bess of Hardwick: First Lady of Chatsworth. Mary Lovell. Abacus. 2005. p. 89
22 Mary Tudor: The First Queen. Linda Porter. Little Brown. 2007. pp. 311–13; Mary Tudor: England's First Queen. Anna Whitelock. Bloomsbury. 2009. pp. 217–25
23 Bess of Hardwick: First Lady of Chatsworth. Mary Lovell. Abacus. 2005. p. 135
24 Ibid. p. 136

6 Mary Marries Philip of Spain

1   Mary Tudor: The First Queen. Linda Porter. Little Brown. 2007. pp. 291–92; Sovereign Ladies: The Six Reigning Queens of England. Maurene Waller. St. Martin's Press. 2006. p. 85; Mary Tudor: England's First Queen. Anna Whitelock. Bloomsbury. 2009. pp. 226–27
2   Ibid. pp. 308–09; Mary Tudor: England's First Queen. Anna Whitelock. Bloomsbury. 2009. p. 229
3   Mary Tudor: The First Queen. Linda Porter. Little Brown. 2007. pp. 333. Sovereign Ladies: The Six Reigning Queens of England. Maurene Waller. St Martin's Press. 2006. pp. 92–93
4   Mary Tudor: A Life. David Loades. Blackwell. 1989. pp. 234–35
5   Bess of Hardwick: First Lady of Chatsworth. Mary Lovell. Abacus. 2005. p. 91; Longleat: Thynne Papers, vol. II, f.227, Sir William Cavendish to Sir

John Thynne 3 March 1554/5. The letter is dated March 1554 because in the Elizabethan period, the New Year began on 1 April (see Appendix).

6 Public Record Office, Kew. C 142/128/91. Frances had a baby girl they called Elizabeth. It was a popular name at the time, but it's interesting to consider that Frances's three older daughters were all named after Tudor queens. Jane Grey was named after Jane Seymour, mother of Edward VI; Katherine Grey was named after Katherine of Aragon; and Mary was named after Mary Tudor. It's possible that Elizabeth Stokes was named after Elizabeth Tudor, but she and two further sons all died in infancy.

7 Mary Tudor: The First Queen. Linda Porter. Little Brown. 2007. p. 338; Sovereign Ladies: The Six Reigning Queens of England. Maurene Waller. St. Martin's Press. 2006. p. 95; Mary Tudor: England's First Queen. Anna Whitelock. Bloomsbury. 2009. p. 255

8 Calendar of State Papers relating to Venice 13 (884). Tudor: The Family Story. Leanda de Lisle. Chatto & Windus. 2013. p. 294

9 Sovereign Ladies: The Six Reigning Queens of England. Maurene Waller. St. Martin's Press. 2006. p. 95; Mary Tudor: England's First Queen. Anna Whitelock. Bloomsbury. 2009. p. 256

10 Mary Tudor: England's First Queen. Anna Whitelock. Bloomsbury. 2009. p. 257-259

11 Tudor: The Family Story. Leanda de Lisle. Chatto & Windus. 2013. p. 295. Similar symptoms to those of pregnancy would be benign tumours on the pituitary gland. 'The Aching and Increasing blindness of Queen Mary', Journal of Medical Biography 8/2 (2000) pp. 102–09

12 Antoine de Noailles quoted in Mary Tudor: England's First Queen. Anna Whitelock. Bloomsbury. 2009. p. 269

13 Mary Tudor: The First Queen. Linda Porter. Little Brown. 2007. p. 342

14 Sovereign Ladies: The Six Reigning Queens of England. Maurene Waller. St. Martin's Press. 2006. pp. 98–99; Mary Tudor: England's First Queen. Anna Whitelock. Bloomsbury. 2009. p. 268

15 Tudor: The Family Story. Leanda de Lisle. Chatto & Windus. 2013. p. 293

16 Mary Tudor: A Life. David Loades. Blackwell. 1989. pp. 207-208; Sovereign Ladies: The Six Reigning Queens of England. Maurene Waller. St. Martin's Press. 2006. p. 65; Mary Tudor: England's First Queen. Anna Whitelock. Bloomsbury. 2009. p. 198

17 Mary Tudor: The First Queen. Linda Porter. Little Brown. 2007. p. 241; Mary Tudor: England's First Queen. Anna Whitelock. Bloomsbury. 2009. pp. 200–01, 229

18 Mary Tudor: The First Queen. Linda Porter. Little Brown. 2007. p. 331

19 Mary Tudor: A Life. David Loades. Blackwell. 1989. pp. 235–42

20 Sovereign Ladies: The Six Reigning Queens of England. Maurene Waller. St. Martin's Press. 2006. p. 113

21 Mary Tudor: England's First Queen. Anna Whitelock. Bloomsbury. 2009. p. 284

22 Bess of Hardwick: First Lady of Chatsworth. Mary Lovell. Abacus. 2005. p. 96; British Library MSS Dept, Private Papers of Rev J Hunter.

23 Ibid P. 95. Longleat: Thynne papers vol. 11, f.252

24 History of the Court of Augmentation, P. 123; Bess of Hardwick: First Lady of Chatsworth. Mary Lovell. Abacus. 2005. p. 97

25 Ibid. p. 98.

26 Ibid P. 99; Trevelyan Papers, part 11. Payne Collier. pp. 21–138

27 Public Record Office: E101/424/10. Bess of Hardwick: First Lady of Chatsworth. Mary Lovell. Abacus. 2005. p. 100

28 Historical Collections of the Noble Families of Cavendish. Collins. p. 12.

29 England Under the Reigns of Edward VI and Mary. Tytler. p. 37; Bess of Hardwick: First Lady of Chatsworth. Mary Lovell. Abacus. 2005. p. 109

30 Longleat; Thynne papers vol. 111, ff.12–14

31 Ibid. ff.15

32 Chatsworth Archives: Hardwick MS 3 f.20

33 Public Record Office. E101/42/10; Bess of Hardwick: First Lady of Chatsworth. Mary Lovell. Abacus. 2005. p. 85

34 The Count of Feria's Dispatch to Philip dated 14 November 1558, in Camden Miscellany XXVIII Camden Fourth Series, Vol. 29 (1984) pp. 330–32. Tudor: The Family Story. Leanda de Lisle. Chatto & Windus. 2013. p. 299

35 Ibid. p. 300

36 Ibid P. 301

7 *Who Will Be Queen of England?*

1 Letters of James V. ed. Denys Hay, calendared by R. K Hannay. 1954. p. 172

2 Chronicles of Robert Lindsay. Piscottie. p. 377

3 Hamilton Papers I. ed. J. Bain. 1890. p. 329

4 Balcarres Papers I.

5 Chronicles of Robert Lindsay. Piscottie. p. 394

6 Letters and Memorials of William Allen. T. F. Knox I. 1882. p. 40

7 Hamilton Papers I PP. 328, 340, 342; C.S.P. Spanish VI (II) P. 189

8 Calendar of State Papers Venetian, VI, pt 3 P. 1571 Mary Queen of Scots. Antonia Fraser. Mandarin. 1970. p. 114

9 Sayings of Queen Elizabeth. Chamerlin. p. 38; Bess of Hardwick: First Lady of Chatsworth. Mary Lovell. Abacus. 2005. p. 136

10 Public Record Office: AO1/283/ 1068.; Bess of Hardwick: First Lady of Chatsworth. Mary Lovell. Abacus. 2005. p. 138

11 Mary Queen of Scots. Antonia Fraser. Mandarin. 1970. p. 114. Images of a Queen. Phillips. pp. 12 et seq, 237

12 Bess of Hardwick: First Lady of Chatsworth. Mary Lovell. Abacus. 2005. p. 139

13 The Arch Conjurer of England: John Dee. Glyn Parry. 2011. pp. 48–49. Tudor: The Family Story. Leanda de Lisle. p. 304

14 Bess of Hardwick: First Lady of Chatsworth. Mary Lovell. Abacus. 2005. pp. 143–54

15 Mary Queen of Scots. Antonia Fraser. Mandarin. 1970. p. 115; Memoirs. Sir James Melville. 1929. p. 49

16 Ibid. p. 169

17 Ibid. p. 168

8 Love Affairs and Poison

1 Longleat: Thynne Papers vol. III, f.27
2 Folger Xd. 428 (19); Bess of Hardwick: First Lady of Chatsworth. Mary Lovell. Abacus. 2005. p. 151
3 Calendar of State Papers Spanish 1559
4 Folger Xd. 428 (75); Bess of Hardwick: First Lady of Chatsworth. Mary Lovell. Abacus. 2005. p. 150
5 Longleat: Thynne Papers 25 April 1560
6 Folger Xd.428 (74); Bess of Hardwick: First Lady of Chatsworth. Mary Lovell. Abacus. 2005. p. 153
7 Ibid. p. 155
8 Public Record Office: C3/159/9
9 Ibid C3/159/9/1
10 Calendar of State Papers 1560. p. 368
11 Sweet Robin: A biography of Robert Dudley. Derek Wilson. For details of Amy Robsart's death see P. 121.
12 English Ambassador at Madrid to Cecil, October 1559, SP. Foreign 1559-60; Arbella Stuart. p. M. Handover. 1957. p. 32
13 British Library. Add MSS 33749, ff. 47,66.
14 Ibid ff.58.49.
15 Mistress of Hardwick. Alison Plowden. BBC. 1972. p. 20
16 Calendar of State Papers: Elizabeth, 1561, P. 369. HMC Salisbury Papers, vol. 1. pp. 87–88, 153
17 Mistress of Hardwick. Alison Plowden. BBC. 1972. p. 20; Calendar of Patent Rolls vol. II, Elizabeth, 15 August 1563. pp. 495–96
18 The Life of Queen Elizabeth I. Agnes Strickland. London. 1904. p. 158
19 A Conference about the Next Succession to the Crown of England. Doleman. 1594. pp. 126
20 Folger Xd.428 (48) Elizabeth Leche to E. St Loe. C. 29 January 1565, and Xd. 428 (35), from James Hardwick to E St Loe dated 29 January 1565
21 Public Record Office: C3/170/13. Lady St Loe's statement to Sir Nicholas Baron, Keeper of the Great Seal of England
22 Public Record Office: PROB 11/48 (244) Morrison, February 1565; Bess of Hardwick: First Lady of Chatsworth. Mary Lovell. Abacus. 2005. P 188
23 Although this monument has not survived, in A Survey of London, John Stow refers to a monument in Great St Helen's Church.

9 Mary Queen of Scots, Darnley and Boswell

1 The Historie of Scotland II. Leslie John, Bishop of Ross. Translated into Scottish by Fr. James Dalrymple. Scottish Text Society. 1895. p. 260
2 Memoirs. Sir James Melville of Halhill. 1929. p. 92
3 Ibid. p. 107
4 Mary Queen of Scots. Antonia Fraser. Mandarin. 1989. pp. 279–81
5 Calendar of State Papers of Spain 1 P. 296
6 Ibid. p. 357
7 Superstition and witchcraft were ever present, even in the delivery room. Margaret, Countess of Atholl, cast spells to throw the pangs of childbirth

onto Margaret Lady Reres who lay in bed, suffering phantom pains with her mistress. When a child was born with a caul over the face as James was, it was believed that the child had special, supernatural powers, and could never drown. This was something that James relied upon later.

8 Tudor: The Family Story. Leanda de Lisle. Chatto & Windus. 2013. p. 339
9 The New Cambridge Modern History, Volume III, The Counter-Reformation and Price Revolution 1559-1610. R. B. Wenham. Cambridge University Press. 1968. p. 228
10 The Comprehensive History of England. Charles Macfarlane and Thomas Napier Thomson. Blackie and Son. 1861. Volume II
11 The Mystery of Mary Stuart. Andrew Lang. p. 255
12 Mary Queen of Scots. Jenny Wormwauld. St Martin's Press. 2001. p. 182
13 Inventairs de la Royne d'Ecosse. Douairiére de France. J Robertson. Bannatyne Club. 1883. p. xxvi
14 A Lost Chapter in the History of Mary Queen of Scots Recovered. John Stuart. 1874.
15 Memoirs. Sir James Melville of Halhill. 1929. p. 154
16 Calendar State Papers Foreign, vol. VIII p. 246
17 Mary Queen of Scots. Antonia Fraser. Mandarin. 1989. p. 397
18 Ibid. p. 407
19 Memorials of Mary Stuart. Claud Nau. Ed. J. Stevenson. 1883. p. 62
20 Mary Queen of Scots. Antonia Fraser. Mandarin. 1989. p. 428
21 Lettres de Marie Stuart. Ed. Prince Labanoff. II. p. 76
22 Ibid. p. 117
23 Memorials of Mary Stuart. Claud Nau. Ed J. Stevenson. 1883. p. 95
24 Lettres de Marie Stuart. Ed. Prince Labanoff. II. p. 91
25 Calendar State Papers Scotland, vol. II. p. 435
26 Ibid. p. 457
27 Ibid. p. 443
28 Tudor: The Family Story. Leanda de Lisle. Chatto & Windus. 2013. p. 345
29 Calendar State Papers Scotland, vol. II. p. 907

10 Bess the Jailor

1 Bess of Hardwick: First Lady of Chatsworth. Mary Lovell. Abacus. 2005. p. 198
2 Calendar of Shrewsbury and Talbot Papers in the College of Arms, ed. G. R Batho, vol. G, f.170. Historical Manuscript Commission publication, jointly with the Derbyshire Archaeological Society.
3 Bess of Hardwick: First Lady of Chatsworth. Mary Lovell. Abacus. 2005. E. Wingfield to Bess, 21 October 1568
4 Public Record Office; State Papers – Domestic. Addenda, 1566-79, P. 39.
5 History of Staffordshire; Somerville, Guide to Tutbury Castle.
6 Bess of Hardwick: First Lady of Chatsworth. Mary Lovell. Abacus. 2005. p. 207, Elizabeth Shrewsbury's letter to the Earl of Leicester from Tutbury 21 January 1569.
7 Letter-books of Sir Amyas Paulet. Morris. p. 108
8 Lettres de Marie Stuart. Ed. Prince Labanoff. VI. p. 176

9   Elizabethan London. Liza Picard. Phoenix. p. 69
10 Hatfield Calendar I P. 400
11 Calendar State Papers Scotland, vol. II P. 632
12 Ibid.
13 Ibid. p. 649
14 Lettres de Marie Stuart. Ed. Prince Labanoff. II. p. 5; III. p. 19
15 Parish of Holyroodhouse or Canongate, Marriages 1564-1800, SRS, part LXIV (March 1914) p. 409, under Paige, Bastian, & Loge, Christen. The register date, circa 20 August 1567, is probably the date the clerk recorded the marriage.
16 Calendar State Papers Scotland, vol. 3. 1903. p. 646
17 The Northern Rebellion of 1569: Faith, Politics, and Protest in Elizabethan England. Krista J. Kesselring. Palgrave Macmillan. 2010
18 According to a report in the *Coventry Telegraph*, 14 April 2014, a rare letter signed by Queen Elizabeth I which sent Mary Queen of Scots into 'the protection of Coventry' at the outbreak of the 1569 Northern Uprising has been put up for sale. The edict is part of a substantial collection of eighty rare artefacts being auctioned by Sotheby's in July 2014 for the Duke of Northumberland.
19 *A History of Coventry. David Mc Gregory. Phillimore. 2003. pp.133–34*
20 Calendar State Papers Domestic, addenda, 1566–79. The state papers and letters of Sir Ralph Sadler, ed. A. Clifford, 2 vols. 1809.

11 Mary's Imprisonment during the 1570s

1   Calendar State Papers Scotland, vol. III. William Boyd. 1903. pp. 94, 107
2   Original Letters, vol. II Lodge. p. 50
3   Calendar of manuscripts at Hatfield House. I. p. 505
4   Historical Manuscripts Commission; Pepys, P. 144. Letter from Shrewsbury to Cecil.
5   Calendar State Papers Scotland, vol. 2. p. 671
6   Illustrations of British History, vol. 2. Edmund Lodge. 1791. p. 52; Lambeth Palace Talbot manuscripts vol. F, fol.9.
7   This letter is reproduced in a catalogue of the antiquities and works of art exhibited in 1861, vol.1, London (1869), pp. 64-65 with its transcription; Labanoff, Alexandre, ed., Letters de Marie Stuart, vol. 3, Dolman (1844), pp. 373-4 translated in Strickland, Agnes, Lives of the Queens of Scotland, vol. 7 (1850) pp. 136-7 and Turnbull, William, ed., Letters of Mary Stuart, Queen of Scotland: selected from the Recueil des lettres de Marie Stuart, Dolman, (1845), p. xxiii. 'Inventions d'ouvrages' is translated as needlework patterns.
8   Emblems for a Queen. Michael Bath. Archetype. 2008. p. 5: HMC Salisbury Hatfield, vol. 1. 1883. p. 564 no. 1721; Calendar State Papers Scotland, vol. 3. 1903. p. 646 no.870
9   Bess of Hardwick: First Lady of Chatsworth. Mary Lovell. Abacus. 2005. pp. 233–34
10 Historical Manuscripts Commission. Salisbury, vol. I. p. 26
11 The healing waters are supplied by nine springs which originate from a source 500 feet below ground, and regularly supply 200,000 gallons per day at a temperature of 82 degrees Fahrenheit (28 centigrade). The water is radioactive

and gaseous, mostly carbon dioxide and nitrogen with a little argon and helium. The water lacks odour, is tasteless, free of organic matter and has a striking blue clarity.

12 Part of this 1573 build is now incorporated into the Old Hall Hotel.
13 Companion Into Derbyshire. Ethel Carleton Williams. Methuen & Co. Ltd. 1947. pp. 61–62
14 *Ibid.*

12 *The Unsanctioned Marriage*

1 The full story of the unsanctioned marriage is in Arbella Stuart. Jill Armitage. Amberley Publishing. 2017.
2 State Papers of Scotland. Elizabeth to James, 30 July 1578, v.314
3 Reference to the allowances are found in State Papers Domestic. Eliz. 1, vol. CLII, pp 42, 43, 53. Also Calendar of Scots Papers, vol. VI, nos 95, 96
4 Historical Manuscript Commission Reports; Salisbury (Cecil), vol. II no. 675
5 Warrant by Mary to Thomas Fowler, 19 Sept. 1579. State Papers Scottish, v. 350
6 See Appendix page on Porphyria
7 For details of the Shrewsbury's quarrel see David N. Durant. Bess of Hardwick. 1977. ch 8.
8 Lettres de Marie Stuart. Ed. Prince Labanoff. VI. p. 37, Mary to Elizabeth. November 1584.
9 Walsingham to Wootton 28 May 1585 State Papers Scottish Ser., i. 496
10 Ibid. 496–97.
11 Full details of the scandal letters Bess of Hardwick. David Durant. 1977. pp. 129–31
12 The Captive Queen in Derbyshire. Derbyshire Heritage Series. Elizabeth Eisenberg. 1984. p. 31
13 Lord Paget's letter dated 4 March 1584 (the letter is calendared as 1583 due to the old dating) State Papers Domestic. 1581–90 Vol. CLIX P. 8. Leicester's letter date 26 June 1584 is from Miss Lloyd's manuscript at Althorp House pp.. 6, 7.
14 Mary's letter to Mauvissiere dated 21 March 1584 is printed in Mary Queen of Scots in Captivity. J. D. Leader. 1880. p. 551; Arbella Stuart. Handover. pp. 63–65

13 *Mary's Final Years of Captivity*

1 Oxford Dictionary of National Biography – Anthony Babington; Penry Williams.
2 Lettres de Marie Stuart. Ed. Prince Labanoff. VII. p. 253
3 The Captive Queen in Derbyshire. Elizabeth Eisenberg. Derbyshire Heritage series. 1984. p. 37
4 Calendar State Papers Scotland, vol. 7. 1913, P. 528 no.493.
5 For the details of Walsingham's involvement in the Babington plot, see Elizabeth I. p. Johnson. 1974. pp. 283–6
6 Queen of Scots: The True Story. John Guy. 2005. pp. 469–80
7 Calendar State Papers Scotland, vol. 8. 1914. pp. 206–07 nos 256, 327, 355, p. 412 no. 439, p. 626 no. 715, p. 632 no. 726.
8 Mary Queen of Scots. Antonia Frasier. 1989. p. 591–652

9 Ibid. p. 590
10 Ibid. p. 591
11 Ibid. p. 592
12 Relations Politiques IV. Teulet P. 163; see also Appendix – Comet.
13 Reign of Elizabeth. Black. p. 308
14 Mary Queen of Scots. Antonia Frasier. 1989. p. 625
15 See Maxwell Scott. Appendix for three contemporary accounts of Mary's execution
16 The Tragedy of Fotheringhay. The Hon Mrs Maxwell Scott. 1895. pp. 417–23
17 Lettres de Marie Stuart, ed. Prince Labanoff. Vol 6, pp. 474–80

14 Suitors and Building Sites

1 Tudor. The Family Story. Leanda de Lisle. Chatto & Windus. 2013. p. 355
2 De Chateauneuf to Henry III of France, 27 August 1587. Quoted by Strickland, p. 215; Arbella Stuart. Handover. p. 77
3 Handover, pp. 82–3; N. Kinnersley to Bess, November 1588; Hunter, p. 90.
4 Leicester and the Court. Simon Adams. 1988. p. 149
5 HMC. Longleat: Talbot Papers vol. V P. 54
6 *Ibid.* p. 55–6
7 CST; vol. 1, P. 202
8 Portrait of an Elizabethan Dynast. David Durant. 1999. p. 152
9 *Ibid.*
10 The England of Elizabeth. A. L. Rowse. 1950. p. 5
11 Levey. Of Household Stuff. p. 8
12 Oldcotes. Pamela Kettle. pp. 14–16
13 Arbella Stuart. B. C. Hardy. pp. 65–66
14 Derbyshire Archaeological Journal vol. XXX. 1908. Brodhurst, vol III. Elizabeth Hardwick, Countess of Shrewsbury, P. 253
15 Arbella Stuart. B. C. Hardy. pp. 75–76
16 Hardwick Hall. Girouard. p. 35
17 Historical Manuscript Collection; Salisbury papers, vol. 15. p. 65.
18 Extracts of Bess of Hardwick's will are printed in Historical Collections of the Noble Families of Cavendish. Collins. pp. 4–15.
19 Historical Manuscript Collection; Cecil Papers, vol. XIV. p. 258
20 Historical Manuscript Collection; Salisbury papers, vol. 12. pp. 529–36

15 The End of the Tudor Era

1 For the continuing story of Arbella see Arbella Stuart. Jill Armitage. Amberley Publishing. 2017.
2 For the Gregorian/Julian Calendar see Appendix 1.
3 British Library; Sloane Manuscript 718, f.39
4 Historical Manuscript Collection; series 5 Frank Bacon Collection. p. 18
5 Bess of Hardwick: Portrait of an Elizabethan Dynast. David Durant. Peter Owen. 1999. p. 223
6 Payments covering the period of Bess's illness and death are taken from William Cavendish's account book MS 29 Chatsworth Archives

Bibliography

Adams, Simon: Leicester and the Court: Essays in Elizabethan Politics, Manchester University Press 1988

Adams, Simon (ed.): Household Accounts and Disbursement Books of Robert Dudley, Earl of Leicester, 1558–1561, 1584–1586, Cambridge University Press 1995

Adams, Simon: 'At Home and Away. The Earl of Leicester' History Today Vol. 46 No. 5, May 1996 Retrieved 2010-09-29 1996

Adams, Simon: 'Dudley, Lettice, countess of Essex and countess of Leicester (1543–1634)', Oxford Dictionary of National Biography online edition. Jan 2008a (subscription required)

Adams, Simon: 'Dudley, Robert, earl of Leicester (1532/3–1588)', Oxford Dictionary of National Biography online edition. May 2008 (subscription required)

Adams, Simon: 'Dudley, Sir Robert (1574–1649)', Oxford Dictionary of National Biography online edition. Jan 2008 (subscription required)

Adams, Simon: 'Sheffield, Douglas, Lady Sheffield (1542/3–1608)', Oxford Dictionary of National Biography online edition. Jan 2008 (subscription required)

Adams, Simon: 'Dudley, Amy, Lady Dudley (1532–1560)', Oxford Dictionary of National Biography online edition. Jan 2011 (subscription required)

Alford, Stephen: The Early Elizabethan Polity: William Cecil and the British Succession Crisis, 1558–1569, Cambridge University Press 2002

Armitage, Jill: Arbella Stuart, Amberley 2017

Armstrong-Davison, M. H.: The Casket Letters, 1965

Batho Jamison, Catherine: A Calendar of the Talbot Papers in the College of Arms, Derbyshire Archaeology Society / HMC /HMSO 1971

Beverley, Anne Murphy: 'The Life and Political Significance of Henry Fitzroy, Duke of Richmond 1525-1536', Ph D. diss University of Wales 1997

Bill, E. G. W.: A Calendar of the Shrewsbury Papers in Lambeth Palace Library, Derbyshire Archaeology Society / HMC/ HMSO (1966)

Black, J. B.: The Reign of Elizabeth 1558-1603, Oxford University Press.

Bossy, John: Under the Molehill: An Elizabethan Spy Story, Yale Nota Bene 2002

Bruce, John (ed.): Correspondence of Robert Dudley, Earl of Leycester, during his Government of the Low Countries, in the Years 1585 and 1586, Camden Society 1844

Bruce, Marie Louise: Anne Boleyn, 1972

Burgoyne, F. J. (ed.): History of Queen Elizabeth, Amy Robsart and the Earl of Leicester, being a Reprint of 'Leycesters Commonwealth', Longmans 1904

Chamberlin, Frederick: Elizabeth and Leycester, Dodd, Mead & Co. 1939

Collinson, Patrick (ed.): 'Letters of Thomas Wood, Puritan, 1566–1577' Bulletin of the Institute of Historical Research Special Supplement No. 5, November 1960

Collinson, Patrick: The Elizabethan Puritan Movement, Jonathan Cape 1971

Collinson, Patrick: Elizabeth I, Oxford University Press 2007

Costello, Louisa Stuart: Memoirs of Eminent Englishwomen, Vol. 1. 'Elizabeth, Countess of Shrewsbury', Richard Bentley 1844

Digby, George Wingfield: Elizabethan Embroidery, Thomas Yoseloff 1964

Doran Susan: Monarchy and Matrimony: The Courtships of Elizabeth I, Routledge 1996

Dowling Maria: 'Anne Boleyn and Reform' Journal of Ecclesiastical History Volume 35, 1984

Durant, David N.: Bess of Hardwick: Portrait of an Elizabethan Dynasty, Weidenfeld and Nicolson 1999

Eisenberg, Elizabeth: The Captive Queen in Derbyshire, Derbyshire Heritage series 1984

Eisenberg, Elizabeth: This Costly Countess: Bess of Hardwick, Hall 1985

Elton G. R.: Reform and Reformation, Edward Arnold 1977

Emerson, Kathy Lyn: Wives and Daughters: The Women of sixteenth century England, 1984

Fraser, Antonia: Mary Queen of Scots, Mandarin Press 1969

Fraser, Antonia: The Six Wives of Henry VIII, New York 1992

Freedman, Sylvia: Poor Penelope: Lady Penelope Rich, An Elizabethan Woman, The Kensal Press 1983

Girouard Mark: Life in the English Country House: A Social and Architectural History BCA, 1979

Graves, Michael: Henry VIII, Pearson Longman 2003

Gregory, Philippa: Three Sisters, Three Queens, Simon & Schuster 2016

Gristwood, Sarah: Elizabeth and Leicester: Power, Passion, Politics, Viking 2007

Guy, John, Queen of Scots: The True Story, 2005

Hammer, P. E. J.: Elizabeth's Wars: War, Government and Society in Tudor England, 1544–1604, Palgrave Macmillan 2003

Hammer, P. E. J.: The Polarisation of Elizabethan Politics: The Political Career of Robert Devereux, 2nd Earl of Essex, 1585–1597, Cambridge University Press 1999

Handover, P. M.: Arbella Stuart, Eyre & Spottsiwoode 1957

Haynes, Alan: Invisible Power: The Elizabethan Secret Services 1570–1603, Alan Sutton 1992

Haynes, Alan: The White Bear: The Elizabethan Earl of Leicester, Peter Owen 1987

Hearn, Karen (ed.): Dynasties: Painting in Tudor and Jacobean England 1530–1630, Rizzoli 1995

Bibliography

Henderson, Paula: The Tudor House and Garden: Architecture and Landscape in the Sixteenth and Seventeenth Century, Yale University Press 2005

Henley Virginia: A Woman of Passion, Random House 1999

Hibbert, Christopher: Tower of London: A History of England From the Norman Conquest, 1971

Historical Manuscripts Commission (ed.): Report on the Pepys Manuscripts Preserved at Magdalen College, Cambridge HMSO 1911

Hubbard, Kate: Material Girl: Bess of Hardwick 1527–1608, Short Books 2001

Hume, Martin (ed.): Calendar of ... State Papers Relating to English Affairs ... in ... Simancas, 1558–1603 HMSO Vol. I Vol. III Vol. IV

Hume, Martin: The Courtships of Queen Elizabeth, Eveleigh Nash & Grayson 1904

Ives, Eric: 'Anne Boleyn' Oxford Dictionary of National Biography, 2004–2014

Ives, Eric: Lady Jane Grey: A Tudor Mystery, Wiley-Blackwell 2009

Ives, Eric: The Life and Death of Anne Boleyn, Blackwell Publishing 2004

Jenkins, Elizabeth: Elizabeth and Leicester, The Phoenix Press 2002

Johnson, I. P.: Elizabeth, 1974

Kettle, Pamela Oldcotes: The Last Mansion Built by Bess of Hardwick, Merton Priory Press 2000

Kilburn, Terry: 'The Wardship and Marriage of Robert Barley, First Husband of Bess of Hardwick' p 197–203 Derbyshire Archaeological Journal Vol 134, 2014.

Labanoff, Prince Alexander: Recueil des lettres de Marie Stuart

Leader, J. D.: Mary Queen of Scots in Captivity, 1880

Leithead, Howard: 'Thomas Cromwell' Oxford Dictionary of National Biography, 2004–2014

Leslie John, Bishop of Ross: The Historie of Scotland, Scottish Text Society 1895

Levey, Santina, Peter Thornton: Of Houshold Stuff: The 1601 Inventory of Bess of Hardwick, National Trust 2001

Levey, Santina: An Elizabethan Inheritance: The Hardwick Hall Textiles, National Trust 1998

Lisle, Leanda de: The Sisters Who Would Be Queen: Mary, Katherine and Lady Jane Grey, A Tudor Tragedy, Ballantine Books 2008

Lisle, Leanda de: Tudor: The Family Story, Chatto and Windus 2013

Loades, David: John Dudley, Duke of Northumberland 1504–1553, Clarendon Press 1996

Loades, David: Intrigue and Treason: The Tudor Court, 1547–1558, Pearson/ Longman 2004

Loades, David: The Six Wives of Henry VIII, 2007

Lovell, Mary S.: Bess of Hardwick: First Lady of Chatsworth, 1527–1608, Little-Brown 2005

MacCulloch, Diarmaid: The Boy King: Edward VI and the Protestant Reformation, Palgrave 2001

Maxwell-Scott, The Hon.: The Tragedy of Fotheringhay, 1895

Melville, Sir James of Halhill: Memoirs, ed. Francis Steuart 1929

Molyneaux, N. A. D.: 'Kenilworth Castle in 1563' English Heritage Historical Review Vol. 3, 2008 pp. 46–61

Morris, R. K.: Kenilworth Castle, English Heritage 2010

Nicolas, Harris (ed.): Memoirs of the Life and Time of Sir Christopher Hatton, Richard Bentley 1847

Owen, D. G. (ed.): Manuscripts of the Marquess of Bath Volume V: Talbot, Dudley and Devereux Papers 1533–1659, HMSO 1980

Pearson, John: The Serpent and the Stag, Holt, Rinehart & Winston 1984

Plowden, Alison: Mistress of Hardwick, BBC 1972

Porter, Linda: Mary Tudor: The First Queen, Portrait 2007

Read, Conyers: 'A Letter from Robert, Earl of Leicester, to a Lady' The Huntington Library Bulletin No. 9, April 1936

Rex, Richard: The Tudors, Amberley Publishing 2009

Rickman, Johanna: Love, Lust, and License in Early Modern England: Illicit Sex and the Nobility, Ashgate 2008

Rosenberg, Eleanor: Leicester: Patron of Letters, Columbia University Press 1958

Rowse, A. L.: Eminent Elizabethans, University of Georgia Press 1983

Rowse. A. L.: The England of Elizabeth, 2003

Skidmore, Chris: Death and the Virgin: Elizabeth, Dudley and the Mysterious Fate of Amy Robsart, Weidenfeld & Nicolson 2010

Somerset, Anne: Elizabeth I, Phoenix 1997

Starkey, David: Elizabeth: Apprenticeship, Chatto & Windus, 2000

Starkey, David: Six Wives: The Queens of Henry VIII, 2003

Strong. R. C. and J. A. van Dorsten: Leicester's Triumph, Oxford University Press 1964

Warner, G. F.: The Voyage of Robert Dudley to the West Indies, 1594–1595, Hakluyt Society p. xli 1899

Warnicke, Retha M.: *The Rise and Fall of Anne Boleyn,* 1989

Watkins, Susan: The Public and Private Worlds of Elizabeth I, Thames & Hudson 1998

Weir, Alison: The Six Wives of Henry VIII, 2007

Weir, Alison: The Lady in the Tower: The Fall of Anne Boleyn, Vintage 2010

Westcott, Jan: The Tower and the Dream, Putnam 1974

Williams, Ethel Carleton: Bess of Hardwick, Chivers 1977

Williams, Neville: Henry VIII and His Court, 1971

Williams, Penry: 'Anthony Babington' Oxford Dictionary of National Biography

Wilson, Derek: Sweet Robin: A Biography of Robert Dudley Earl of Leicester 1533–1588, Hamish Hamilton 1981

Wilson, Derek: The Uncrowned Kings of England: The Black History of the Dudleys and the Tudor Throne, Carroll & Graf 2005

Appendices

Appendix 1: The Julian/Gregorian Calendar

Julius Caesar introduced the Julian calendar in 45 BC with each new year beginning on Lady's Day, 25 March. Queen Elizabeth died in the early hours of Thursday 24 March 1603. As the Elizabethans still used the Julian calendar, with the New Year beginning on 25 March, the queen died on the last day of the year 1602. However, in February 1582, the calendar that we recognise was established by Pope Gregory XIII and the New Year was to begin on 1 January. To rectify the ten-day time difference that had occurred, the day following 4 October 1582 was to be 15 October, with the intervening days being dropped. Disregarding papal authority, England ignored the new calendar and until 1751 English time continued ten days behind that of the Catholic states of Europe. This may cause slight confusion when dating events throughout the period covered by this book.

Appendix 2: The Act of Attainder

Under the Act of Attainder anyone could be sent to the Tower and shut away. The word 'Attainder' meant tainted. A bill, act or writ of this kind declared a person or persons guilty of a crime and allowed for the guilty party to be punished without a trial as long as royal assent was gained. Habeas Corpus guaranteed a fair trial by jury and the prevention of unlawful or arbitrary imprisonment, but an Act of Attainder bypassed this. It was mostly used for treason and was a convenient method used by the Crown to remove nobles who were deemed to be getting above themselves. Such a move suspended a person's civil rights and guaranteed that the person would be found guilty of the crimes stated in the bill. For serious crimes such as treason, the result was invariably execution. The guilty person's family would find that his/her property was confiscated by the Crown as he/she had no right to make a will. All titles held would go to the Crown. In this sense, the attainted person's family was also held to be guilty as they were also punished, though not to the same degree.

Appendix 3: How News Was Gathered

News travelled slowly and verbally, which invariably meant it became garbled in the spreading. Many inhabitants, particularly outside the capital, relied upon the hearsay of itinerant priests, wayfaring entertainers or the occasional roving merchant. The word 'news' came into literary use in 1551 when the occasional news pamphlets started to appear, but most people relied upon letters, rumours or bruits as their main means of knowing of events. The court was a notorious hotbed of gossip where reports contradicted each other, letters were written to obfuscate and the inevitable family loyalty and/or conflict frequently came into play. Most gentlemen and merchants of standing employed agents in appropriate places to keep them informed of current affairs. Gilbert Talbot employed the services of a man named Peter Proby, who also sent reports to the earls of Hertfordshire, Pembroke and Derby. The letters that contained these reports were a vital means of communication and some booksellers made a business of supplying written newsletters to those wealthy enough to afford a subscription.

Understandably, people like the queen and Walsingham needed a network of reliable informants, intelligence gatherers who had to mix and mingle in a sort of secret service. They were known as spies. Their information had to be up to date and not 'such things that come to every man that harkens to news', and their motives were not wholly reprehensible. Information was currency and only paid on results, so they usually had other jobs as diplomats, merchants, servants and tutors.

Appendix 4: The Royal Ancestry of John of Gaunt

John of Gaunt's legitimate male heirs, the Lancasters, included Kings Henry IV, Henry V and Henry VI. By his first wife, Blanche, his other legitimate descendants included his daughters Queen Philippa of Portugal and Elizabeth, Duchess of Exeter; and by his second wife, Constance, his daughter Queen Catherine of Castile. His long-term mistress and third wife Katherine Swynford had five children who were specifically barred from inheriting the throne – the phrase *excepta regali dignitate* (except royal status), was inserted in Letters Patent with dubious authority by their half-brother Henry IV. Descendants of this marriage included Henry Beaufort, Bishop of Winchester and eventually Cardinal; Joan Beaufort, Countess of Westmorland, grandmother of Kings Edward IV and Richard III; John Beaufort, 1st Earl of Somerset, the grandfather of Margaret Beaufort, mother of King Henry VII; and Joan Beaufort, Queen of Scots. The three succeeding houses of English sovereigns from 1399 – the Houses of Lancaster, York and Tudor – were descended from John through Henry Bolingbroke, Joan Beaufort and John Beaufort, respectively.

Philip of Spain's claim to the English throne was derived from that first marriage, with Philippa of Lancaster being one of his ancestors. The claim may have been remote but it was just as valid as that demonstrated in 1485 when Henry Tudor, a descendant of John of Gaunt's third and very dubious marriage, had claimed the English throne.

Appendix 5: The Cavendish Dynasty after Bess

As the Cavendish heir, Henry Cavendish inherited Chatsworth House but sold it to his brother William. Henry died in debt in October 1616 and is buried at Edensor. His illegitimate son Henry became the Lord Waterpark. His descendants are the Cavendishes of Doveridge. The family seat of Doveridge Hall was demolished about 1938. William Cavendish added the prefix Lord to the name of Cavendish. He chose to spend his vast fortunes to gain a further title, Earl of Devonshire. Later William, the 4th Earl, was to raise this to a dukedom in 1694. The title has passed down the family. Chatsworth House and Hardwick Hall remained the principal seats of the Cavendish family until Hardwick was taken in lieu of death duties. Charles Cavendish, Bess's third son, died in 1617 almost as wealthy as his older brother William. In 1607, he took Bolsover Castle and the Welbeck lands from his stepbrother Gilbert Talbot, and rebuilt Bolsover Castle in the medieval style with battlements, turrets and vaulted rooms. His descendants were the dukes of Portland and the dukes of Newcastle. Of Bess's three daughters, the dukes of Kingston-upon-Hull and eventually the Earl Manvers came from the line of her eldest daughter, Frances Cavendish, who married Sir Henry Pierrepont. Bess's youngest daughter, Mary, married Gilbert Talbot and became Countess of Shrewsbury. Mary's oldest daughter, also Mary, married William Herbert, 3rd Earl of Pembroke. Her middle daughter, Elizabeth, married Henry Grey, 8th Earl of Kent, and her youngest daughter, Alethea, married Thomas Howard, 2nd Earl of Arundel, whose descendants took the title dukes of Norfolk. Despite all Bess's efforts, nothing came of the triumphant marriage of Elizabeth Cavendish and Charles Stuart, Earl of Lennox, in line to inherit the thrones of both England and Scotland. Arbella Stuart, their only child, was deprived of her title, not permitted to marry and died aged forty, a captive in the Tower of London. Bess, Countess of Shrewsbury, is buried in Derby Cathedral, where up until 1848 over forty of her descendants were buried beneath her in the family vault. Rather unexpectedly, her sons Henry and William are buried at Edensor Church, and Charles at Bolsover.

Appendix 6: The Line of Succession

Elizabeth I refused to name her successor, but now the heir to the throne is acknowledged and the line of succession established. The first six in line still need the queen's permission or approval to marry. After the current monarch comes her eldest son, Charles, Prince of Wales, followed by his son Prince William of Wales, Duke of Cambridge, followed by his son, George of Cambridge. Shortly after George's birth, in July 2013, the Succession to the Crown Bill 2013 changed the succession laws so that the right of male primogeniture no longer applies; males born after 20 October 2011 no longer precede their elder sisters in the line of succession. The birth of Princess Charlotte in May 2015 thus made her fourth in line to the throne, and she will remain in that position even if she has a younger brother. The Bill removed the disqualification of those who marry Roman Catholics and also repealed the Royal Marriages Act 1772, so that only the first six people in line to the throne require the sovereign's permission to marry. This means that Princess Beatrice and Princess Eugenie, the queen's granddaughters who are seventh and eighth in line after their father and cousin Harry, no longer require the queen's permission to marry.

Appendix 7: Porphyria

Mary Queen of Scots complained of a continual pain in her side and head that sometimes persisted for weeks. As well as the acute pain, she had periods of vomiting, mental instability, uncontrollable weeping and discoloured, purplish urine. She was easily moved to tears of frustration, hysteria and anger. One minute she could be kind and generous, the next cruel and callous. She showed a certain amount of eccentricity and behaved in a self-destructive manner that no one could explain until recently, when modern medical research has revealed that she was suffering from the hereditary disease of porphyria. The Scottish queen was just one of the many members of the royal family who suffered from this condition, which is believed to have run through the generations. There is a striking similarity between Mary's symptoms and those of her niece Arbella Stuart. Both were considered unstable and both had the accompanying symptoms of acute pain and muscular weakness. For many years Queen Elizabeth I suffered from some form of mental instability, although at this distance in time it is impossible to diagnose her condition. She could be charming, witty and graceful, but she could also be rather paranoid and, increasingly, bitter. Porphyria is more common in women and often lies latent in men who can pass it on to the next generation, but James also suffered from the same wide range of symptoms as his mother and cousins. James's son Henry, Charles I's youngest daughter Henrietta and her daughter Marie Louise died of this fatal disease. More than a century later, the strange and tragic illness of George III is well documented but was not diagnosed as porphyria until the 1960s; it is believed that most of his children suffered from the symptoms of porphyria too. Queen Victoria is suspected also. In her lifetime it was referred to as 'the hereditary malady'. She passed the fatal gene on to her daughter Vicky, granddaughter Charlotte and great-granddaughter Feodora. More recently, Prince William of Gloucester was diagnosed and Princess Margaret may also have been a sufferer. The physical suffering they endured as well as the bouts of mental derangement made them gravely ill, but one of the remarkable features of the illness is how quickly the patient can recover. Looking for a common ancestor, the finger points to Margaret Tudor, eldest daughter of Henry VII, and 13x great-grandmother of Queen Elizabeth II. (Rőhl, W. and Hunt, Purple Secret, pp. 297, 306.)

Appendix 8: The Comet That Heralded Mary Queen of Scots' Death

Between midnight and one o'clock on the night of Sunday, 29 January 1587, Mary's rooms at Fotheringhay Castle were illuminated three times by a great flame of fiery light bright enough to read by. The guards on duty stationed beneath Mary's chamber were blinded by the light's unexpected intensity and brilliance, and, understandably tense, these superstitious people considered this to be some sort of evil omen. It was probably a comet, a body of rock and ice moving on its eccentric orbit through space and passing close to the earth. In earlier times, the appearance of a comet in the night sky was considered a supernatural warning presaging disaster. Unlike the familiar charted stars and planets, a comet's appearance was an erratic, unpredictable and frightening disturbance in the natural course of events and led to supposition that the comet was a kind of heavenly message that mankind dare not ignore.

The association between comets and disaster is seen in many cultures. The ancient Romans believed that the appearance of a fiery comet marked the assassination of Julius Caesar. Halley's Comet was believed to presage the Norman Conquest in 1066. The appearance of a comet is linked with the outbreak of the Black Death in the fourteenth century, and according to legend Pope Calixtus III later identified this comet as an instrument of the devil and in 1456 formally excommunicated it. It's therefore not surprising that this was considered a supernatural warning, which in Elizabethan England was traditionally associated with the death of a famous person. As Shakespeare wrote in Julius Caesar, 'When beggars die, there are no comets seen; the heavens themselves blaze forth the deaths of princes.'

Appendix 9: James of Scotland and the Berwick Witchcraft Trials

When Anne of Denmark set sail for Scotland to marry King James, the voyage ran into terrible storms which the admiral of the escorting Danish fleet blamed on witchcraft. Determined not to be thwarted by the evil powers, James left Scotland for the first time in his life and braved the supposed black arts. He was confident that he wouldn't drown and could successfully defeat the evil powers because he had been born with a caul covering his face. This was believed to give him psychic powers and among other things prevent him from drowning. The wedding ceremony took place on 23 November, and after spending the winter at the Danish royal court they arrived back in Scotland on 1 May 1590, but by this time James was more interested in witchcraft than a wife. During his stay in Denmark he had been a witness at the witchcraft trials when six women confessed that they had sent devils to climb up the keel of Anne's ship, and had been guilty of sorcery in raising storms that menaced her voyage.

When James heard this he decided to set up his own tribunal, the first major witchcraft persecution in Scotland, and very soon more than 100 suspected witches in North Berwick were arrested. Many confessed under torture to having met with the Devil in the church at night, and devoted themselves to doing evil, including poisoning the king and other members of his household, and sending storms in an attempt to sink the king's ship. The incident had given James a confidence in his own ability and he was convinced that few earthly princes had been permitted to put the prince of darkness to the test and defeat him. Apparently James learnt that the Devil had announced to the witches at North Berwick that the king was the greatest enemy he had in the world (Newes From Scotland 14 and 17).

James was sure that not only was he divine, but he was unique in having divine protection. In trials that lasted two years, he personally supervised the torture of over seventy women accused of being witches. James became obsessed with the threat posed by witches and, inspired by his personal involvement, in 1597 he wrote the *Daemonologie*, a tract which opposed the practice of witchcraft and which provided background material for the playwright William Shakespeare when he wrote *Macbeth*.

James was intensely superstitious, and laid great stress upon the fact that he was born on 19 June; he first saw his wife on 19 November; his son Henry was born on 19 February, his daughter Elizabeth on 19 August and his younger son Charles on 19 November.

Appendix 10: Bess's Legacy

With typical thoughtfulness, in 1601 Bess had compiled an inventory of the contents of Hardwick Hall because 'it hath pleased God to give me leave to perform some buildings at my houses at Chatsworth, Hardwick and Oldcotes in the county of Derby, which I greatly desire should be well preserved and the furniture continued at my said houses for the better furnishing thereof, into whose possession soever, of my blood, the said houses shall come'. It wasn't just the valuables; the list covered all the paraphernalia of items in general use 400 years ago. The passage of four centuries has scattered many of Bess's treasures, but some remain at her beloved Hardwick Hall.

In the High Great Chamber, the six pieces of tapestry hangings of the story of Ulysses, 11 feet deep, still line the walls. Two inlaid tables survive, as do a drawing table gilt carved standing upon sea dogs inlaid with marble stones and wood; the walnut table made to mark the triple wedding of the Talbot and Cavendish family; the chest of oak, walnut and marguetry with two arched panels inlaid with distant buildings seen through an arch, the keystones of which bear the initials GT (George Talbot) and which chest has drawers in the lower section, an innovation that marked the evolution of the chest of drawers. The thirteen Gideon tapestries acquired from the Hatton family in 1592 'contained one thousand ells and a half of arras of the story of Gideon'. They had cost Bess £326 15*s* 9*d* 'whereof for making a new arms was abated five pounds'. Bess paid Mr Shelton's man 30*s* 4*d* for changing the Hatton coat of arms to Hardwick, converting does into stags

Locations Mentioned in the Book

Many of the places mentioned in the book can still be visited. Although not complete, here is a list of properties to add to your enjoyment.

HARDWICK OLD HALL

The birthplace of Bess of Hardwick, now managed by English Heritage, stands in the grounds of Hardwick Hall. This roofless medieval manor house was transformed into an impressive Tudor mansion by Bess prior to building the new hall. Visitors can still ascend four floors to examine surviving decorative plasterwork, as well as the kitchens and service rooms.

BARLOW

A rural community on the Derbyshire–Yorkshire border. Bess was a child bride of Robert Barlow, Lord of the Manor. The present Barlow Woodseats Hall, a privately owned, Grade II listed manor house, was built in the first half of the seventeenth century on the site of the former manor house.

BARLOW CHURCH

The first church on the site of the Parish Church of St Lawrence, Great Barlow was probably Saxon but the history of the present church dates to the early twelfth century. The Barlow family added a chantry chapel to bury their dead and for prayers to be said for their souls. Now known as the Lady's Quire, it is here that the young Robert Barlow, the first husband of Bess of Hardwick, was interred.

CODNOR CASTLE

Young Bess of Hardwick lived here with the Zouche family in the 1530s. This thirteenth-century castle near Ripley, Derbyshire is now a ruin, access is very limited and not encouraged. It is a Scheduled Ancient Monument, Grade II listed building, and since 2008 the site is officially a building at risk.

CHATSWORTH HOUSE

The original Tudor mansion, built in the 1560s by Bess, was in a quadrangle layout approximately 170 feet from north to south and 190 feet from east to west with a large central courtyard. The front entrance was on the west front, which was embellished with four towers or turrets. The south and east fronts were rebuilt around 1696 for William Cavendish, 1st Duke of Devonshire, and is a key building in the development of English Baroque architecture. The first and sixth dukes both inherited an old house and tried to adapt it to the lifestyle of their time, which resulted in the interior reflecting a collection of different styles. Although it's not obvious, the Tudor building is incorporated into the main building; the Great Hall, which in the medieval tradition was on the east side of the courtyard, was where the Painted Hall is today. The Elizabethan garden was much smaller than the modern garden. Its main visual remnant is the belvedere, known as 'Queen Mary's Bower', where Mary Queen of Scots was allowed to take the air. Chatsworth House has remained the principal seat of the Cavendish family, but the house and grounds are open to the public. It is one of Derbyshire's premier tourist attractions.

HARDWICK HALL

A magnificent statement of the wealth and power of Bess of Hardwick, Hardwick Hall has been described as a huge glass lantern because of its many windows. It dominates the surrounding area and is remarkable as being almost unchanged since Bess lived there with her granddaughter Arbella. This perfectly preserved house and estate is now owned by the National Trust and is a showpiece.

HARDWICK OLD HALL

Now mainly roofless and in ruins, incorporated into this structure is the original farmhouse where Bess of Hardwick was born. Bess purchased the estate and rebuilt it before commencing work on New Hall. Visitors can see the kitchen and service room and still ascend four floors to view the surviving plasterwork. An exhibition in the West Lodge describes Bess's adventures in architecture and how she transformed her birthplace from a medieval manor house into a luxurious Elizabethan mansion. Managed by English Heritage and owned by the National Trust.

RUFFORD ABBEY

The original abbey, from which Rufford takes its name, was built around 1170 on behalf of the Archbishop of Lincoln, Gilbert de Gaunt, as a Cistercian monastery. It was part of the great Yorkshire Abbey of Rievaulx founded in 1146. It was converted to a country house in the sixteenth century and was where Elizabeth Cavendish met and married Charles Stuart, Earl of Lennox. Part of the house was demolished in the twentieth century, but the remains, standing in 150 acres of park and woodland, are open to the public as Rufford Country Park.

WORKSOP MANOR

Despite Shrewsbury's concerns over money, between 1580 and 1585 he went to enormous expense building a new house at Worksop. The new Worksop Manor was a magnificent mansion, designed by Robert Smythson. It was very tall, with a narrow tower in the centre of each façade capped by a domed lantern, and on the ends of the long façades were projecting square bays. The long gallery, 224 feet long and 38 feet wide, was famous throughout England, and ran along the top floor giving magnificent views over the earl's parkland; it was described by Robert Cecil in 1590 as 'the fairest gallery in England'. The master mason was Giles Greves who had also worked on Chatsworth. This is where Gilbert Talbot, 7th Earl of Shrewsbury, entertained King James I in 1603.

Until the early part of the seventeenth century, when it passed through an heiress to the dukes of Norfolk, Worksop Manor formed part of the ancient estates of the Talbots. In the autumn of 1761 the original manor house, which contained about 500 rooms, was destroyed by fire. Although a new manor was commissioned to replace the previous building, only one wing was completed and work stopped in 1767. The wing was demolished in the 1840s, and after a number of years the surviving parts of the house – the stable, the service wing and part of the eastern end of the main range – were reformed into a new mansion. It is now in private ownership.

SHEFFIELD CASTLE

After a short and bloody siege during the Civil War, Sheffield Castle was demolished in 1648. The buried remains lie under the Castle Markets and surrounding areas. Prior to the building of the Brightside and Carbrook Co-op Society Store in 1927, an excavation uncovered the base of one of the castles gateway bastion towers, as well as part of the gateway. These remains are Grade II listed and are preserved under the city's Castle Market. The visible remains are in two rooms – one is open to the public, subject to booking a tour, the other is walled and the only access is via a manhole in the market's food court. The remaining ruins approximately 32 feet above the River Don are those of the eastern gate tower. During excavations in 1999 and 2001 by Sheffield Archaeological research and consultancy unit, drilling was done in the upper food court delivery yard and flag stones left *in situ* mark the castle boundaries. A landslide at the back of the Edward Street Flats uncovered a large stone supporting wall. The stone blocks were quite substantial, which suggests they were previously used in the building of Sheffield Castle. Parts of the Old Queen's Head on Pond Street which dates back to 1400 is believed to have been the lodge of Sheffield Castle. Pond Street is named after the stew ponds in this area that supplied the castle kitchens.

SHEFFIELD MANOR

Sheffield Manor extended over the whole of the Park Hill from Heeley to Darnall and Handsworth to the River Don, covering an area of nearly 2,500 acres. It's still known as The Manor. After the sixteenth century, Sheffield Manor House became increasingly neglected and fell into a slow decline. In 1671, a Yorkshire historian named Nathaniel Johnson was allowed access to The Manor and was able to rescue thousands of letters and documents of the Shrewsburys and Mary Queen of Scots. This unique collection of papers had been abandoned there and many were damaged by damp and nibbled by mice, but Johnson ensured their survival. The contents of the manor were taken to Worksop Manor where they were destroyed when the house burnt down later in the eighteenth century. Over a period of weeks during 1709, most of the manor was demolished, the materials carted away for re-use in building projects. One of the towers was adapted to house what was probably the first local pottery producing a wide range of brown slipware, but this tower blew down in a particularly furious gale in 1793. The Turret House, originally built as a porter's lodge, is now the only remaining roofed building on the site. It escaped demolition because it had been incorporated into a complex of barns and farm buildings which throughout the eighteenth century formed a picturesque ruin, much loved by local artists. The cellars and base of the towers which survive today hardly reflect the grandeur. The austere, three-storey turret tower is all that remains and was originally built as a porters lodge.

Each floor has two rooms interlinked with a narrow winding staircase at the corner running up all three floors. On the top floor is Mary's room, where an effigy stands in a corner. Excavations in the 1970s revealed the footing of buildings that date back to the twelfth century. At least six building phases have been identified prior to the early sixteenth century. By the end of the fifteenth century, quite an extensive complex of buildings were in existence but no sign exists today above ground. The earliest standing walls that survive date from the fourth earl George Shrewsbury's days when the buildings were considerably extended and upgraded. The Manor Castle Inn, 239 Manor Lane, was built around the ruins of the former Sheffield Manor. It was not until the early nineteenth century that any significant development of the town of Sheffield extended across the Sheaf and encroached onto the lower slopes of Park Hill.

SOUTH WINGFIELD MANOR

South Wingfield Manor has become more synonymous with Mary Queen of Scots, who was a prisoner there. Now a vast, impressive ruin arranged around a pair of courtyards, South Wingfield Manor has an impressive undercroft, Great Hall and 72-foot-high tower. Managed by English Heritage, visits must be pre-booked.

TUTBURY CASTLE AND PRIORY

The small, picturesque town of Tutbury lies on the banks of the River Dove on the border of Derbyshire and Staffordshire.

Tutbury Castle was a fortress, large enough to be more like a fortified town, and was the most hated prison of Mary Queen of Scots. Largely in ruins, what used to be a south tower with a winding staircase, two chambers and the high tower are all that remains. It is a Scheduled Ancient Monument in the ownership of the Duchy of Lancaster and is open to visitors.

Tutbury Priory was the home of Henry Cavendish. The original priory occupied an area of 4 acres on the hillside below the castle, with the monastic buildings lying on the north side of the church. The foundations of the cloister, dormitory and apartments were still visible *circa* 1832 in the field adjoining the church to the north. Now only the parish church of St Mary remains standing, and that has been much reduced in size.

DERBY

Mary Queen of Scots stayed in Derby on her 17-mile journey between South Wingfield Manor and Tutbury Castle. The ancient St Mary's Bridge, which she would have crossed, still spans the River Derwent. Babington Hall, owned by the infamous Babington family, was where the Scottish queen stayed in January 1585. It was demolished in 1826 and now the site opposite the Babington buildings on the corner of Babington Lane is marked by the carved family crest, a baboon on a tun or barrel, on the gable of the present building.

LINLITHGOW PALACE

This was the traditional lying-in place of Scottish queens and where Mary Queen of Scots spent the first seven months of her life. Her father, James V, had been born there, and he later improved the earlier castle and made it in a quadrangular form. By the standards of the day it was magnificent and Mary of Guise compared it very favourably to the castle of the Loire. The palace today owes much of its beauty to that period of building, but the room where Mary was born is roofless.

HOLYROOD CASTLE, EDINBURGH

Darnley's former apartments were here and this is where he murdered David Rizzio. There is a plaque on the floor of the old queen's apartments that commemorates the event.

FOTHERINGHAY CASTLE

This ruined motte-and-bailey castle dates back to 1100. The flat top of the inner bailey was a 160-foot-by-213-foot rectangle some 23 feet above ground level surrounded by a 230-foot-diameter motte. Despite its size and importance, little can now be seen but earthworks and some masonry in farmland. Mary arrived here on 25 September, and her trial and execution were held in the Great Hall. By 1635, less than fifty years after Mary Queen of Scots was executed in the castle's great hall, it was reported as being in a ruinous state, having been allowed to fall into disrepair as the fixtures and fittings were sold off and the building materials used in other locations. It was gradually demolished, and in the 1820s, when stone from the walls was being stripped for reuse, Mary's ring was found. It is believed that it rolled off during her death throes and was swept away unnoticed. It can now be seen at the Victoria and Albert Museum in London. By 1864, the final traces of the walls had disappeared and now all that remains is a small selection of tumbled stonework with an abundance of thistles enclosed by railings. The thistles have been attributed to Theodore Napiere, a Scotsman who every year would travel down from his native Scotland to the castle site to lay a wreath on the spot where Mary was executed. Dressed in full Highland garb, his annual visit on 8 February started in 1901 until it was stopped due to complaints that he was trespassing. In the nearby church, most of which was pulled down in 1533, is a chair from Fotheringhay Castle, reportedly the one which Mary sat in just before her execution. There is also a display of artefacts and pictures.

TALBOT HOTEL, OUNDLE, NORTHAMPTONSHIRE

The village of Fotheringhay lies 4 miles north of Oundle, where you will find the Talbot Hotel. When Fotheringhay Castle was demolished some of the interior fixtures and fittings were purchased by William Whitwell, the landlord of the hotel that stood on the site at the time. He was able to rebuild his hotel in grand Elizabethan style, installing the great horn windows from Fotheringhay into the inn's ancient walls. But the most significant item purchased at the time was the great oak staircase from Fotheringhay Castle down which Mary walked on her way to face her executioners. Local legend also maintains that on the polished wood of the balustrade is the imprint of a crown left by the ring on Mary's finger as she clutched the balustrade for support on her way to the block.

HATFIELD HOUSE

The seat of the Cecil family, the Marquesses of Salisbury. Princess Elizabeth was confined here for three years in what is now known as the Old Palace in Hatfield Park, 30 miles north of London. The Old Palace was built by the Bishop of Ely, Cardinal Morton, in 1497 during the reign of Henry VII, and the only surviving wing is still used today for Elizabethan-style banquets. Legend has it that it was here in 1558, while sitting under an oak tree in the park, that Elizabeth learned that she had become queen following the death of her half-sister, Queen Mary I. She held her first Council in the Great Hall of the Old Palace of Hatfield. The town grew up around the gates of Hatfield House. Old Hatfield retains many historic buildings, notably the Old Palace, St Etheldreda's Church and Hatfield House. St Etheldreda's Church was founded by the monks from Ely, and the first wooden church, built in 1285, was probably sited where the existing building stands overlooking the old town. In 1851, the route of the Great North Road (now the A1000) was altered to avoid cutting through the grounds of Hatfield House.

THE TOWER OF LONDON

A grand palace early in its history, the Tower of London served not only as a royal residence but also as a prison from 1100 until 1952. Despite its name, The Tower has twenty-one towers which together form the Tower of London castle complex covering an area of 18 acres.

It is officially a castle and one of several royal palaces located on the north bank of the River Thames in central London. It was founded towards the end of 1066 as part of the Norman Conquest of England, and built for William the Conqueror in 1078 as a symbol of oppression.

As well as a castle and prison, it has also served as an armoury, a treasury, a menagerie and zoo, the home of the Royal Mint, a public records office, and the home of the Crown Jewels of England. The general layout established by the late thirteenth century remains despite later phases of expansion, but during the eighteenth century the royal lodgings in the Bell Tower were dismantled; a lawn now covers the spot. The Tower of London has played a prominent role in English history and is still a very popular tourist attraction.

PALACE OF WESTMINSTER

When William II built the Palace of Westminster between 1097 and 1099 it was the largest, most impressive hall in England, sitting proudly on the banks of the Thames in central London. It was remodelled and extended by various royal residents until its role as a royal residence ended abruptly in 1512 when fire gutted the privy chamber.

Henry VIII decided to move to a nearby building in Whitehall, and in the late fifteenth century the Palace of Westminster became the home of the main Courts of Law. It hosted many high-profile trials such as that of Guy Fawkes and his co-conspirators in the Gunpowder Plot, tried and executed in 1606. The Courts of Law only vacated the building in the 1800s after a fire in 1834 destroyed most of the old structure.

Inside today's Perpendicular Gothic building is the Great Hall, otherwise known as Westminster Hall – all that remains of the medieval Old Palace and the place where Parliament has convened regularly since the reign of Henry III.

THE PALACE OF WHITEHALL

In the fourteenth century, the archbishops of York built a house, known as York House, conveniently close to the king's palace at Westminster. When the Palace of Westminster was destroyed by fire in 1512, Henry took over the house, renaming it Whitehall and extending the whole to 23 acres. The Palace of Whitehall became the main residence of the English monarchs in London from 1530 until 1698.

In 1581, Queen Elizabeth built the Banqueting House, which James I replaced in 1609 as an appropriate setting for a new and elaborate form of court entertainment, the masque. The building burnt down in 1619, but James immediately rebuilt it; a major fire in 1698 finally ended its days of grandeur.

HAMPTON COURT PALACE

Hampton Court Palace, along with St James's Palace, is one of only two surviving London palaces out of the many owned by King Henry VIII. Hampton Court roughly 12 miles south-west and upstream of central London on the River Thames at East Molesey, Surrey. In 1515, Cardinal Thomas Wolsey undertook the redevelopment of a former manor house, adopting new Renaissance architectural styles. Wolsey had always been a favourite of Henry VIII, who coveted this grand new building, and on Wolsey's fall from grace he confiscated it; he forced Wolsey to accept Richmond Palace in exchange. Wolsey died two years later. Henry enlarged Hampton Court Palace, but in the following century, William III rebuilt and extended it further. Work ceased in 1694, leaving the palace in two distinct contrasting architectural styles, domestic Tudor and Baroque.

Although classed as a royal palace, it has not been inhabited by the British royal family since the eighteenth century, George II being the last monarch to reside there. Today, the great palace by the river is open to the public and is a major tourist attraction.

RICHMOND PALACE

The current Richmond Green was originally a common where villagers pastured their sheep, but around 1501 Henry VII built a palace to replace the former Sheen Palace, built on the site of a manor house. The town of Sheen, or Sceon to use its Saxon spelling, had grown up around the royal manor, but by command of King Henry VII the name was changed to Richmond. The palace was given the name Richmond Palace after Henry's earldom and ancestral home at Richmond Castle in North Yorkshire. Richmond is a Norman name, Riche Mont meaning strong hill – a rather strange name for a town that is virtually flat on the bank of the River Thames.

Richmond Green became a medieval jousting ground alongside the palace. The district we now call Sheen developed in the nineteenth and twentieth centuries and was never in ancient times within the manor of Sheen. In 1502, the new palace witnessed a betrothal between Henry VII's daughter Margaret and James IV of Scotland, Arbella's great-grandparents. In 1509 Henry VII died there, and in the 1520s Cardinal Wolsey took up residence after being forced out of Hampton Court by Henry VIII.

In 1540 Henry gave Richmond palace to his fourth wife, Anne of Cleves, as part of her divorce settlement. Once Elizabeth I became queen Richmond Palace became her favourite home. She enjoyed hunting stags in the 'Newe Parke of Richmonde' (now the Old Deer Park), and died there on 24 March 1603. James preferred the Palace of Westminster to Richmond, but it remained a residence of the kings and queens of England until the death of Charles I in 1649. Within months of his execution, the palace was surveyed by order of Parliament and was sold for £13,000. Over the following ten years it was largely demolished, the stones and timbers being reused as building materials elsewhere. By the eighteenth century all that remained of the palace was the gatehouse and local street names, including Old Palace Lane, Old Palace Yard and The Wardrobe, in the area between Richmond Green and the River Thames. The gateway with Henry VII's arms above still faces Richmond Green. To the left of the gateway, fragments of the old palace remain, including two half-towers. Old Palace Yard, inside the gateway, was originally the courtyard of the palace. The largely reconstructed Wardrobe, once a store for furniture and hangings, still incorporates some of the Tudor brickwork. What remains of the Old Palace are now leased as private residences.

SHREWSBURY HOUSE

Shrewsbury House, Chelsea, the London house of the Shrewsbury family, lay beside the river, west of the present day Oakley Street on Cheyne Walk, and adjoining the palatial residence set up by Sir Thomas More. Shrewsbury also possessed Coldharbour in the City below London Bridge, but neither house remains.

Index